CRE

MW01008539

From
Kathy
Laramby
5/06

Created for Commitment

A. Wetherell Johnson

Tyndale House Publishers, Inc.
Wheaton, Illinois

All Bible references are taken from
the King James Version of the Bible
unless otherwise indicated.

Trade paper edition
Library of Congress Catalog Card Number 82-50707
ISBN 0-8423-0443-6
Printed in the United States of America

05
15 14 13 12

I dedicate this book to fellow-workers,
to whom I shall ever be grateful.

I thank God for profound impressions
given during training days in London
and for fellow-workers in China,
who under great difficulties
shine like stars in a dark sky.

I thank God for fellow-workers
in Bible Study Fellowship
during those early days in San Bernardino,
and for others those first years
when the Headquarters were in Oakland.

How I would love to name in the book
these who have given so much
to the Lord and to me in this work,
but this would be impossible.
However, they are in my heart forever.

Finally,
I praise God for the Board of Directors,
and most especially for my friend and co-worker,
Miss Alverda Hertzler.

I pray that all of them who read this book
may be conscious of my deep gratitude.

A. WETHERELL JOHNSON

CONTENTS

Part IV Guidelines for the Christian Life

FOREWORD

Audrey Wetherell Johnson is a remarkable woman. Vision, faith, humility, and tenacity mark her out. She is utterly committed, body and soul, to her Lord, and will go on working for him till she drops. She has honoured me by asking me to introduce her book to the world. It is a privilege thus to pay my respects to one of the noblest Christians I know.

Wetherell Johnson is English, which is greatly in her favour so far as I am concerned. Furthermore, she embodies a most winning though now rare type of English charm, a compound of gaiety with courtesy, liveliness with gentleness, modesty with forthrightness, dignity with determination, a playful girlish sense of the absurd with a serious adult sense of the tragic. "Ladylike" was the old English word for it, but in modern England that word is almost defunct because so few remain whom it fits (and I have never heard it used in North America at all). Once in England a person like Miss Johnson (as most Bible Study Fellowship members call her) would have been described as a gentlewoman, but that word is quite dead now. Yet I hope I convey something by saying that as Agatha Christie's sharp-minded Miss Marple is a gentle-woman turned detective, so Wetherell Johnson is a gentlewoman with her wits about her who fulfills a leadership role for God.

She tells her story as such stories were conventionally told two generations ago, in the pre-Freudian era, when it was not fashionable to approach autobiography-writing as an emotional binge on which one must make a point of letting all one's feelings hang out. But do not on that account dismiss her book as old-fashioned and quaint; learn rather to read between the lines. The correct human description of the life of this woman, who after devoted missionary ministry and grueling internment in China became teacher of tens of thousands of students and hundreds of leaders in the Bible Study Fellowship, is heroic. By that divine strength, which is Jesus' resurrection life in his faith-full servants, Wetherell Johnson has learned to love the unlovely on three continents, to welcome what comes, however rough, with a believer's smile, to keep going through murderous physical pain, and to spend herself absolutely in spreading the knowledge of God and his infallible Word. But for her it has all been ordinary step-by-step obedience, and so she presents it. God called; God guided; God enabled; God is faithful; what more need be said? Her perspective does not make for dramatic storytelling, but the joy in God which shines through her non-harrowing narrative of sometimes harrowing things is beautiful to see.

"One thing I do," wrote Paul, "forgetting what lies behind and straining forward to what lies ahead, I press on toward the goal for the prize of the upward call of God in Christ Jesus" (Phil. 3:13, 14). I do not know anyone today of whom this is more obviously true than Wetherell Johnson, "a mother in Israel," a woman greatly beloved. Her life story has spurred me on; may it have the same effect on all its readers.

J. I. Packer

PREFACE

I am grateful to several friends who have been employed in typing assistance for the manuscript of this book. In the early days, Mrs. Betty O'Connell came. Later my friend and former co-worker, Miss Marguerite Carter traveled from California to stay two months in San Antonio to type long hours for the bulk of this book. Lastly Mrs. Jan Kuhn has assisted on different mornings of a week to complete the manuscript. I owe more than I can express to my friend and fellow-worker, Miss Alverda Hertzler, who faithfully proofread a large part of the book and often gave valuable advice.

The task of preparing this book has been unusually difficult because of illness, and I have been aware of the constant help of God. To His hands, and for His use, I now entrust it.

A. Wetherell Johnson

INTRODUCTION

Man searches for his own fulfillment in life in many ways, but where is lasting fulfillment to be found? A career comes to an end; attaining to a great position of wealth or power fails to satisfy one's deepest longings. Surely there must be something more to life! Has life on earth any meaning if death is its final end? Many people experience a sense of frustration by life's seeming emptiness and brevity.

I trust this book will give some answers to people who today are living in the same position in which I found myself at twenty years of age. Following my education in atheistic philosophy in Paris, I slowly came to realize that in spite of all my outwardly busy life of a good career, parties, and friends, I was inwardly experiencing a life of profound dissatisfaction. This book is a story of how I found a purpose for living which far exceeded all my longing.

In view of the tragic world situation of today and stories of deep loneliness and despair of many who have come to me for counsel, I long to share on a wide scale how I was given comfort, joy, and profound fulfillment.

The first chapter relates some tragic events in my mother's life, and an unusual story of her faith.

During my own early years in England and education in

France, I experienced some real difficulties as well as many exciting opportunities.

Later, while living in China, I was in danger of death from illness, also from bombing in World War II. The rigors of nearly three years in a Japanese internment camp finally culminated in a riot of prisoners because of specific brutality. This brought more than 2,000 of us face to face with death as Japanese guards held their guns aimed on the crowd, ready to fire.

When American planes dropped, not bombs, but parachutes with packages of food, and our prison gates were opened to freedom, our joy knew no bounds.

After a year in Europe, I returned to China, and lived under the Communist regime until the Communists began to force aliens out of China. Although I was expecting to return to England, I decided to visit America since I had many friends there. However, my stay was prolonged because of the need to recuperate after the strain of living in China during the Communist takeover.

Little did I know that this enforced rest was to lead to numerous invitations to speak to students at Inter-Varsity camps as well as to those in colleges and seminaries. I also spoke at large conferences such as Mt. Hermon and The Firs Conference Center.

One day after speaking at a church service, I was surprised when five ladies asked me to give them a course in Bible study. How could I have ever anticipated that granting this request would eventually lead to an organization which would spread over the United States, and even into England, Canada, Australia, and lately, New Zealand!

Many agnostics, unchurched people and others of various faiths, crowded into Bible Study Fellowship classes, where they found answers to deep problems and frustrations through personal Bible study.

Friendships formed over many years with dedicated class leaders, and individual class members have greatly enriched my life. Although I am now retired, I continue to be thrilled because of hundreds of letters from men and women who feel constrained to write engrossing stories of how God has changed their lives through their study of the Bible.

What I would have missed had I not cried out as an agnostic to God and discovered that I was "created for commitment" to Him and to His purpose for my life.

I
The Early Years

sold in 1935. It is now a well-known college.

While Maude was in this governess position, a son of the Cope family fell in love with her. John Cope was a staunch Anglican; Mother was a young Christian. She decided to go to the vicar of Mr. Cope's church to seek confirmation concerning the spiritual belief of her would-be fiancé. She inquired whether the vicar considered him to be "born again." He replied, "But, my dear Miss Wetherell, Mr. Cope is a steward in my own church; of course, he is a Christian." Mother took the vicar's word as her answer.

The marriage took place soon after this interview. It was a true love match. They bought a beautiful new home called "Wiggington Park" in Tenterden, Surrey. It comprised a lovely estate with a lake surrounded by beautiful woods. As the young couple began to furnish their new home, Mother wanted to place a Scripture text on the wall of one of the main reception rooms. Her husband replied, "Oh no, my Dear, that would not be suitable in the drawing room. Display it, if you wish, in your own boudoir." Gradually there were other indications which made Maude Cope realize that, although her husband assiduously attended church with her, he did not "know her Lord" through personal experience. As time went on and two boys and two girls had been born (Claude, John, Katherine, and Marjorie), Mother became increasingly, but quietly, concerned for her husband's salvation.

One summer her husband sent her with her four little children and their nurse to enjoy the cool breezes of the beach. At that time he had business in London and stayed in their townhouse. One particular Sunday Mother was led into intensive, expectant prayer for her husband's conversion. After hours of fasting and prayer, the phrase "And Nehemiah prayed before the God of heaven" (Nehemiah 1:4) came to her mind so forcibly that she was convinced God was speaking to her. Also, she discovered that her prayers were being turned into praise, for the Holy Spirit had given her that inner knowledge that God had already answered her prayer.

Meanwhile, that same Sunday evening, her husband was

pacing the London streets, lonesome for his wife's company. He passed a mission hall and for the first time in his life decided to go in. The unusual text chosen by the preacher was "And Nehemiah prayed before the God of heaven." Mr. Cope was deeply moved and returned to his London townhouse. Upon going to bed he noticed a copy of a devotional book on the bedside table. To his amazement when he opened it he discovered that the text for that day was "And Nehemiah prayed to the God of heaven." Unable to resist any longer the pressure of God's Holy Spirit, John Cope knelt in prayer by his bed and gave himself totally to his Savior.

Shortly after this he returned to their home at Tenterden. When he met his wife and family in the horse carriage, he did not say anything to Maude about his experience. But when she arrived home, the first thing Maude Cope noticed in a prominent position on the wall of the drawing room was a text from the Bible. After sending the children upstairs with their nurse, he took his wife into his arms and poured out the glorious news of his conversion and of the sense of peace and joy which filled his heart. Then Mother told him her side of the story, the miracle of the same verse from Nehemiah being given to them both.

They planned together how they could use their large home for the Lord. They would invite neighbors to informal drawing room meetings where well-known Christian leaders would present the gospel message. Many found the Lord there.

Their marriage union became infinitely closer, but eventually the Lord took Maude Cope's husband to Himself. The family of Mother's in-laws at Bramshill House did not share their son John Cope's new-found belief. Nevertheless, at his death, they warmly invited my mother and her four children to live with them, guaranteeing full financial support and adequate education for the children. At this time the four children were in their late teens. Mother was a widow who could only look to the sale of her home, Wiggington Park, for their livelihood. However, such was her trust in God and concern for the spiritual welfare of her four children that she turned down the gracious offer. She chose to believe that the Lord would provide for her needs in His own way.

By this time she had become closely acquainted with many Christian leaders of that era. One, for example, was Andrew Murray. (Mother once told me that such was Andrew Murray's close walk with God, that even in a prayer meeting when everyone was kneeling at prayer with closed eyes, one *knew* when Andrew Murray entered the room, for a deep awareness of the Holy Spirit's presence impressed hearts.) Other key persons with whom she enjoyed relationships were Evan Roberts of "Welsh Revival" fame, Mrs. Jessie Penn-Lewis, and another particularly close friend was Dr. F. B. Meyer.

When Mother became a widow, Dr. Meyer invited her to act as a deaconess in his church, giving her a wide Christian ministry, including teaching a large evening men's class. My sister, Katherine, told me that many times Mother would call her children out of bed to pray for someone who had received the Lord that evening and for other needs as well.

God wonderfully provided for an adequate education for the children by friends, so that they were able to attend private or boarding schools which would have been chosen for them by her husband.

I believe the spiritual inheritance parents give to their children is very important. Twice my mother had chosen to give up financial affluence to give her children spiritual influence. This was the greatest inheritance I could have had.

T W O
AN ENGLISH CHILDHOOD

When I call to remembrance the unfeigned faith that is in thee,
which dwelt first in thy grandmother Lois, and thy mother
Eunice; and I am persuaded that in thee also [II Timothy 1:5].

Following John Cope's death, my mother took her family to live in Leicester where the four teen-aged children went to school.

After my mother had been a Christian worker in Dr. Meyer's church for some time, she met Henry Johnson, who fell in love with her. Later they were married. At that time the two teenage sons, Claude and John Cope, chose to accept their grandparent's invitation to live with them at Bramshill House. The two girls, Kitty and Marjorie Cope, elected to remain with their mother and new stepfather in Leicester.

I was born Audrey Johnson in Leicester at the end of 1907.

Soon after my birth my father was invited to join a missionary work in France. He was eager to go, but my mother had no sense of call in that direction. However, as an obedient wife she went to France with her husband, accompanied by Kitty and myself.

Their situation in France did not work out satisfactorily. Neither of my parents knew the French language. The work also involved a great deal of travel. My mother became seriously ill, and it was finally decided that she should return to England to recover, leaving my sister Kitty (then about eighteen) to look after Father and me. Kitty loved children and was a true mother to me. Indeed in my early years I considered her my "ideal Christian."

One of the blessings God gave me as a child which greatly influenced later years was that of close friendships with key Christians in Switzerland to whose homes we were often invited. Especially interesting was Father's friendship with the well-known Swiss artist, Paul Robert. His outstanding murals still beautify the two-story entrance hall at the art gallery in Neuchâtel. Others of his paintings can also be seen at the Lausanne Art Gallery. Their greatest interest to the Christian is that all of these exquisite paintings represent different aspects of our Lord's return. Mr. Robert had an immense and beautiful estate with glorious wild flowers where I played to my heart's content. From this early beginning, my love for Switzerland has continued through my life.

When I was about five I loved to ride on top of the hay cart on Mr. Robert's estate. Once, not knowing I was there, laborers tossed the hay with me in it into a huge barn. My sister Kitty frantically searched for me, and God directed the laborers to the middle of the hay. I was unconscious. Life was almost extinct, but a child quickly recovers.

My mother was never able to return to France, her health continuing to be very frail. (I thought it was amazing to see the spiritual ministry she accomplished in England in spite of this.) Father had a passion for travel and later joined the French "Scripture Union," traveling throughout France, Africa, and Switzerland. God blessed his ministry.

My sister Kitty and I stayed in France until the outbreak of World War I in August 1914. At that time all English persons in France struggled to board the few boats leaving for England. Although I was only seven, I will never forget the frantic mob which fought to get into the last boat leaving the shores of France for England. Actually the ship was crowded with twice as many passengers as its official capacity allowed. I vividly remember all the terrifying, squeezing pressure of grown-ups. I can still hear my sister, who was afraid I would be downtrodden by the mob, pleading, "Please be careful. There is a little child here. Do not trample over her." We reached London late at night "sans" all luggage, but with my teddy bear, from which I was inseparable.

From this time on, I lived with my mother and two sisters. Our home was situated in one of the most beautiful and historic places in England, Kenilworth in Warwickshire (famous for its castle ruins). Although my half sisters, Kitty and Marjorie Cope, belonged to another father, I never felt any estrangement. There was always a tender love between Mother, two young women, and the mischievous little "Snipit," as I was then nicknamed. The love of God was the foundation of the home, and with all the humor, a soft-speaking atmosphere was all-pervading.

Kenilworth is an exquisitely beautiful village immortalized by Sir Walter Scott's historical novel. There is a famous castle ruin there (perfect for a little girl's playground) with fields, woods, an old church, and a clocktower in the village center.

Our cottage backed on to the fields and woods. Once when I was about nine, temptation became too great. Some bulls were quietly lying in the field, so I climbed on the back of one. To my dismay the bull got up immediately and started to run, leaping over the hedge, with me clinging desperately to its horns. Away along the village lane it ran until we reached the clocktower, where my sister Kitty's horrified eyes watched her unpredictable young imp of a sister being rescued and scolded by a policeman who happened to be there.

Later we moved to the suburbs of Birmingham. My father remained in France, visiting us between speaking engagements. Therefore our home in England mainly consisted of my two half sisters, Marjorie and Katherine (Kitty) Cope and Mother. We were a fun-loving family with a simple recognition of the Lord's presence all the time. Mother's connection with some of the spiritual giants of our day often brought them into our

home for meals. Many are the spiritual truths a child unconsciously imbibes by quietly drinking in godly conversations!

My favorite guest was Dr. F. B. Meyer. As we met him at the
station, I heard him ask, "What news have you had from
Heaven today?" When he died I felt I had lost a close relative. I
wrote the following in a book of memories:

DR. F. B. MEYER AS I KNEW HIM

A rather fragile looking man, with a very fresh com-
plexion, clear blue eyes, a face wrinkled like a russet
apple. His expression was that of a gentle radiancy. You
felt that you had come into contact with a man who lived
with God, and who was a friend of God. His voice was
quiet, yet it reached into every part of the large hall or
chapel. While he spoke, there came a sense of stillness,
and we seemed to hear the strong, virile voice of God
which reached to the deepest part of one's being.

When we lived near Birmingham, I was sent to boarding
school, which was good for social contacts with children of
my own age. This was still during World War I.

Although I knew the Bible from many church meetings and
could have told someone else how to be saved, I had no
personal assurance of salvation. Moreover, I believed that I
was a scamp and that everyone around me was good. I was
always afraid of being left behind when the Lord came and
believers were raptured, especially when it thundered.

My sister Kitty and I at one time shared the same room. I'll
never forget once waking up in the middle of the night. She
wasn't there. The house was absolutely quiet. In panic I said to
myself, "There! It's happened. The Lord has come, taken my
beloved family, and I will have to make out alone during
seven years of tribulation!" The family at that time believed in
a "pre-tribulation rapture," and I suffered under a guilty
conscience.

My upbringing was lovingly strict. Sunday was a day kept

apart for the Lord. In that age Christians did not attend shows or dances, although we would attend Shakespearean plays and others of similar standard, as well as many musical recitals and symphonies. My sister Marjorie majored in music, studying under Dame Myra Hess. I went to sleep every night to the replaying of Beethoven, Brahms, Schumann, and Bach. Classical music became one of my best loved treasures.

At one of my schools there was a mathematics teacher who was a good friend of my mother's. Somehow the word reached her that I had been selected to play the part of Orlando in Shakespeare's "As You Like It." She reported it to my mother, who was already concerned over my great love of drama. This resulted in my being told that I must not accept the part. For a long time I could not forgive "Jacko bird" (so named because she "hatches things") for her interference. However, I realized later the overruling of God, for it stopped my life going in a direction opposite of His purpose.

Books were also an integral part of daily life. Before I could read, Kitty read to me every day such books as Mark Twain's *The Prince and The Pauper*, Kipling's *Jungle Book*, and A. A. Milne's *Winnie the Pooh*. As a result, from the time I could read, I was never without a book. Robert Louis Stevenson, Dickens, Sir Walter Scott, Jack London, Victor Hugo, Alexander Dumas, and many others were absorbed before I was twelve. Later I became fascinated with John Ruskin and Thomas Carlyle, and later still, C. S. Lewis. (It is interesting that many psychologists declare that if one reads aloud to a child in the early years, it is almost an inevitable result that as he grows older he will become a reader.)

One day at school I was introduced by my peers to an undesirable magazine called "Peg's Papers." I hid it under my mattress and devoured it in order to be "in" with the gang. I was delighted with my secret hoard. But, alas, my sister Kitty discovered it. At that time we were studying Tennyson at school. I was enraptured with "The Lady of Shalott." I returned home and said, "Kitty, have you ever heard of anything so beautiful as:

Lying robed in snowy white
That loosely flew from left to right
The leaves upon her falling light
A gleaming shape she floated by
To many towered Camelot.

Kitty replied, "Let me tell you something. If you continue to read trash like 'Peg's Papers,' you will lose all your love for beauty in literature and lose one of God's great gifts of joy." This scared me so that never again was I able to indulge in reading trashy magazines or really empty books, although now I do read "non-religious" books for a "change of pace."

I have already stated that although I presumed I was a Christian and probably made several "decisions" due to a Christian environment, I had no deep assurance of personal salvation nor was I truly committed to God. One reason was that in comparison with people I knew who were so good, I felt utterly unworthy. Another reason was that there were sins in my life which required honest confession.

A key transaction with God came when my family was away and I stayed in a friend's home. God was strongly convicting me of the sin which had to be confessed to the family. The root probably could be traced to a desire for popularity with my peers. I knelt and searched in my Bible for all the salvation texts I knew. These I "claimed," but without any intention of putting right the conspicuous sin which required confession. I remember the date still. I remember climbing into bed saying to myself, "There, I'm now saved on the grounds of John 3:16."

However, God is not mocked. I was not obeying Him as Lord, nor was there any true repentance or definite turning around of my entire life to Him. This was most dangerous. I was deceiving myself. Therefore, in spite of all the texts I claimed, I had no assurance of belonging to Jesus Christ the Savior.

Little did I know then that within months I would be in

France, deep in the study of philosophies, and that faith in the Bible and the Lord Jesus would be "taken away," leaving only an agnostic outlook and pity for my family who believed "biblical myths."

THREE

EDUCATION LEADING TO AGNOSTICISM IN FRANCE

Take heed therefore how you hear: for whosoever hath, to him shall be given; and whosoever hath not, from him shall be taken even that which he seemeth to have [Luke 8:18].

Although because of the pressure of my father's ministry in France he was not able to come home to England often, he always hoped that when I was grown I would live with him and share his ministry as a Christian worker in France. In my late teens he decided that I should leave England for Paris to "finish" my education there and become completely bilingual.

Before making this decision, he had met and had offered spiritual help to a remarkable woman by the name of Mademoiselle Mercedes Heldwein. She had a most unusual background. Her father was one of the engineers of the Trans-Siberian Railway, then in the making. Her mother had been a lady-in-waiting to the Queen of Spain. She herself had done graduate work and had degrees from three universities: Berlin, Madrid, and the Sorbonne in Paris. She was a brilliant woman who had also edited a French journal for a period of time.

However, she had a sad history. She had had a disastrous love affair in Berlin, and it continued to haunt her. One day in Paris she decided to commit suicide. She threw herself into the Seine. But her fur coat kept her unwillingly afloat. A Salvation Army officer pulled her from the water and took her to a training home. Such was her ignorance of Christ that when she was present at a small Salvation Army Workers meeting in which they prayed, she looked around to see to whom they were speaking! She had never been exposed to any relationship with God.

When my father talked to her about spiritual matters, he realized her need for new work, and suddenly conceived the idea that she might be willing to act as tutor and chaperone for his only daughter Audrey. At the same time she would be able to forward his large correspondence. Hopefully some of Mademoiselle's brilliance would rub off onto his daughter! In any case, she would become completely bilingual.

I remember arriving at the Paris station to be met by my delighted father. He had brought Mademoiselle with him to meet me. I saw a beautiful, slim, and very cultured-looking lady.

Soon after we arrived at the home he had rented for us, Father left again to travel in his strenuous ministry. Mademoiselle and I were alone to get to know each other. I admired her brilliance and unusual education, and longed to feel accepted by her. However, although she wrote Latin and many other languages with unusual expertise, she spoke little English, and I only had a smattering of French at that time.

She quickly organized an educational program and engaged extra tutors and classes for me. She was very conscientious in making me *work*, probably for the first time in my life! My family had spoiled the youngest daughter, and although Mother said that "sunshine went out of the house" when I left home, I know that through that front door many problems went out too.

My key interests in England were reading, music, and sports. I would play tennis for days at a time during vacations, and gloried in being on the school team of English "net ball." Also, I had a profound love of beauty in nature, but study and

34

success were not very important to me. It meant too much *work*.

Mademoiselle insisted on high standards of study and discipline. I was never allowed to sit in an easy chair, and all letters to home were read by her. Mademoiselle had no time for sports, and was not very musical. Indeed, after I had studied under a classical musical teacher for a short time, Mademoiselle told my father that she could not stand my practicing. I was therefore forced to give up a major delight until I returned to England.

She took me to visit her non-Christian family, all of whom were very sophisticated; one was a well-known actress in Italy. She also knew key men and women in Paris social circles such as the director of the Mercedes car manufacturing company, professors from universities, and journalists from France, Czechoslovakia, Germany, Spain, and even Japan.

She was often invited to become a part of French intellectual salons. There would be from thirty to fifty intellectuals at these salons, who discussed many areas of life: politics, art, literature, and world affairs on broad terms. Mademoiselle was perfectly at home with them, and they looked up to her. She had once said to me shortly after I arrived in France, "If you have anything intelligent to say [in French!] speak up. If not, it's best to keep silent."

I was accepted at these salons as her "silent" shadow. I bravely tried to eat the snails presented to me as hors d'oeuvres, not to speak of raw oysters in their shells, under her watchful eye. Once the waiter offered to me a plate of what looked to an English person like a special bean. (I had never before seen green olives.) I took a large helping of them. After I had eaten one, I knew I could not eat any more. What was I to do? I surreptitiously slid them into my handkerchief while Mademoiselle was turned the other way. Later, absorbed in the general conversation, I absentmindedly pulled out my handkerchief before the assembled company. Suddenly all the green olives tumbled out on the floor. That was it! I flushed until I was as red as a beet and almost in tears. I will never forget how a dear Japanese university professor said to the guests, "I think Mademoiselle Johnson is feeling faint. Mademoiselle, won't you let me take you outside to fresh air." ("Faint" with a crimson face!) Bless him, he saved the evening for me with his kindness. For once Mademoiselle Heldwein made no comment over my *gauche* behavior.

At the many salons to which I was invited I listened to all the conversations eagerly, for it opened my eyes to the sophisticated secular world around me of which I had not previously much experience.

At the same time, my studies were concentrated on history and philosophy and psychology, reading books of Fredrich Wilhelm Nietzsche, who set forth such ideas as "Two great European narcotics are alcohol and Christianity" and "I call Christianity the one great curse." He was greatly sought after in his day but died a madman. I also studied the writings of the romantic humanist, Jean Jacques Rousseau, and Hegel and Coue, together with such a true *savant* as Blaise Pascal. I studied Buddhism, Confucianism, and ancient Greek philosophers. Who could help but enjoy the wit of Voltaire, but this only involved a great danger of being open to some of his philosophies. It was Voltaire who prophesied that some day Bibles would no longer be widely read, yet in God's providence Voltaire's own house in Paris was later used for group distribution of Bibles after his death.

All my studies were on a secular level. Slowly, unknown to anyone except myself, I began to discover that I no longer believed in the bodily resurrection of Jesus, nor in His virgin birth. As for the impossible stories of "Jonah and the Whale," "Elijah and Elisha," and "Adam and Eve"—surely these were just legends or myths. My dear parents of a previous era simply believed in myths. I never spoke to my father about this change. He would have been horribly angry.

I have many beautiful memories of France. I recall drinking coffee and eating croissants by the ocean early in the morning on the shores of Brittany with Mademoiselle and an English young man, watching the great white waves which looked like sea horses and then plunging into them with delight. I'll never forget one day which we spent in one of the beautiful forests near Paris. I was happy to roam on my own, while Mademoiselle and her friend, Mr. Ralph Banning, were sitting on a log of a tree, talking. I came across a carpet of yellow primroses and wild lilies of the valley under beech trees clad in their spring leaves and felt as never before how much I belonged to this beautiful earth.

Then there were historic trips to the Louvre, Tomb of Napoleon, Les Tuillieries, La Conciergerie, the Palace of Versailles, Montmarte, and Notre Dame. I would sing the French National Anthem with other students with as much fervor as if I had been French!

Once I might have been rescued from my deepening unbelief. This was when Father took Mademoiselle and myself to Switzerland to the home of Mr. and Mrs. Hugh Alexander, founder of a Bible school in Geneva, who begged Father to let me continue my education in Switzerland with them, which I would have loved. However, Mademoiselle was adamant that we should go back to Paris. Father did not know at that time that she had a young man in Paris and needed me with her until her situation was settled.

Suddenly that time came. Almost without warning, Mademoiselle told Father she was engaged to marry Mr. Banning and therefore needed to leave for Bournemouth in England immediately, where he lived. This meant that Father needed to send me back home to England also, to be with my mother.

It is an interesting fact that after only a few months in France, I felt compelled to write a confession of the particular sin (of which I wrote in the previous chapter) in a letter to my family in England. However, at this period, the confession was a matter of personal integrity. It did not result in any attempt to enter into a real relationship with God.

To *knowingly* refuse to obey God when He speaks to you as

He did to me in England is a serious matter. It invariably has dangerous consequences. My attitude of agnosticism resulted in months of desperation in England as I considered the meaninglessness of life lived without any philosophy in which I could believe.

F O U R
CHANGES IN A
YOUNG ENGLISH WOMAN

And that from a child thou hast known the holy scriptures,
which are able to make thee wise unto salvation through faith
which is in Christ Jesus [II Timothy 3:15].

When I returned to England, I found that many things had
changed. My sister Kitty had married a Jewish man who had
been led to Christ by a Jewish Christian, a former rabbi.

I also had changed. Indeed, my mother hardly recognized
the rather silent and reserved girl who returned from Mademoiselle's disciplined life. Mademoiselle, for reasons unknown to
me, had never encouraged any personal relationships with my
peers. No friends were ever invited to our home, and I was not
allowed to visit any home of students with whom I studied.

Mademoiselle had instilled in me a passion for study, and at
that time I wrote essays in French far more easily than in
English. Sometimes when speaking to my mother, she would
interrupt me after a few minutes, saying, "My dear, do you
realize you are talking to me in French, not English?"

During that time I tried to hide from Mother the greatest
change in me, one far greater than the continental sophistica-
tion that had been instilled in me while in Paris and greater
even than my propensity to speak French. I dearly loved my

mother and knew that my unbelief would have brought her great grief. Even so, Mother had profound gifts of insight, and I am sure she prayed earnestly for me in those days.

I refused all speaking engagements expected from a grown woman of our family. I could not bear any sermon which mentioned "the blood of Jesus" and was willing to attend churches only of the most liberal persuasion.

My father believed that most women were unbusinesslike. He also expected and wanted me to marry. Since I had had so much liberal arts education, he insisted that I take a complete course at a good business college. This I did. It was very much against the grain of my temperament, but I graduated quite well.

Largely because of influence I was later offered a very interesting position as registrar at a public high school where I was included as a member of the faculty. I was closely associated with the headmistress and enjoyed the work, even the bicycle trip to and from home which took one hour each night and morning.

It was not difficult to renew old friendships. However, no one knew that I was living an inner life of quiet despair. While I was in France, the heavy study left no leisure for thought or emotional introspection. However, in England, I had time to recognize that when I gave up belief in the Lord Jesus Christ and the Bible, I had no philosophy to fill the vacuum that remained. Life was utterly without meaning. What did it matter how one lived if one is "snuffed out" at the end with no assurance of immortality? What use was it "to live to make a better world" if in any case all humanity could be "snuffed out" at death?

After several months I knew that sooner or later I must share my religious change with my mother. My problem was that if I did not live by Christian philosophy, I must discover which philosophy I believed in.

One night I felt desperate. My emotions were very intense. I can fully identify with young people of today who even commit suicide because of despair over the meaninglessness of life without purpose.

I locked my bedroom door and went over to the window looking at the starry sky. I was "agnostic," not atheistic, because I could not fail to be aware of the mathematical precision of the stellar universe without some vague conviction that surely there must be a Master Mathematician behind it all. I opened the window and said aloud, "God, if there be a God, if You will give me some philosophy that makes reasonable sense to me, I will commit myself to follow it."

Following this, I walked back and forth considering in turn the various philosophies with which I was acquainted. My thoughts were continuously interrupted by a Bible verse which banged at my mind like a hammer knocking in a nail. "Believest thou that I am the Son of God?" Again and again I tried to thrust it out of my mind. "Of course not, I have already settled that question." Yet none of the philosophies made viable sense, and I could not rid myself of that persistent question from the Bible.

Finally I sat down and said to myself, "Why do I not believe that Jesus is the Son of God?" The reply that immediately came to mind was, "Because there is no such thing as a virgin birth." At this point God met me in a mysterious way which I cannot fully explain. I began with the mystery of life. "I know I am alive, but no one has ever satisfactorily traced the beginning of life." Suddenly God's mysterious revelation was given to me. I can only say with Paul, "It pleased God to reveal His Son in me." I could not reason out the mystery of the Incarnation, but God caused me to know this was a fact. I knelt down in tears of joy and worshiped Him as Savior and Lord, with a divine conviction of this truth which could never be broken.

However, this did not mean to me at first that I was obliged to accept the Old Testament literally. Adam and Eve, Jonah and the Whale, Elijah and Elisha, David, Joshua, Moses—could not these persons and events be partly legendary?

How did I come to a reasonable decision? I reasoned within myself, "If Jesus is the Son of God, He will not lie. He knows all wisdom and is Himself Truth. He will not accommodate Himself to the culture of His day in anything that is not true. If He is the Son of God, He may not tell us all the secret things which belong unto the Lord our God (see Deut. 29:29). But what the Lord Jesus Christ taught I am bound to believe."

I believed that the disciples who wrote His words in the four Gospels were His true followers, and that He had promised that His Holy Spirit would bring all things to their remembrance. Therefore the four Gospels were reliable records of His teachings.

I decided to read His words and teaching concerning the Old Testament Scriptures, given in the Gospels of Matthew and John; I read both of these Gospels completely that night. I discovered that our Lord made explicit statements concerning the inerrancy of the Old Testament Scriptures ("the Scripture cannot be broken"—John 10:35) and also spoke of Old Testament persons and events as really happening in history. Jesus did not believe them to be legends! I studied these New Testament passages carefully:

> Adam and Eve, Matt. 19:4, 5 (implied)
> Noah and the Flood, Matt. 24:37–39
> Abraham, John 8:39, 56–58
> Isaac and Jacob, Matt. 22:32
> David and the Shewbread, Matt. 12:4, 5
> Solomon, Matt. 12:42
> Jonah and the Whale, Matt. 12:40, 41
> Isaiah, Matt. 15:7, 8

However, knowing my temperament, I knew that my initial enthusiasm for reading the Bible could quickly wane. I might stay up late a few nights, get up early a few days, but I would not be able to keep it up. Yet I believed that somehow this was important to my life and my faith. What discipline could I adopt to make myself get up early every morning continually until it became a new habit of life?

I decided on a correspondence course of Bible study. It would cost me hard-earned money, but that would compel me to follow through, answer the questions, and send them in. And then I would learn from the correct answers sent back.

Eventually, I took five correspondence courses, all of them difficult, from well-known Bible scholars. I dragged myself out of bed in the morning (with strong tea to wake me up) until God changed my sleeping habits. (Later my metabolism was changed so that early morning became my prime time.)

I studied with three key questions in mind: (1) What does this Bible passage say? (2) What did it mean to the people of the day when it was written? and (3) What does it mean to me?

Following this, I would kneel to Christ Jesus as Savior and Lord, yearning to know Him through my study of "all the counsel of God" (Acts 20:27). I might have said, "Here I stand, so help me God. I can do no other," as Luther said in totally different circumstances. However, I could not have conceived at that time that life with the Lord would be so *joyous*. I knew it would be *right*; I knew it would be *safe*; I knew He would be *faithful*. His grace was sufficient for all sense of inferiority and any other lack, but I never realized how *joyous* it would be.

I love the last chapter of C. S. Lewis's autobiography where he says he came to Christ because it was the only thing he could do. It was reasonable, and it was right, and commitment was his bounden duty. Following this, Lewis said, "But I never expected to experience the joy that has come with commitment."

FIVE

COMMITMENT TO GOD'S WORD AND SERVICE

Brethren, I count not myself to have apprehended: but this one thing I do, forgetting those things which are behind, and reaching forth unto those things which are before, I press toward the mark for the prize of the high calling of God in Christ Jesus [Philippians 3:13, 14].

As I look back upon past events, I can see how the hand of God has worked in my life. I am astounded at what the Holy Spirit has taught me through the ordinary occurrences of each day. Five truths, particularly, have been taught me at various times, and they constitute what I call God's Path of Life.

The five truths are:

1. The authority of the Scriptures
2. The power at the Cross of death to self
3. The fullness of the Holy Spirit
4. The sufficiency of God's love
5. The abundance of God's grace

One doesn't just learn these things once for all. I had to be re-educated again and again, each time on deeper levels. And these truths didn't come all at the same time. At different times of my life, sometimes during a particular crisis or event, God would see fit to open my eyes to another aspect of His glory.

That first truth was the key element in my conversion. God gave me confidence in the authority of the holy Scripture; I came to know I could trust the Bible to be the true revelation of God Himself.

This was the first of those five special truths God would teach me throughout my life, although of course I didn't know at the time that's what it was. To me, it was simply an assurance that since God loved and cared for *real* human beings in history, He could love and care for me too.

I did not share my conversion experience with my mother nor anyone else for many years. I was now a committed Christian, and I feared that the news of my former agnosticism would grieve her. It would also perplex friends who knew about the family's godly upbringing.

Still, I knew that my commitment to Christ needed to be openly confessed. I immediately accepted an invitation to speak to a young people's group. Since I wanted to avoid telling my "testimony," especially the parts about France, I decided to speak on a text. I thought it would be easy, but I finished with embarrassment in less than five minutes, recognizing too late that speaking for God needed careful preparation.

After several other more successful speaking experiences and after considerable personal time spent studying the Bible, God presented me with a choice between two types of Christian work. One was to teach an "up and outers" class (which met in the drawing rooms of wealthy homes), and the other was a "down and outers" class, which was to be held in the worst slum area of Birmingham—Floodgate Street. The police would patrol it only in pairs. (Eventually a famous writer, H. V. Morton, wrote on its disgrace to England; it has since been completely renovated.) This was the class God led me to take. It consisted of factory girls, extremely poor, who only knew the word "Jesus" as a swear word. I was warned that they were a rough crowd and that it would be very difficult to gain their confidence.

I began by getting them to tell me something about themselves, and included suitable things about myself. After this I told them what the Lord Jesus meant to me, and could mean to them if we could cosily (!) just talk together, read a few Bible verses, and sing. Knowing they would not want to pray aloud, I closed with a simple prayer. The class took hold. Little by little they brought their friends. Since it was after 11:00 P.M. before I could return home, Mother was often anxious. However, after class we would walk the street, ten in a row, arm in arm, singing as we went.

The ring leader of the crowd was a girl called Gladys. One night I said to them, "You cannot use your tongue to speak of Jesus or pray to Him and use it also as a swear word, or use it in unclean jokes." I tried to get them to have a morning prayer time and reading of the Bible. I was in blissful ignorance at that time of the real circumstances in which they lived.

I'll never forget Gladys saying, "Hey, Miss, we sleep twelve in our bed! I got out early and tried to kneel, and me brothers threw their boots at me, so I can't do it!" There were echoes of agreement around. (I realized I should try to visit their living quarters to understand them.) Meanwhile I replied, "Gladys, God created you to love you and for you to get to know Him by reading about Him. I know He wants you to do this sometime in your day. As to how or when, you ask Him, and He will help you find a place and time."

I will never forget her answer the following week. She sidled up to me and said, "Oh, Miss! God did it. I found an open church at lunch time, and went in there. And Miss, He told me to give you these." She thrust into my hand a bunch of shocking pornographic cards. Gladys was extremely popular in her factory, partly because at lunch time she produced different cards, which provoked lewd jokes and stories appropriate to the salacious subjects of the cards.

I took them from her with a sense of awe. The cards were pornographic, but I was touching something sacred. I knew that Gladys was giving up one of her main causes of pleasure, namely her popularity and leadership with the factory girls. She chose instead to read the Bible and pray in a church during lunch time. The cards might be unclean and pornographic, but God knew that she was exchanging her "treasure" for His treasures. Christ Himself was now the treasure where her heart was (Matt. 6:21).

By this time Mother and I were living alone, and she had let the lower part of her house to a young couple, while we lived in our roomy upstairs. One night the front doorbell rang at 3:00 A.M. I rushed down with an instinctive premonition. Yes! It was Gladys. She said she couldn't go on. She wanted to commit suicide; her home situation was terrible and brutal. Could God help her? Of course I brought her indoors, and upstairs I comforted her. Later I walked back to the streetcar with her. Next morning our lower house tenants were furious. How could Miss Johnson consort with such persons? They said, "Why, we'll all be murdered in our beds one night!" (Gladys ultimately triumphed and eventually married a good man.)

Never have I loved a class so much as this first one. My life had been very sheltered. Therefore I was shocked when visiting the girls' homes to find that the furniture consisted almost entirely of wooden crates for tables and chairs, and mattresses on the floor. On discovering that strong drink was responsible for both the poverty and brutality, I began to wonder whether one should continue casual drinking of wine (learned in France) and support such a dehumanizing traffic.

A Miss Frances Brook was at that time a conference leader, and she exercised a considerable influence on my life. She wrote a moving book of poems called "My Home is God" and a hymn (well-known to Bible Study Fellowship leaders)— "My Goal is God."

I had just attended one of her conferences in Llandudno, Wales, where the theme was the power of the Holy Spirit. Traveling back from the conference by train, very much desiring the fullness of the Holy Spirit, I started to read Miss

Brook's book. It spoke of the glorious life lived in the fullness of the Holy Spirit. I had seen this in others, and as I read, thought, "This is just what I want." However, the book continued, "But if you would have the fullness of the Spirit, you must yield to a deep working of the Cross."

Paul writes in Galatians 2:20, "I have been crucified with Christ; nevertheless I live, yet not I, but Christ liveth in me." Romans 6:5 states, "If we have been united with Him in His death, we will certainly also be united with Him in His resurrection" (NIV). I can see myself today in that train, riding home from the conference. I shut the book by Miss Brook and said, "Oh! That's morbid!" As a young woman, I had been exposed to a great emphasis of teaching about the Cross and death to self in the religious circles where I moved, and I wanted none of it.

However, in the mercy of God, Good Friday was approaching. When I arrived home, Mother had news that a member of the "Officers Christian Union," an intelligence officer, Captain Alan Cooper, was to hold an all-day conference at a nearby Baptist church. That was more than fifty years ago, yet the message left such an impression on my soul that I can remember all the points and most of the illustrations of his three sermons that day. They were given in the power of the Holy Spirit, and God stamped them indelibly upon my soul. Captain Cooper never knew it, and has long since gone to Heaven.

The text was John 12:24 ("Verily, verily, I say unto you, except a corn of wheat fall into the ground and die, it abideth alone: but if it die, it bringeth forth much fruit").

I know that the "grain of wheat" is the Lord Jesus Himself. He chose to do His Father's will at Gethsemane (although He prayed, "If thou be willing, remove this cup from me: nevertheless not my will, but thine, be done"—Luke 22:42). The Cross of punishment for my sin was torture to "the grain of wheat" who died. But the result was His resurrection and the redemption of a new humanity. Our Lord Jesus links His servant to Himself, for John 12:26 declares that "If any man

49

serve me, let him follow me." I have been enabled to receive the indwelling Christ through the Holy Spirit into my cleansed heart because the Lord Jesus became that "grain of wheat" which fell into the ground and died. This "grain of wheat" (the Lord Jesus within the heart) urges the believer to be identified with Him in death to self-will. Self-will is that old nature which refuses God's will when it opposes my own. But "*if it dies*" (i.e., if I choose to apply the power of Christ's death to my self-nature), Christ through the Holy Spirit will empower me to bring forth fruit in the lives of others. We need to remember that the "power" of Christ's Cross gives us the power to be willing to die to self.

I thought of a grain of wheat. Within its covering of chaff is the "kernel" (life). We all know that when any grain of wheat falls into the earth, a secret work of nature takes place. Hidden forces (in the earth) work upon its shell (the outer chaff) until it is "broken." After this, nothing can hinder the kernel from springing up into "first the blade, then the ear, then the full corn in the ear." A single kernel of wheat has the potential to cover fields and fields of wheat only *if* it falls into the ground and dies. Otherwise it remains still one grain of wheat, but *alone*.

I came to recognize that this denial of self—taking up the Cross or choosing to be identified with Christ in His death (which leads to identification with the power of His resurrection)—is far more stressed in the Gospels than believers of today realize.

Before the second World War, there was a grave in Germany sealed with a granite slab and bound with strong chains. On it an atheist had inscribed, "Not to be opened throughout eternity." Yet somehow a little acorn had fallen into some crack, and its outer shell "died." Years after, everyone saw a huge oak tree which had completely broken up the slab, still having the inscribed arrogant words. The new life of the acorn had openly displayed the power of life.

This call to the believer to be united in Christ's death in order that one might also experience the resurrection life is

reiterated in II Corinthians 4:10, 12: "Always bearing about
in the body the dying of the Lord Jesus, that the life also of
Jesus might be made manifest in our body [body means in
real life on earth]. . . . So then death worketh in us, but life in
you."

This death to the self-life could be illustrated by a "pressed"
or "squeezed" sponge, which when squeezed by pressure
pours out the water of life upon others.

Actually, this lesson of crucifixion and resurrection with
Christ has to be learned again and again. I have found that the
use of a chart helps me to remember it and make it a working
part of my spiritual life.

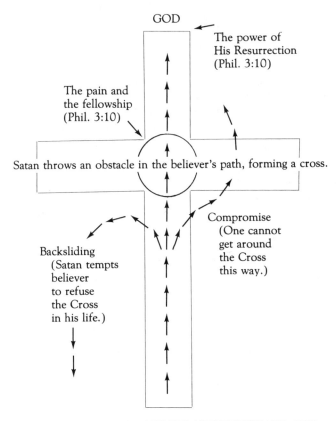

GOD

The power of
His Resurrection
(Phil. 3:10)

The pain and
the fellowship
(Phil. 3:10)

Satan throws an obstacle in the believer's path, forming a cross.

Compromise
(One cannot
get around
the Cross
this way.)

Backsliding
(Satan tempts
believer
to refuse
the Cross
in his life.)

THE BELIEVER'S WILL SET STRAIGHT TOWARD GOD

51

It becomes clearer in the illustration. God's will is a direct path from the believer to God. Satan, who knows just where self-will is strongest or most sensitive, places some obstacle across the direct path to God, thus forming a cross.

The believer comes to the obstacle and sees that to cross it will hurt. Some believers say, "Oh, I can't manage this," and they turn back. That is *backsliding*. Others say, "There has got to be a way around this." That is *compromise*. One never does get around the pain of the Cross if one wishes to experience Christ's resurrection power.

At the end of the conference on that Good Friday, Captain Cooper said to his audience (a group of about 400), "Are there any of you who are willing to commit yourselves to identification with Christ in His death by prayer aloud? Are you willing to say, for example, 'Lord, I am willing at whatever cost, for Thy death to be worked out in me, in order that Thy resurrection life may also be manifested?'"

Being a very reserved young Englishwoman at that time, I was not apt to make public decisions or lift up my voice in a large audience, especially a religious meeting. My religious upbringing had been in the Anglican Church denomination. However, the Holy Spirit's pressure was so strong that I prayed aloud the prayer and commitment suggested.

Right there and then, I realized there were changes needed in my lifestyle—some things had to go. There was something I had to do which would represent a "death to self" in my life. After this I began to experience the promise of John 12:24.

I began preparing for the misson field, thinking it was to be Africa. I took a course in nursing. I shall always remember the night—several years after the experience of that Good Friday— I went into the room in the nurse's dormitory where I stayed. There were six other girls in the room with me. They were very, very worldly, "hard-nosed" and tough. I listened to their talk, their swearing, and the room was blue with smoke. I said to myself, "Prayers in bed tonight," and heard my own promise to God, "Lord, I am willing at whatever cost that Thy death be worked out in me. . . ." So I knelt down. Immediately there was a dead silence, then suppressed giggles. You can imagine that actually I said my *real* prayers in bed! However, the following week, as I was walking along the corridor, one of those seemingly hard, tough girls said to me, "Johnny [they used to call me Johnny], tell me about your religion. I want it!''

You see? The fruit was borne by the seed that first had to die!

S I X

PREPARING FOR
A MISSION FIELD

*Now the Lord had said unto Abram, Get thee out of thy
country, and from thy kindred, and from thy father's house,
unto a land that I will shew thee* [Genesis 12:1].

I asked God what he wanted me to do. He seemed to thrust
the question right back at me: "What would you above
all things like to do?" I replied, "I love Your Word above all
things. I would love to spend my life teaching others to find
what I have found."

I was deeply interested in the Sudan in Africa, not without
personal motives, for I had been dating a young man who was
fascinated by that region. Had I gone to Africa, I would
undoubtedly have been married.

This was why I took up nursing, realizing the particular
necessity for medical work. I loved this life and the babies,
mothers, and fellow students. Once, in the hospital, I decided
to pay back some scores on my confreres. While I was on
night duty, I went around to all dormitories at about 2:00 A.M.
calling everyone down to the Labor Room. Sleepy students
asked, "Johnny, what's going on?" "Triplets," I replied.

Half asleep, they emerged to find outside the Labor Room a
basket of three kittens just born. Needless to say there was a

sequel. Next day as I was trying to sleep, an alarm clock went off after an hour. I looked everywhere for it to turn it off; it was under the bed! I had just gotten back to sleep when another alarm went off—at the bottom of the wardrobe. It went on and on. I believe there were ten different alarm clocks in all. I was duly punished!

I graduated with a C.M.B. degree which allowed qualified nurses to deliver babies on their own (without a doctor's help, except in abnormal cases). This meant undertaking for the period of pregnancy as well as the actual delivery in the home of the patient.

Later I became responsible for a large district in Bracknell, Berkshire. Within two years I had delivered over 600 babies on my own without anesthetics. God helped me in that I managed to avoid any tear (which called for a physician to stitch the torn area). I thank God that I never lost a baby. There were several breech cases and many twins. This was challenging, but of course in hospital training I had already witnessed and helped to deliver over a thousand cases.

Most of the babies were born at night. I used to boast that whenever a husband knocked at my door, I would be with him within four minutes! (Perhaps that is why I have suffered from insomnia ever since that period.)

Although I never used this training after going to the mission field, I am grateful for it. I believe this close contact with individuals was God's gift for understanding people. It helped in knowing how to present the Word of God to differing temperaments and personalities.

Bracknell was an exquisitely beautiful place, with woods covered with bluebells in spring. Only the English know how unspeakably lovely is a wood carpeted with wild hyacinths (called bluebells), especially their fragrant scent. I always stopped to listen to the nightingales sing at night as I was returning home.

I had dear friends in Bracknell. There was one married couple; the husband and I would argue theological points for hours on end. Since he knew more than I knew, but let me discover the truth in argument, I owe much to him concerning conservative theology.

I was teaching a small class, absorbed in Andrew Murray's books, when the same longing for the "fullness of the Holy Spirit" engrossed my thinking once again. Andrew Murray did not "speak in tongues," but he greatly emphasized what he called the baptism of the Holy Spirit, a deeper experience than that of original conversion, when one is indwelt and sealed by the Holy Spirit (see Eph. 1:13).

I longed to be the best God wanted me to be. I was headed for the mission field (I thought Africa) and longed for a deep experience of the *fullness* of the Holy Spirit. My friend, Phyllis Webster, and I prayed together often about this. She went to India after I had left for China, and she died there. It is wonderful to have a friend of your own sex with whom you can pray freely. She was a real prayer partner for me.

One day as I was thinking about this question while walking along the main street of Bracknell, an older friend, Mrs. Sandwith, happened to meet me. She was quite wealthy, and with her husband occupied a lovely home on a large estate, so large that they had built a Pentecostal chapel on it. I did not attend their chapel (I was not interested in "tongues"), but we were good friends and often enjoyed informal friendship at meals and in the evenings.

As we met, to my surprise Mrs. Sandwith said, "Audrey, God seems to have told me that you are seeking after something you do not have. You are really hungering for a fresh touch from God." I was startled, for no one except Phyllis knew my longings and how much the subject of the fullness of the Holy Spirit was filling my thoughts. I looked at her with big eyes but said nothing. She went on, "We have a marvelous man from America staying with us, Mr. W——. To have him in our home is like having an angel. He lays hands upon people; they speak in tongues, and he heals the sick. All the time he talks about the baptism of the Holy Spirit. Would you be interested in coming to talk with him early in the morning before church in our drawing room?" We made the appointment.

When I went home and talked to my friend, Phyllis Webster, I said, "Phyllis, I want you to pray for me. I'm going out into the woods early in the morning to pray too. Please don't pray that I will, or will not, speak in tongues. Just pray that I will know if God wants this for me, because I want God's full purpose." I knew that because of the Christian circles in which I moved and my family background, there might be criticism. However, I told myself, "If this is the way God wants me to take, and it means the loss of friends and misunderstandings, that is part of the Cross."

This was a period in Christian history (particularly since 1906 and the Welsh Revival), when what was known as the "Pentecostal Movement" was taking root in England and all over the world. Many Christian leaders questioned the experiences and perceived fallacies which they believed would lead to error. Therefore, my thinking had been influenced somewhat against the movement. However, at this point, I began to wonder if I was "missing something" and felt the need to investigate further.

The next morning at about 6:00 A.M. I went out into Bracknell woods. The lovely pale yellow primroses made a carpet of delight. I prayed from 6:00 A.M. to 8:30 A.M. when my appointment was due. I searched the Scriptures, saying, "Lord, I am hungry at any cost for You. If this is of *You* and *Your purpose* for me, I'll go through with it, but please make sure I am in Your will." Meanwhile, Phyllis prayed for me for a solid hour. It is not easy to pray for one person and one subject for a solid hour, and I attribute a lot to that persistent prayer.

I met Mr. W—— in the Sandwith's drawing room. It was a very large room with a huge fireplace, and armchairs on opposite sides. I sat in one, Mr. W—— in the other, and we started talking. To find a point of contact, we spoke of persons of whom we both knew—C. T. Studd, Mrs. Penn-

Lewis, Dr. F. B. Meyer, and of Andrew Murray and Dr. Campbell Morgan. Except for Mr. Murray, these were persons I knew personally and of whom he had heard. Then Mr. W—— replied, "Yes, they are wonderful people. The Holy Spirit is very much *with* them to influence them, but *not in* them." I said, "Wait a minute. They must have the Holy Spirit if they are Christians." He replied, "Oh, Sister, *with* them, but not *in* them. They do not have the baptism of the Holy Spirit." Well, this greatly disturbed me. I said, "But I have the Holy Spirit in me." He answered, "Sister, *with* you, but not *in* you." I asked, "What about Romans 8:9, 'If any man have not the Spirit of Christ, he is none of His'?" His answer was, "Oh, but Sister, you cannot understand the Epistles written after Pentecost until you have had the experience of the baptism of the Holy Spirit."

By this time I was really confused! I only knew the Word of God for doctrine, and knew that I had received Christ through the indwelling Holy Spirit. Mr. W—— then said, "Sister, you are too preoccupied with doctrine. You will have to let go of it. You are too proud, Sister...." But I thought, "I have nothing else for my spiritual foundation than the doctrinal statements of Scripture."

He realized we were getting nowhere, and I was deeply puzzled and shaken. He said, "Would you be willing to pray with me?" I replied, "Oh, certainly. I am delighted to pray with you."

It was a very large drawing room. He sat in one armchair about 20 feet away from me. I sat in the other. I bent my head and closed my eyes to pray. The next thing I knew, he had silently, without warning, walked across to my chair. Suddenly his two hands were on my head. There was no request, no preparation—everything was totally unexpected and in total silence. I was startled, but at the same time felt what can only be described as a physical "tingling" which began at my head and went right through the rest of my body. At the same time I had an almost overpowering emotional craving at the core of my personality to let myself go, to *take it*. All of me wanted to yield to this strange "tingling power." I sent up an arrow prayer to God. "Lord, if this is of You, I yield. If not, I claim the precious blood of Christ to cover me. Help me!" Immediately it was gone—just like that! I had my answer, and a profound peace filled my being. I knew that Mr. W—— was surprised, for he had felt the impact in his hands. We said goodbye and I left. I had my answer, and it was final.

I trust the reader will not misunderstand me. I believe Mr. W—— was a saved man. I believe in healing in answer to prayer. I believe that many persons have been saved through the charismatic movement. And I believe in the fire of Pentecost. But, remember, wherever there is true fire, Satan is apt to introduce a counterfeit fire. The Christian must be wary of the dangers of a psychic, psychological release that is misunderstood as baptism of the Holy Spirit.

Could it be that Mr. W—— became deceived, perhaps unknowingly, by some counterfeit fire? Could he have been confused in his scriptural doctrine by Satan, whose methods are very subtle?

Later that night I sat in my apartment by the fire reading a book written by Mr. W—— and given to me by Mrs. Sandwith. It included a story of Mr. W——'s experience of raising a presumably dead person. Like Elijah, he had apparently stretched himself seven times upon the body. She revived from "death" and walked downstairs and played beautiful music which filled the house. Suddenly as I read, I felt something evil in the room. *What is the matter?* I wondered. I could not explain it. Suddenly I threw the book into the fire, and immediately the sensation of evil was gone. God's presence comforted me.

SEVEN
GOD'S CALL TO CHINA

*I know thy works: behold I have set before thee an open door,
and no man can shut it; for thou hast a little strength, and has
kept my word, and not denied my name* [Revelation 3:8].

Whenever I went to a particular conference concerning
missionary work in the Sudan in Africa, I could never reach
the assurance from God that this was His place for me. I was in
touch with a fine evangelical mission, and my heart was deeply
involved in it in many ways. Yet every time I paced the
grounds of the conference center the same uneasiness would
return concerning the *place* where God wanted me for my life
work.

I decided to take magazines from different countries of the
world, and concentrate upon knowledgeable prayer for a
different country every day of the week. I had long since read
the complete life story of Hudson Taylor, and more recently a
very interesting autobiography of three women missionaries
who worked in far Urumtsi, the capital of Chinese Turkestan.
The title was *Something Happened*. It is a fascinating, very well-
written book. Miss Mildred Cable was the daughter of an
English judge, converted as a child through the Scripture
Union Mission. Miss Evangeline French, the eldest of the trio,

was educated in France and at one time was connected with the nihilist marxist group in Geneva. Miss Francesca French, her sister, was a quiet author. After conversion, the innovative, exuberant Evangeline was the first out to China before 1900 and nearly lost her life in the Boxer uprising, when thousands of missionaries were killed. Later she was followed by Miss Mildred Cable, and finally her sister Francesca French.

Profoundly impressed with the book, I decided to attend one of their meetings in London. The speaker was Miss Mildred Cable. She spoke of the absolute paganism in China, the danger of the travels, and the glory of seeing God change lives after only *one* hearing of the gospel. I sat enthralled. Deep down in my heart, it seemed God was saying to me, "This is what I have for you. Why do you keep trying to get Me to call you to Africa?"

There were certain commitments which needed to be handled with integrity. I promised God that if these could be handled in His righteousness, I would apply to the China Inland Mission. Apart from these problems, complete joy and assurance filled my soul.

After sending in my application, I was invited to have an interview at the China Inland Mission headquarters in London (now known as the Overseas Missionary Fellowship). I went with some trepidation, having heard that only one in six was accepted. My interviewer was Mr. Roland Hogben, who was in charge of candidates at the C.I.M. Bible Institute. One question he asked was, "Miss Johnson, I see that you do not believe that hell is an *everlasting* punishment." I explained I thought that after a long period hell would be extinguished. He replied, "Do you not know that Matthew 25:46 uses the same Greek word for 'everlasting' in regard to eternal life and everlasting punishment?" This was enough for me. Immediately I accepted his argument.

Later he said, "Miss Johnson, I see that you currently teach Bible classes. Supposing you knew of no changes in lives as a result of your ministry, what would your attitude be?" Impulsively I replied, "No results—no fruit—I'd die!" I felt sure I had blundered and tried to restate it, "Well, perhaps God would not want me to know. It is His work. . . ." Mr. Hogben replied, "Miss Johnson, your first answer was the right one. You go to China to get results, changed lives, new birth. You are satisfied with nothing less." It was a good interview, and I sensed, favorable. I never forgot his admonition.

Incidentally, to give the reader a picture of this man who deeply influenced my life, I heard of one girl who (thinking about furlough) asked, "How long does one stay in China?" Mr. Hogben replied, "Miss, you go to China to die there." Needless to say, this was a mission joke repeated by students to all candidates.

After returning home I received a letter from the C.I.M. stating that my application and interview were entirely satisfactory. They invited me to study at the C. I. M. Bible Institute in preparation for work in China. However, there was a disquieting clause. I had worked very hard in my nursing work in Bracknell and was possibly "under par" when the C.I.M. doctor carried out the physical examination. The letter warned that after completing training, there was a definite possibility that I might be turned down on physical grounds.

This was a real shock to me, for I had felt sure that this was God's direct call. Like Hezekiah (II Kings 19:14), I took the letter and laid it open on the bed. Then I knelt and prayed. "Lord, surely You called me—yet if so, why this letter? Will You not give me now a text from the Bible which I could take as Your confirmation?" Straightway a phrase from the text at the beginning of this chapter came to mind. "I have set before you an open door and no man can shut it." For the moment I could not think of the book from which that text was to be found. I asked God for something I had never asked for before nor since—namely that He would enable me to turn to the text. I took my shut Bible and let it fall open where it would; it fell open at Revelation 3:8. As I looked at the comforting words, "I know thy works," "a little faith," "not denied my name," this was all the confirmation needed.

Years later in 1936 a group of graduates, including myself, were due to sail for China. At that time I was overcome with three situations of tragedy and ill because of the pressure. Again the doctor advised I should not be sent out. But the God who gave me His word overruled in ways which will be explained later.

The China Inland Mission Training Institute was different from seminary or Bible school training in several ways and similar in others.

First, only potential candidates for missionary work in China were accepted. Far more students were in training during the period when I was there than actually went out to the mission field.

Every student knew that he or she would certainly be under observation and appraisal. The emphasis would be on character, reaction to situations, aptitude in language, academic Bible teaching, and good interaction with fellow students and those in authority. Therefore we were always aware that our ultimate status was precarious. It was a common saying among students that we would not know we were really accepted until we were aboard ship and actually sailing out of port for China!

Second, the China Inland Mission established certain goals for the training of candidates:

1. The purpose of training was to deepen a true dedication to God Himself. It also emphasized the habit of private and public prayer.

2. It was important that students should be trained in thoughtfulness toward other persons of differing temperaments and dispositions. In China one could be living in very close quarters with a senior missionary with whom one might not have any natural affinity. Probably there would not be another missionary nearer than 200 miles or more.

3. Students needed to be able to adapt to a sudden change of situation—for example, a crisis of war.

4. Most of all we needed to have a thorough knowledge of

Bible content, as well as the ability to communicate God's revelation in the Bible to Chinese who had never even heard the name of the Lord Jesus Christ.

Consideration for others was instilled by our living conditions. Students slept three to four persons in a room. The rising bell tolled early. The early morning personal devotional time of reading and prayer was important to each person, therefore *noiseless dressing*, and movements considered not disturbing to other roommates were essential. I was one of four in a room. We had little time for conversation as the morning and evening "quiet time" and sleep constituted about the only times we were in our rooms.

But, oh, the joy! There was an attic where boxes and trunks were kept. I discovered it, and as far as I know, no one else but myself went there for the urgent need of having some time alone. I could prostrate myself in an agony of prayer or kneel against a box. As far as the students were concerned, "Audrey, as usual, had disappeared."

I remember once being absolutely overcome by a repeated sin. As I prayed to God, the verse came to mind, "In all afflictions He was afflicted." I replied, "No! Lord, You never knew the *guilt* of sin." He replied, "But what about II Corinthians 5:21? 'He hath made him to be sin for us, who knew no sin.'" I suddenly realized afresh all that my Lord endured emotionally, as He *identified Himself* not only with my sins, but the sins of the world. Therefore He also felt the *guilt* of sin, and enters into what the believer feels when he is guilty before God. This was a great revelation to me.

One of my concerns was in regard to my half sister, Marjorie. Certain similarities of temperament meant that we had an unusual affinity. She was already married with two children; however, she was suffering from a nervous breakdown. We in our family all tried to keep this from Mother, who was too frail to carry any such burden, especially when I was living away from home. I *understood* Marjorie. Indeed, I even prayed that God would transfer her trouble to me (for I felt I was younger and stronger). I greatly feared the pressure of the depression might overwhelm her. However at the beginning, no one in the C.I.M. knew about this. As is typical with students, I feared the authorities might think this problem ran in the family and question my ability for missionary work. Actually the China Inland Mission superiors were extremely understanding and fair to all students who might suffer under special burdens.

Having written of the strong discipline necessary to avoid "casualties on the field," I need to include the *joys* in the atmosphere of the presence of the Lord, and fellowship with students, all aiming for the same sphere of service in China. Morning prayers were very special. Mostly they were led by the faculty, occasionally by a fellow student, and sometimes by a returned missionary. In the Prayer Room there were texts, which I continue to see in my mind. On one side: "In me there dwelleth no good thing" (Rom. 7:18). On the other side were the words, "Ye are complete in Him" (Col. 2:10).

Our days were filled with hard study. Dr. Russell Houghton, a leading seminarian of the Anglican Church, taught the Theology class. Mr. Roland Hogben taught Bible Content and Homiletics (teaching techniques). We studied the Chinese language instead of the usual emphasis on Greek and Hebrew, and also studied Chinese History. All of us had work assignments in churches or organizations for which we prepared written messages, which were handed in to Mr. Hogben, who returned them on Saturday.

My work assignment was speaking and counseling in a home for delinquent girls. This reminded me a little of my beloved Floodgate Street class, and I loved the girls.

Another distinctive characteristic of the C.I.M. Training Institute was that the men and women students were strictly segregated. The men candidates lived in a college-type house at Newington Green, which was also the compound for the mission headquarters. The women candidates lived in a house called Aberdeen Park, which also housed the women faculty. The China Inland Mission had adopted the policy that engaged couples going out to China should not marry until they had been on the field two years. This was a wise policy. The Chinese language is very difficult to learn and to write. The customs of that day needed considerable adaptation for Western missionaries. Since both husband and wife were given full missionary status, it was considered too hard immediately to set up a home, have children, and adapt to Chinese ways—all at the same time. After two years, the wife and husband would have completed some of the first stiff C.I.M. examinations, would have become acclimated, and would have taken part in evangelical meetings and other work. Marriage then was strongly recommended, for it was good for Chinese to see and visit Christian homes.

Mr. Hogben changed forever my former method of Bible study. He forced us to discover biblical truths for ourselves. We studied all the books of the Bible. Mr. Hogben would give about five leading questions for the following week. No commentaries were allowed *before* the teaching session. He would know when someone's answer parroted one well-known scholar's Bible notes, and he would say, "Ah! Dear Mr. Scofield!" He never missed a trick! Having taken Mr. Scofield's correspondence course, I had become almost ultra-dispensationalist in interpretation of Scripture. Under Mr. Hogben's biblical tuition, I first veered strongly in the opposite direction and later found a balanced conception of different views of eschatology (prophecy).

I'll always remember one assignment. "Read all of Jeremiah, answering the following questions." One question was, "Discuss the personality and temperament of the prophet Jeremiah. For every character trait use passages to prove your point." There were four other similar questions—and we had other assignments from other faculty members as well!

Mr. Hogben was very strict about avoiding allegorical meanings unless it was clear that a passage was intended allegorically. The word "type" was not to be used indiscriminately; it was suitable only if it was applied to a symbol confirmed in the New Testament. We were encouraged instead to use the term "illustration" to refer to something symbolical.

I remember when I had prepared a message for the women of my assignment class on Sunday. As was the procedure, I had filled out my homiletics form and submitted it to Mr. Hogben for his evaluation and approval. My theme was "I will *make* you," taken from Genesis 12:1. I used it to describe how God remakes our character. Mr. Hogben tore it apart, saying, "You are completely out of context. God's promise to Abraham was *not* on the subject of a changed character. For that, you must go to the New Testament." He was right.

To this day I believe that much church teaching today suffers from generalizing (allegorizing) specific passages, often promises given to the Jews which are not meant to be generalized in that way. They lose their original meaning and distinction. Consider, for example, Genesis 13:14–17: Abraham's promise related to the *land* he was walking upon. It cannot honestly be twisted to mean the Church, but means Israel as a nation.

(Little did Mr. Hogben know that apart from teaching Chinese in the China Bible Seminary, his strict but extraordinarily helpful homiletics would be taught to teachers of thousands of students in Bible Study Fellowship through the years. I trained teaching leaders in this method of homiletics at headquarters' orientation classes. Much of the clarity and blessing of their teaching can be traced back to this training which I have not found in any other book on homiletics. Mr. Hogben would tell us to avoid being like the preacher who went under deeper, stayed under longer, and came up dryer than anyone else.)

Every Friday night it was a "must" for all candidates to attend Dr. G. Campbell Morgan's Bible study class. He was an outstanding expositor of Scripture, and a most loveable man of God.

Another difference between most seminaries or Bible schools and the C.I.M. Training Institute was in financial matters. Ever since the departure of Hudson Taylor for China with his wife and children and sixteen missionary recruits, God miraculously sent in the appropriate money without any appeals, and always without debt.

Never have C.I.M. missionary candidates been asked to look for financial supporters. Missionaries never let anyone know if they were short of money. They were sent out by God; He would provide. In my day there were nearly 2,000 missionaries on the field. Sometimes monthly remittances would be on the short side. In that case headquarters encouraged each mission station to have a day of fasting and prayer, and always God supplied our need.

When I went into training, I was informed of the cost of board and tuition. However it was made clear to me that if money did not come in for this, I was *not* to consider it a debt. I knew better than to let anyone know of my situation. Mother and many friends concluded that the training was free. Mother had a legacy left to her by a friend, and would gladly have helped me had she *known*. But that was not "living by faith." Also I felt it was not living by faith to fail to discharge any expenses the mission might pay on my behalf. I had some money saved from my previous positions, but this was not sufficient. I prayed, and friends who knew nothing of my need were led of God to send gifts. When I sailed for China, all those expenses had been completely met.

God trained me in the way of faith in other ways. Sometimes I was so short of cash I had no money for stamps. I prayed, and a little sum was sent in to me for a birthday or some other special day. Most of my clothes were sufficient. However one day I looked at the soles of my shoes which were full of holes. I remember lifting my foot and saying, "Look, Father, I've worn through my shoes." One hour after this, a student, Mona Miller, called me to her room. She had just received a box of clothes from a mother whose daughter had died. Mona said, "Audrey, the only thing is, these shoes are too large for me. Would they fit you? Would you have use for them?" They were an *exact* fit!

Another time, all students were to attend a mission conference away from London. I had no money for a ticket, but concluded that in answer to prayer some postal order would arrive at the last minute. It did not. The situation reached the place where I was standing in a long line at the station ticket office, knowing I had no money to pay for the ticket. Then my roommate, Betty Pedley, came over to me and said, "Audrey, I feel so embarrassed. All this week I have had the impression I must give you this money. I don't know why. Please don't be offended, but I felt constrained to speak to you about it." Needless to say I told her the story and joyfully purchased a return ticket. There were needs at the conference too, but God saw that she and I lacked nothing.

Although I had come from a family who knew the principles of "living by faith," as a young Christian I thought debts were allowable within the family. I liked good clothes, concerts, and traveling. It did not seem to matter if I was somehow in debt to Mother. One day she said, "Audrey, the Bible says, 'Owe no man anything except to love one another.' Do you think it is consistent with a committed Christian life to be in debt to me every month?" From that day forth I have never been in debt.

At the mission headquarters this kind of dependence upon the Lord for financial needs increasingly led to confidence concerning spiritual and situational needs. This area of training has also formed the basis for Bible Study Fellowship policies which will be discussed in later chapters. I have always remembered the verse: "My God shall supply all your need according to his riches in glory by Christ Jesus" (Phil. 4:19).

There were many joyous occasions during training days, such as periods of time when I could be with my sister Kitty and her family of three, David, Ruth, and Margaret. We delighted in being together in the lovely English countryside. Marjorie and her husband also had two girls. I saw much of my mother, who rejoiced in my call to China.

In 1935 we expected to sail in September. However, there

was a crisis in China when C.I.M. candidates were murdered, and this kept the women candidates back. For me, this meant waiting another year. But during this time I was privileged to work in the beautiful French mountains of Haute Savioe.

EIGHT

DELAYED SAILING—
MINISTRY IN FRANCE

*And I was with you in weakness, and in fear, and in much
trembling. And my speech and my preaching was not with
enticing words of man's wisdom, but in demonstration of the
Spirit and of power* [I Corinthians 2:3, 4].

In 1935 World War II was not far away. Already Germany
was in the hands of the Nazis. Civil war tore into Spain. In
China the Communist armed rebellion disrupted the entire
country. Meanwhile, in 1933 the Japanese army had landed
troops near Shanghai and threatened Peking and Tientsin in
the north. Generalissmo Chiang Kai-shek had difficulty in
unifying the country, but the Lord was greatly moving within
the Chinese Church, and new believers were spreading the
Good News all over this heavily populated land.

But there were tragedies. Some of our missionaries were
held captive in Communist hands. In South Anhwei, John
and Betty Stam were suddenly caught by Communist troops,
tried, and condemned to die as imperialist spies. A Chinese
woman managed to hide their baby daughter and bring her to
safety. In her clothes a letter was found. It was her parents' last
message to friends and relatives. "All our possessions and
stores are in their hands, but we praise God peace is in our

hearts. The Lord bless and guide you. And as for us—may God be glorified whether by life or death." They were be-headed along with a Chinese friend who tried to intercede for them.

That same year Miss Mildred Cable, through whom I received God's call to China, and the Misses French were arrested and held for months by Communist forces. Miss Cable wrote, "We are in a Satanic whirlwind."

The general unrest was so serious in 1935 that only *men* students were allowed to sail from home countries. Since my anticipated sailing was delayed for these reasons, it seemed of God that I was invited by the Thonon Mission, in France on the border of Switzerland, to help them, as they were short of missionaries. The C.I.M. thought this would be good experience for me.

Thonon is situated opposite Switzerland on the lovely lake of Geneva. Missionary work was in progress under the leadership of Mr. Orr in the town, but there were also many expeditions into the high mountains of Haute Savoie, where villages were isolated from the outside world and from the gospel.

I stayed with a godly couple who had ministered before in Africa. They had to leave Thonon-Les-Bains for a brief time; therefore I was needed to "take their place." Another younger missionary, Marjorie, was my close companion. We held small meetings for adults. My particular function was to run a Girl Guide troup (similar to Girl Scouts), and lead these girls to the Lord. I had never been a Girl Guide, and tying knots, and other specific accomplishments related to the movement were a mystery to me. Therefore, all day I would study these practical things in order to be able to teach them at night.

After the practical session we would have Bible study. I remember once turning out all the lights and holding a small candle alight. Then the girls (about thirty of them) followed me in single file. Following this I spoke on John 8:12. "I am the light of the world: he that followeth me shall not walk in darkness, but shall have the light of life." Those who kept in the circle of candlelight could follow in the light; all the others were walking in a physical darkness. God brought several of those Catholic girls to a real conversion and commitment to Christ.

The expeditions into the mountains with my fellow missionary, Marjorie, were a different proposition. This was long before Pope John advocated that Catholics should study the Bible (which brought thousands into Bible Study Fellowship classes in the sixties). However, in the high mountains of Haute Savoie, the priest and church were the *only* means of religious teaching, of material help in time of need, and the life of the villagers revolved entirely around the church. Therefore, we of the Thonon Mission had to tread warily.

A bus took us up part way; after that we climbed. The scenery was indescribably beautiful. At first I clung like a limpet to Marjorie and her experience. The villagers were totally ignorant. We would talk with them at the well about the need "to think more about God and be blessed by Him." This received a ready response. However, once when we knocked at a house, a woman wanted to shut the door on us, and *feared* even to *touch* the little New Testament we wanted to give her, fearing she would be excommunicated for even touching it.

At this time the Lord challenged me. He knew I was terrified to knock on doors without Marjorie, but I knew that He wanted me to do just that and prove His sufficiency. So we separated. Most of the villagers were at home because it was winter and snowing outside; all the work was done in the house to get ready for the spring.

I knocked tremblingly at my first house. I said I had come to talk to them about God. A gracious welcome was given me. My French was adequate. They questioned me: "Are you a nun?"

"No, I am not a nun, but I love God and believe in Jesus Christ."

"Do you believe in the Virgin Mary?"

"Of course, here is the history in Luke's Gospel." As I

pointed to the verse about the Virgin Mary, I underlined the text.

"Do you believe in confession?"

"Yes, I believe in confessing my sins to God." I turned to I John 1:9, underlining all verses as I went along.

Then I talked to them of the love of God, the joys of prayers answered, and that this New Testament would tell them more—a good book to read when one was not busy in the winter. As I spoke I underlined many passages. Then I left the New Testament with them, amid gracious goodbyes.

We heard that they came to love that little book they had never seen before, so much that they simply kept quiet about it, yet truly received the Lord. One passage I had underlined was John 5:24:

> Verily, verily, I say unto you, He that heareth my word, and believeth on him that sent me, hath everlasting life, and shall not come into condemnation; but is passed from death unto life.

I had given them other specific salvation texts. Had they informed the priest of what had happened, the book would have been taken away from them.

It was to me a thrill to prove God sufficient for my timidity, and to work for months in different villages of the mountains.

However it was hard to live so near to Switzerland, yet not to visit the beloved mountains of my childhood. But even had there been time, I had no money for this. One day I wistfully said to the Lord, "It may not be Your will, but I can tell You of my desire. Would You let me see Switzerland before I leave for China?" Very quickly an answer came. The missionary whom I had temporarily replaced knew my passion for mountains. She sent to the director, Mr. Orr, a sum of money to take the few missionaries in Thonon to see the mountains of Switzerland.

One of the places we visited in Switzerland was Lucerne. I

remember being enraptured as I stood on the bridge and looked at Lake Lucerne, Mt. Pilatus, and Mt. Rigi. I thought that going to China meant that I would *never* again see the mountains and lakes of Switzerland. Little did I know that in the Lord's goodness I would go there on furlough, speaking in many Swiss towns, and also that in later years I would be climbing those mountains year after year when I was taking students to Dr. Francis Schaeffer's "L'Abri."

News reached me that the women candidates, if accepted, would probably sail in September of that year. I returned to England in early spring to prepare for sailing. I had asked my father for his approval about my going to China, and at first he refused. He had always wanted me with him in France. Finally, under the Lord's direction, I wrote him a special letter which he said "would break a heart of stone," and he gave his full approval for my sailing.

When I returned to England, bad news awaited me. First was the news that my sister, Marjorie, was now temporarily in a nursing home in London. Second, there was a family situation which seemed serious and very much troubled me. Third, there was the tragic suicide of a lady who was a close friend and confidante. This affected me profoundly. She was a most earnest Christian, probably about fifty years of age. She had prayed for Marjorie, had visited her in my absence, and had greatly helped me personally.

I happened to run into her just after my return to England, and was dismayed at her white face and look of anguish. She asked me to spend the evening with her. However, this was impossible, as the C.I.M. was holding one of their important meetings in Albert Hall (the largest in London), and all candidates were expected to be present. The meeting ended late, after which I went by train to Pinner, which was my sister Kitty's home.

All that night was spent in prayer for my friend, who had done so much for me. I could not rid myself of the tragic look on her face. Never will I forget the next early morning when I was still concerned, that my sister Kitty's little son David came into my bed, gaily demanding "a million kisses." Everyone in the home was welcoming me back to England. A picnic was arranged for that morning. Somehow I felt this profound concern was getting to be an obsession. My friend's condition would clear up. My immediate duty was to give myself totally to my family, so I completely laid aside the prayer burden.

Imagine my dismay when I heard that my friend had paced the floor *all night*, and finally in the morning had committed suicide by inhaling gas. The hurt and questioning of why God allowed this was too deep to tell anyone about—least of all, my family. When I returned to Aberdeen Park, I was still deeply distressed and wondering what I could say to Marjorie, still in the nursing home, who had been faithfully encouraged by my friend while I was in France.

When I went to visit Marjorie, I had a second deep concern. She normally was a happy, humorous, and very unselfish person; now I found that her temporary illness had made her very depressed. That afternoon she knelt at my feet holding me and saying, "Audrey, I need you. Doesn't your own flesh and blood mean more to you than Chinese you have never met?" I thought, "Was God speaking to me to stay in England?"

I went back to Aberdeen Park and my secret place—the attic! When I brought my sister Marjorie's need before the Lord, He gave me back a stern word: "No man, having put his hand to the plough, and looking back, is fit for the kingdom of God" (Luke 9:62).

That was enough guidance. However, in view of my friend's suicide and my sister Marjorie's need, there remained one other continuing anxiety which could not (and cannot) be confided to anyone else.

These three anxieties resulted in physical strain. When the time came for a final physical examination, the doctor strongly advised against my going to China. The home director, Rev. Aldis, was a very understanding person. He called me into his office and asked, "Miss Johnson, the doctor feels you are suffering under some severe strain. Would you be willing to give me your confidence, which I promise to keep?"

I told him in some detail of my situations. He said, "It is my experience that God does not often trust a person of your age to go through three such traumatic situations at the same time. I do not believe this will happen in your life again. Disasters occur in believers' lives, in youth, middle age, or in later years. But always God provides green pastures. I am sure precious, joyous times are in store for you. . . ."

Finally he said, "In view of your record, and of what you have told me, I am going to take responsibility for sending you to China. I am sure God will vindicate this decision."

Truly God had confirmed His earlier promise to me. He had opened the door (Rev. 3:8), and no man could shut it. In my Bible I wrote, "No reserves, no regrets, no retreats."

God fulfilled Rev. Aldis's words, for never again in life did He call me to go through such soul-shattering experiences. Of course, for every believer there may be devastating difficulties, but through these, one learns to lean more fully upon Him.

Finally, all candidates went before the mission board. They questioned us on theology, views on the fullness of the Holy Spirit, our call, etc. I never will forget one General Mackenzie who was an outstanding Christian and totally unpredictable. I was startled when out of the clear blue sky he suddenly said, "By the way, Miss Johnson, what is the message of Micah?" I don't remember exactly what I replied, but Mr. Hogben was there, and I managed to weather it somehow. Then came another, "Miss Johnson, why did Ezra [Ezra 1:9] take twenty-nine knives and no forks?" Completely thrown off guard, I did not remember that Persians did not eat with forks! Fortunately, the C.I.M. did not consider this lapse so grave so as to prevent me from sailing to China!

After our acceptance, there were many meetings where candidates gave testimonies, until we all knew each other's by heart.

Finally there was a farewell meeting, again in Albert Hall,

for eighteen new workers, where we all had to give our testimonies. My dear mother sat in the front row, and as it happened, that was the last time I saw her.

Our belongings were packed in wooden, tin-lined boxes (about three feet cubed). They were used for commerical tea boxes and considered the maximum weight which a Chinese coolie should carry. It was arranged that we eighteen new missionaries would travel in charge of senior missionaries, Mr. and Mrs. George Scott, whom we loved dearly. Imagine our excitement when we were ready to sail for the destination to which God had called us even though emotionally it was hard to leave England and our loved ones.

The Johnson family before Audrey's birth. From left: Mother, Kitty, Marjorie, and Henry Johnson.

Left: Audrey and her teddy bear, from which she was inseparable, 1914.
Right: Leaving Southhampton for Shanghai, 1936.

The Cope family residence, castle near Basingstoke.

Audrey was born in Leicester and grew up in lovely Kenilworth.
Basingstoke was the location of the Cope family mansion.

II

The China Years

NINE
SAILING TO SHANGHAI

*And when he putteth forth his own sheep, he goeth before them,
and the sheep follow him: for they know his voice* [John 10:4].

We sailed on a late afternoon in September on the H.M.S.
Ranchi. People streamed out of the station across a very large
pavement, up a wooden gangway onto the coffee-colored
steamship. There were many people on board; and amid the
noise, bustle, and photograph-taking, dark-skinned Lascars
(East Indian sailors) in red turbans ran up and down the
gangway with baggage. All my family and friends were on the
dock or in my cabin to see us off. Only my dear mother was
not there. The emotional and physical strain would have been
too much. We had said good-bye previously, and she was
being well cared for at home. Always my last memory of her is
sitting in the front row of Albert Hall and slowly walking out
to catch a train.

Suddenly a bell was rung and there was a cry: "All friends
ashore, please." The last good-byes began. Our friends waited
on the pavement below, and all the passengers were at the
rails. There were silly little messages like, "Don't forget to give
my love to . . ." which do not mean anything at all, but one
must say something to relieve the tension. Then began the

long wait for the ship to sail. Someone on shore started singing "Jesus Shall Reign," and then "Crown Him with Many Crowns," and finally "The Whole Wide World."

There was no mourning on the faces of those who were going forth at His bidding. Both those who were going and those left behind were radiant with the joy and peace He had especially given for this occasion. Slowly the ship moved out into the darkness. There were shouts of "Good-bye C.I.M.," "Good-bye Church Army," and an attempt to sing "God Be with You. . . ." We passengers strained our eyes to see the last waving of the handkerchief attached to the hand of the shadowy figure we believed belonged to us. Soon we could make out only the last outline of the shores of England, and we sailed out into the unknown. We were on our way to China at last, not knowing whither, but knowing Him Who is all-sufficient. Our Father was with us. To any who might be fearful of answering God's call to lands overseas let me give my testimony, one which others share with me, that at the moment of the last farewell He gives a peace that passes all understanding.

I shall never forget an aged couple, Mr. and Mrs. Pearce, at the leave-taking. They were poor. They had spent all their savings to send their only son, Jim, to medical college. Doubtless they expected he would be with them in their old age. He was sent to far Kansu on the borders of Tibet. Their faces were absolutely radiant. I could not help thinking of Abraham giving up his only son. Later when all missionaries had to leave China, I felt grateful to God that Jim's parents were still alive. God honored their faith and also gave them back their Isaac.

Before long, the ship was sailing toward the Red Sea. I never forgot that hot, steamy passage. The temperature was unusually high according to the steward. I looked over the desert (the wilderness of Exodus) with its sand dunes, baked rocks, and here and there a thorn bush. I watched a caravan of camels with an Arab in front march slowly through that haze of heat. On the opposite side we had seen the pyramids built by

Hebrew slaves. I tried to imagine Moses leading a million cantankerous women, children, and men on and on through forty years of that barren desert. I imagined I saw a cloud of God's glory above leading them. The unimaginable amount of water He gave them from the rock and the manna, "that small round thing like hoar-frost upon the ground," every morning. I marveled at the miracles of God's grace and preservation of His people and tried to picture the tent of worship and the setting up of all the family tents. Probably no one who reads Exodus can fully enter into that miracle of absolute dependence upon our faithful God who revealed Himself so clearly that throughout Israelite history and Psalms this miraculous preservation and protection was never forgotten. Think for instance of Deuteronomy 29:5: "For forty years God has led you through the wilderness, yet your clothes haven't become old, and your shoes haven't worn out" (TLB).

Why should we ever draw back when God calls us to go through a "wilderness of trial"? He is with us, leading us, for a future and a hope, and He will supply our need—(see Jer. 29:11 and I Pet. 1:7, 8).

It would take too much space to describe all the ports at which we stopped, although all were interesting.

Bombay was the port which interested me most. We went for a drive through the Hindu, Mohammedan, and outcasts' quarters, as well as the district of the wealthy. I have never seen such color. The sky was very blue, without a cloud. The buildings were dazzling white, or blue, and one Parsee hospital was orange-colored like a dark marigold, with green trees growing up beside it. There were palm trees and coconut trees with yellow fruit. There were long avenues of feathery trees with pink, mauve, and yellow blossoms. We passed palaces of pure marble, one of which was a green palace where the Maharajah lived with his twenty wives. We caught glimpses of shady courtyards with many flowers and also a golden temple.

But it was the Indian people themselves who attracted me most. The women are so short, very erect, and graceful, with lovely, soft black hair and large, expressive brown eyes. They dressed in saris of every brilliant hue imaginable—magenta, pale blue, gold, pink, crimson, and emerald green. The men wore white mostly, with multi-colored turbans.

There were little beggar children with nothing on at all, curly hair, and a winning smile. With all this beauty one could not but realize something sad and tragic underlying it all. We saw some Hindu priests with evil faces and matted, ragged long hair, begging. One even *felt* the evil sometimes—for as Paul says in I Corinthians 10:20, "The things which the Gentiles sacrifice, they sacrifice to devils and not to God: and I would not that ye should have fellowship with devils."

At 10:30 each morning we all met for reading and prayer for China and other mission fields represented on the ship, in a corner of the second class dining room. Then in the evening, when there was a cool breeze blowing and the light of the moon made a shining pathway right across the sea, we gathered around in deck chairs on the top deck and sang choruses, closing with "Light that groweth not pale . . . ," and prayer. Some of us stayed up there a little longer to lay hold of the peace of the quiet waters for ourselves before retiring. I would stand alone late in the evenings on the ship's deck with an intense feeling of meditation: crises at home.

C.I.M. missionaries led an active life on board the H.M.S. *Ranchi*. Some of us took turns in running a children's hour at 3:30 P.M. for about twenty-seven children. We then played games. Afterwards they sat on a rug for the story, which varied from fairytales to Bible stories according to the leader. We would finish the session with, "Joy, Joy, Joy," and "Wide, Wide As the Ocean." Parents sat around and listened too.

Below the deck, the ship was decorated with multicolored lights, and most of the passengers danced to the strains of the ship's band until 5:00 A.M. We missionaries were marked men and women. We dressed differently and did not dance or join football sweepstakes. Opinions differed about us. Many parents were grateful to have their little ones kept happy for an hour or two every day. One person was heard to say, "Oh!

Missionaries! I don't believe in them. They are simply a public expense and go out to have a good time." Now and again God gave us an opportunity, generally in private conversation, to speak of Him to a receptive soul. As usual, it was often so unexpected and sudden that one is reminded of the need *always* to be filled with the Spirit, so that He may speak His words in natural conversation.

Our trip halfway around the world took several weeks, but it seemed too short a time to absorb all the fresh experiences that were encountered along the way.

The day came when we finally sailed into Shanghai. It is hard to give first impressions of Shanghai, partly because on the surface it seemed largely cosmopolitan and Westernized, partly because it would be some time before we would have a chance to see the city close up. Later on I would know the narrow back streets, the begging lepers on the pavement, and the strange experience of sitting in a rickshaw while a Chinese man would pick up the rickshaw's two shafts and pull me along.

We received a very warm welcome. Immediately we were taken to the new C.I.M. headquarters. Its compound enveloped a fine building—the largest mission premises in the world at that time. Even the twelve stenographers had a flat of their own.

All of us were offered opportunities to see Christian work in the Shanghai area. I was most interested in going with five others to the largest women's Bible seminary in China, the China Bible Seminary, whose principal was an American, Miss Ruth Brittain. (Little did I know how close a connection would be developed between the two of us.) I was enthralled by my first sight of the seminary. It was run on the same faith principle as C.I.M. and registered between 80 and 100 women. The students were native Chinese, from twelve of China's provinces, and after a year's study they could work for a year with missionaries at inland stations. Then they returned for further training.

We went all around the buildings, then into their dining

room with its little square Chinese tables, benches without backs, and bowls and chopsticks. Their so-called "milk" was actually made from soybeans. These are ground, and the milk is said to be nutritionally equivalent to cow's milk. It tasted burnt to me, but I grew to like it. We saw the stone mill where the soybeans were ground like wheat is ground.

Although I had attended prayer meetings ad infinitum, I was very impressed with the spiritual quality of what was called the "Prayer League" here at the seminary. Every evening, kneeling on concrete floors for more than an hour, they prayed for graduates in the field. A secretary would read out the requests and list them, leaving a space for answers. (Later, in the years when I was on the faculty of China Bible Seminary, I had to prepare a summary of the League for the board. I counted about 2,000 requests for that year and 1,500 recorded answers, not to speak of people who forgot to tell us when their prayers were answered.)

When we returned to mission headquarters, we found it full of people. Everyone was very kind, and we were invited out to tea.

Everyone seemed to belong to a group. There was a group of seventeen American girls just arrived. Groups of senior missionaries were going or returning from furlough. There seemed to be a group of four housekeepers and another of administrators. We were a group too, of about fifty persons going to the women's language school.

One small event occurred before we went on to language school, which left a deep impression. We new missionaries were warned not to give money to beggars lest we be mugged. However, I passed a leper lying on the pavement. He was covered with leprosy, one arm had gone, the other leprous pink-red and lying by his begging cap. I couldn't resist putting a few coins into the cap. Then I remembered how the Lord Jesus touched the leper. Therefore, I deliberately and lovingly touched his leprous arm. I shall never forget the *physical* repulsion which penetrated my physically healthy body. Then

I realized the emotional, mental, and spiritual repulsion which must have flooded the heart of the Lord Jesus when He, the Holy One, "became a leper" as He was *"made sin"* (II Cor. 5:21). Yet He was willing to *touch me* to make me whole.

TEN

THE LANGUAGE SCHOOL AT YANGCHOW, INLAND CHINA

And we know that all things work together for good to them that love God, to them who are called according to his purpose [Romans 8:28].

All C.I.M. women missionaries were immediately sent to the language school at Yangchow. Yangchow became for us a happy home but involved us in very heavy Chinese study. We lived in a long, grey two-story building with a roof that in Chinese fashion turned up at the corners. It had a sunny veranda running the full length of the house. Onto this opened tiny, square, whitewashed rooms that two students shared as study and bedroom combined. Our language school home was set in about two acres of ground with many trees such as bamboos, firs, and others of graceful Chinese variety, with beautiful golden Orioles flying in and around them.

Often in the early morning I would slip out and let the quietness of it all grip my soul until I was quiet enough to hear what God was wanting to say. "Be still and know that I am God!" I often thanked Him for that garden when the Chinese language appeared to be the most inscrutable language under the sun, and Satan came armed with his usual doubts. I realized there that the God Who made the stars and all the glory of the rising sun was also sufficient for every need of mine for the furtherance of His kingdom.

A massive stone wall encircled the city of Yangchow with its hundreds of grey tiled roofs and the green curved roofs of temples. In the distance one could hear the creaks of the junks (which sounded like wails) as they passed slowly down the canal. From our veranda, we heard the continuous squeaking of wheelbarrows, which were never oiled. (It was considered bad luck if one's wheelbarrow did not squeak.) All day we would hear the singsong of water carriers carrying buckets of water hung on shafts over their shoulders. We watched from our veranda the children playing. In their billowy gowns, they looked to us like walking pillows. Some of the children wore pants, overlarge, tattered, and torn. This impression struck my fancy and compelled me to write a poem:

> The funniest little aspect did I see
> Is the Chinese children's idiosyncrasy
> Their baggy trousers rippled fore and aft,
> They stoop to conquer, and feel a draft.
>
> Built for comfort, not for style
> They must be air-cooled all the while
> And think! It saves so many stitches
> And how handy for scratching when it itches!

As we novices walked through Yangchow's narrow streets, people stopped to stare at the unusual sight. Little children called us "foreign teachers" to our faces and "foreign devils" to our backs. We passed along the main street with its shops without glass fronts, each having its own distinguishing banner of red, green, or yellow. It was very colorful. There was one shop that sold water. We wound our way along streets that would be called alleys at home; even four of us could not walk abreast. On either side of some streets were high, grey, stone walls, each sheltering a courtyard and the home of several families, with the oldest matriarch at the head.

Some of it made me think of New Testament days. I could imagine the funeral cortege of the widow's son passing out through the gate of the city wall to the graves beyond. I imagined the Lord standing there: because He could not bear her sorrow, He brought that son back to life. Another vivid scene that also reminded me of Palestine was the constant jostling of crowds in the little cobblestone alleys. Whenever a rickshaw passed, people were squeezed against the open shop fronts, or into doorways. Once we stopped for a few minutes to buy some little thing, and a crowd gathered around us so quickly that police had to keep the traffic moving.

There were over half a million people in Yangchow, and we passed hundreds of clay-matted straw houses, dirty and smelly, dark inside and sparsely furnished. Each displayed a paper idol over the door to keep out evil spirits. We met men and women pulling heavy barges along the canal bank, work done only by animals in England. Yet each person was thankful to do it for a coin or two. No wonder the Chinese of 1936 often made the mistake of thinking the missionary rich. They saw our clean homes, which kept out the rain and had plenty of fresh air and light. They noted our clothes, which to us were simple, but to them seemed expensive.

All through my years in China, I never got over these depressing sights. However, He who preached the gospel to the poor walked among crowds such as these. He was always filled with compassion as He walked in their midst, and *He did something about their suffering.* I was so very glad that "as the Father sent Him to earth," even so He sent me (John 17) to this land where there is desperate need, granting me His Power to "open the blind eyes, to bring out the prisoners from the prison, and them that sit in darkness" (Isa. 42:7).

There were fifty-two of us students at the language school. We were a mixture of English, American, German, Swiss, Danish, Swedish, and Australian recruits. We called one another by our first names and invited each other to come for cocoa and an "apology" for a cookie at night. We felt like one big family. There was a very happy spirit of freedom and fellowship among us.

A large part of language study consisted in reading aloud with a Chinese teacher. I would stand at a small table until he came in, clad in a long grey gown and silent shoes like bedroom slippers. He always wore a little round stiff black hat with a button on top. We both bowed to one another and then sat down about three feet apart. He read a sentence first. Then I read it again trying to imitate exactly the tones and sounds he made. Afterwards we tried to make a little conversation. He ate lots of garlic!

Later we had a conversation class held in a whitewashed room where about seven of us sat on stools against the wall facing our teacher who wrote Chinese on a blackboard. We used these words in sentences of our own. Occasionally funny things happened. For instance one student tried to say she went into a shop and sat on a stool. Instead, she actually said she sat on the proprietor! Again, another student spoke most rudely about someone else's hair being dirty, when she wanted to say it was long. The difficulty was that both words have the same sound, but one is aspirated and the other is not. This is but a simple example of many of the subtle intricacies of the Chinese language.

Language school was not without its fun and fellowship by any means. For one thing the interrelationship with different nationalities was a good education. We learned that our English words and expressions could be misunderstood. In England the word "bug" always means a "bedbug" and is never used except in that concept. "Lousy" is only used in its strict sense. Imagine my first meal when an American at my side said, "Will you please put a 'bug' in the Director's ear concerning. . . ." Once when I was ill at a hospital a sympathetic doctor shocked me by saying, "I expect you feel real lousy, don't you?"

The warmth of the outgoing Americans and Canadians

helped the reserved English. We loved the German, Norwegian, and Swedish students.

When one is working hard all day on a most difficult language, listening and trying to understand with very little let-up psychologically, there sometimes comes a time when there is an explosion of fun. Perhaps this was the reason my sense of mischief overwhelmed me one night. Just before leaving language school, another student and I changed all the fifty-two students' night attire from their beds to one another's rooms. Absolute pandemonium and laughter prevailed as fifty students wandered around wondering in whose room their night wear was located.

However, there was an aftermath. I was called on the carpet by Miss McQueen, our principal. "Really, Audrey, what will the *Chinese* think of such unruly behavior from missionary teachers? Where is your dignified position?"

It so happens that by temperament, I am a quick-moving person. I walk quickly, and when young would usually go upstairs two steps at a time. Again and again our Language School teachers would stop me. "You *must* walk slowly. The educated Chinese are dignified and expect their teachers to be the same." A class of schoolchildren or college students would always stand before the teacher was seated. In giving anything to a friend or superior, *two* hands would always be used.

Gradually God tamed our spirits in different ways to become as like to the Chinese in manners, movement, eating habits, and dress as possible. This was a policy of the mission. After all, when our Lord Jesus came to earth, He became human, like to us in all things except sin: "Wherefore in all things it behooved him to be made like unto his brethren, that he might be a merciful and faithful high priest in things pertaining to God, to make reconciliation for the sins of the people" (Heb. 2:17). Paul said, "I am made all things to all men, that I might by all means save some" (I Cor. 9:22).

After the first two sets of examinations in the Chinese

language had been weathered, the day finally arrived when each of us would be designated by Mr. Warren, acting director on the China field, to a missionary station. The place was teeming with excitement. Students found themselves designated to the four corners of China. The reader should remember that today there are about 1 billion Chinese, and as in 1936, *most of them have never heard the word "Jesus."* In my day the Chinese worshiped demons and ancestors according to the Confucian ethic. Because of this great need in inland China, the C.I.M. policy was to penetrate all of inland China with the gospel. This is why the mission was named China Inland Mission.

Actually, I was the last student to be interviewed by Mr. Warren, in April 1937. I was surprised when I learned that it was to south China (in Kiangsi Province) and not to north China to which I was designated. I knew that all my doctors had stated that I should not live in a humid and hot climate and that Kiangsi Province was noted for that kind of climate. However, I did not doubt that God Himself had ordained this for His own purpose, and later events confirmed the wisdom of the original appointment. I recalled the verse: "And we know that all things work together for good to them that love God, to them who are called according to his purpose" (Rom. 8:28).

To have the kind, experienced Scottish woman, Miss McQueen, whom I had admired for so long as principal of the language school, as my first senior missionary was indeed a privilege. Also, another American student, Miss Margaret Sells, a delightful young missionary full of humor, was designated to the same station.

The other students were all waiting for me, and I was hugged and teased (because of going to the principal's station) and congratulated. Mr. Warren asked for a nurse. He had a strangulated hernia—fatal, if left over twenty-four hours. However, he insisted on finishing the twenty-five remaining designations before returning to Shanghai, giving each student five minutes while he was in bed. What a rugged saint he was! His prayers were moving in their simplicity and father-liness. Before he left, he said he had a word from the Lord which he must deliver to us all, and that was a never-to-be-forgotten scene. We were all in our sitting room, and Mr. Warren was carried in on an improvised bed. There was a solemn stillness, and our eyes were fixed on the old saint with his shaggy white hair, lying propped up with pillows. His New Testament was in his hand. His face looked like what John's face must have looked like after Patmos.

He spoke to us on the passage, "What is that to thee? Follow thou Me." We realized we might be hearing him for the last time, certainly for many students traveling to far west China. He prepared us for the hardships, but spoke of the joys—and above all, reminded us that whatever happened, "I will never leave thee" (Heb. 13). Then we all formed two lines to the front gate singing, "Praise the Savior, Ye Who Know Him" as he was carried down with his hands upraised to say good-bye and to offer us his blessing. A litter was prepared and he was carried through the city of Yangchow to a sleeping compartment on the train to Shanghai C.I.M. hospital.

It turned out that Mr. Warren's operation was successful. I shall never cease to thank God for the spiritual enrichment of such dedicated saints who were leaders of the China Inland Mission.

E L E V E N
MY FIRST INLAND STATION

Other sheep I have, which are not of this fold: them also I must bring, and they shall hear my voice; and there shall be one fold, and one shepherd [John 10:16].

Margaret Sells and I, who were traveling with Miss McQueen, had to wait until all the other language school students had left. Miss McQueen, "captain of the ship," could not leave until all her charges had been seen safely on their way; therefore I didn't arrive at my first station until the beginning of June 1937.

It is imporant to mention here that at this time in Chinese history the country was ravaged by a Communist rebellion. Kiangsi Province perhaps suffered the most; thousands were killed, and many homes were burned to the ground. Some missionaries were captured by the Communists and a few murdered. It was in 1934 that Central Government troops finally broke through, and the situation greatly stabilized.

Still, when Miss McQueen, Miss Sells, and I went to Yu-Kiang in Kiangsi Province, throughout China missionaries were still being captured and held by the enemy.

Nevertheless, there was one way in which our welcome in Kiangsi was a warm one. Never had I felt so hot and wet, except when traveling through the area of the Red Sea. A wonderful Chinese meal was set out for us on a small table under the trees. The food was covered by big blue flies, which the Chinese kept swatting away. Finally we sat down in Chinese fashion, with the wife of the host serving us. We were just three missionaries with the Chinese host, who was the only man. By this time we were well used to chopsticks, rice, sweet and sour pork, and fish. At this table there was a huge codfish complete with head and *big* eyes.

We were able to enjoy the conversation. For some unknown reason, I happened to be seated next to the host. Suddenly he used his own chopsticks to place in my bowl of rice the greatest delicacy of the feast; namely, one of that cod's huge eyes! He smiled, thinking how honored I would feel. Honored! Looking longingly at the chickens feeding underneath the table, I smiled at my host and I looked at Miss McQueen and knew what I had to do. I thanked God I possessed a large throat—one swallow and it was over. Never again did I have such a "treat," for this delicacy belonged to that region only! A true missionary always eats what is put before her like the Chinese; she is supposed to "become Chinese." God helped me to keep down that ugly cod's eye.

At Yu-Kiang we were a very happy family; I felt that no one in China could have been blessed more in this way. Kiangsi was one of the first few inland provinces of China to be entered by a missionary. It was and no doubt still is a large and densely populated region. There are still thousands there who have never yet heard the name of Jesus.

While we were in our main station, Yu-Kiang, we also took trips by boat to outstations such as Ugan. Never will I forget my first Sunday in Ugan. Imagine a very large whitewashed building, like a barn with four wide-open windows and two doors. The benches were backless and very narrow. On the walls were colored posters and texts. At one end there was a long blackboard. There was a wooden platform (where a sleeping baby was stretched full-length), and a plain reading desk. Among the congregation were coolies, without any shoes, farmers in their coarse blue cotton trousers and open jackets and a few educated men in long white or grey silk gowns. The women sat apart: mothers who thought nothing of feeding their infants in the middle of the service, and beggar women in from the street. An invalid boy lay on a long chair; children with ghastly sores were munching a watermelon. Newly married girls wore fragrant white flowers set against the glistening coils of their black hair. The atmosphere was hot and sticky. Most of the people had arrived about 7:00 A.M., and had walked five to ten miles to get to the place of worship.

At last, when the preacher was ready, someone rang a little hand bell, and the morning service began. The hymn was "Jesus Loves Me, This I Know." The evangelist sang the first line, and the congregation repeated it after him; and so on, line by line. It was not what most Westerners would call singing, but it was praise, as incense sweet to the Lord. My eyes filled again and again, not with sadness, but because the singing was so heartfelt, so utterly unlike the tuneful, yet often empty singing of many of our home churches. Then the evangelist would call everyone to prayer. Each person prayed his own prayer—aloud. Imagine the thunderous sound of some 400 voices speaking different words in different tones, and all at the same time! It was quite an experience for a young missionary, and one I shall never forget! I was in the company of God's very elect.

Just behind me was a little woman who had a blind husband. She heard the gospel, and went home and began to pray that God would open his eyes. Following this, although often against his will, week after week he was brought to morning service, and daily her believing prayer went up to our heavenly Father. In Luke 18:1, the Lord said that we "ought always to pray and not to faint." She prayed daily for two years; one day, without any warning, her blind husband could see! The Ugan folk had a simple, living faith. They gave up their superstitious, often injurious methods of treating diseases, and instead of invoking demons, they told their Father of their trouble. Again and again a miracle was wrought, and a demon-possessed girl was set free or a sick man healed.

Sitting next to me was a little woman with a face brown and wrinkled like a russet apple, and quiet, shining eyes. She had not long belonged to the Lord and had already endured much persecution for her faith in Him. She was very poor. However, when the offering for forwarding the Lord's work was taken, she offered the equivalent of a man's wage for a month. "Not a mite would I withhold" was no empty phrase to her, for she gave the money which a Chinese will keep safe when everything else has gone—the price of her coffin and funeral! The morning message had been on "Love." Later Miss McQueen talked to her saying, "And you love Him, don't you?" She replied, "Oh, yes! But it was He who loved me first." What an honor and a privilege to sit next to such a lover of the Lord.

The next day a family came in from another village where at the fifth-month feast, according to custom, a collection was taken for the idols. Here for the first time a little company of Christians dared to say they could not give. The whole village to a man rose up in arms. Then followed the usual persecutions—taunts and reproaches, and bit by bit, mysterious disappearance of articles from the homes, until at last the family bullock was taken, without which they could not plough the land, and upon which they depended entirely for their living. We had prayer. After that the bullock was returned, but the persecution was keener than ever, even to a threat to burn down the wooden Jesus Hall they had just finished building with much sacrifice of time and money.

The humid heat was unimaginable. We would bathe, put on a fresh set of clothes, but in ten minutes we needed to do it again. There was rather a funny episode at prayers in Yu-Kiang. Of course, we always went to all the evening meetings during the week. Sometimes after a full day of Chinese study, we were pretty sleepy from the heat even before we arrived.

The sleepiness was not helped as we went into a small barn-like structure to sit on very narrow backless benches. Nor was the heat problem helped by numerous oil lamps set on a long table, with mosquitoes in abundance!

This particular night the evangelist started off with a chorus that he explained in detail, sermonizing on every line. Following this we had another hymn with another sermon. Then at 9:45, (to our despair) he opened his Bible to I Corinthians 15, and *started* the evening message! Margaret Sells whispered to me, "I thought they said the Chinese went to bed early!" Oh, dear! How we ached and ached to sleep! Needless to say, we were honor-bound to sit up straight and pretend to be intelligent, even if it was in order to "save your face" and the "face of the other missionaries." ("Saving face" is a Chinese expression.) We knew we would be in that place three times a week. How we envied the small boy sleeping peacefully with his head on his arm at the table facing us. But even his peace was short-lived, for he had a bad dream and began to moan. Someone came from behind and pinched his nose, tweaked his ear, and shook him thoroughly to wake him up.

The following morning we had Acts 20:1-12 for our reading. It was pertinent to read about that poor man, Eutychus, and to learn the lesson: We must not blame the apostle for continuing his speech until midnight, but let not the "lesser lights" use this incident as an example and an excuse for going on too long! Which of us, had we heard the great apostle, would have wished him to stop? Several things may have accounted for the fatal drowsiness of Eutychus. First, the many lights that exhausted all the air. (Yes!) Perhaps some of the windows were not made to open. (Yes!) Probably Eutychus was a "tired slave" whose day's work was ended. (Yes!) Possibly he was illiterate, (as we were in Chinese!) and could not follow "our beloved brother Paul" in the "things hard to be understood." (Yes!)

It has been said, "Sleep, like fire, is a grand friend, but a dangerous enemy when uncontrolled." This was illustrated, and our compulsion to laugh was hard to control that same evening when one of the "lesser lights" did continue even longer than usual, and Bessie Huntimer, sitting against the door, suddenly fell backward when it opened from behind!

I was sitting next to Miss McQueen, who never moved a muscle!

NEAR DEATH

The Lord, he it is that doth go before thee; he will be with thee; he will not fail thee [Deuteronomy 31:8].

At the beginning of summer I came down with the most violent form of dysentery (the same kind that resulted in J. O. Fraser's death). I thought I had eaten something which disagreed with me, and said nothing of it to anyone. Finally I had to go to Miss McQueen, who immediately tried to get in touch with a doctor, but none was available at a reasonable distance. She took me into her own room to nurse me herself. For six days I had nothing but water, and after that was in bed for a long time. But I could not have received more kindness anywhere.

However, although eventually on my feet again, I kept having pains and sickness. When these became acute, in spite of mild remonstrances from me, Miss McQueen decided to escort me up to the Shanghai C.I.M. hospital. Traveling was interesting. First I was taken over the hills by sedan chair. As the Chinese ran up and down hills with the sedan chair, it felt rather like being on a roller coaster at a fair, and I hung on to the rails for dear life. Miss McQueen arranged for sleeping berths on the train to Shanghai. I felt utterly spoiled and thankful to God for her kindness.

After X-rays and tests, an operation to remove my appendix was ordered; it was to be at 4:00 A.M. After having been well bathed by the nurse, I prepared for sleep. But underneath my ear was a thump, thump, thump! Not usually nervous regarding physical upsets, I could not think why my heart would thump because of an appendix operation. I pulled up my pillow and to my horror, there was a large black bat struggling! I was really scared of bats and was sure he would get in my hair—but a good little missionary would never think of calling a nurse! I pushed off the bat, paddled energetically about the room on bare feet, chasing him until I finally got him out the window. Next day at 4:00 A.M., during the operation, one nurse said to another, "Did you bathe her?" "Yes." "Well, just look at those dirty feet!"

No one, least of all myself, expected any trouble from an appendectomy. However, the operation was followed by a "post-operation obstruction." I was in incessant and acute pain, and could not eat, or even drink a teaspoon of water. Therefore, all kinds of what might be old-fashioned methods today were used to keep me going. My doctor, Dr. Ranson, also ordered morphine at regular intervals. I made the mistake of telling my nurse, Miss Woosely (now with the Lord), of the delightful release from pain and the pleasant kind of visions which accompanied this drug. Miss Woosely was very conscientious, and since I was a young missionary (who she thought might become addicted to the drug), refused to give me the medication ordered. This I resented. Integrity made it impossible for me to tell Dr. Ranson my circumstances, although every time he came (several times a day), I asked for it, and he ordered it again. I was in an agony of pain that I have never endured before nor since.

However, I had the Lord. He says in His Word, "Come, let us reason together." Therefore, I reasoned with my Father in this way: "Lord, if I were being martyred for You and China by this suffering I would gladly bear it. But this is so unreasonable. You know I would never become addicted to morphine. Surely it is not Your will that I should endure this unbearable pain unnecessarily, especially as the doctor does not want me to bear it. Why do You allow this to happen?" His reply in my mind was one that I shall thank Him for all my life. He answered gently, "My child, I know exactly the extent to which you suffer. This decision does not come from Me, but I allow it for your eternal benefit. . . . I want you to prove now the truth that My grace will exactly balance the extent of your pain. Try Me." Of course, I knew the text He was applying to my circumstance, which was written in regard to Paul's thorn in the flesh: "My grace is sufficient for thee; for my strength is made perfect in weakness" (II Cor. 12:9).

Once when the great Dr. Spurgeon was apparently very concerned about difficulties in his church, again and again this text was given him, but he ignored it for quite a time. Suddenly, remembering the phrase, "My strength is made perfect in weakness," he burst into laughter and said, "I should think it is, Lord." I had no laughter, but my whole attitude and restlessness changed. When the doctor came, the nurse said, "She is like a different person." The pain was the same.

The situation turned out to be so serious I was not expected to live. A cablegram was sent to my mother, with the message, "Second operation necessary. Recovery doubtful." Code numbers were used in those days, and the numbers somehow got rearranged. The numbers decoded read, "Johnson opened, most of the contents missing!" Of course, the error was discovered and corrected before reaching Mother.

I was too ill to have an anesthetic at the second operation. I felt everything. Everyone was very kind, but no one, including the doctors, expected me to live afterwards. When I could not swallow even a teaspoon of water, uncomfortable tubes were inserted in my mouth and elsewhere in my body, and I just lay there expecting to die. This time I again prayed to the Lord, asking Him to clarify my confusion. "Lord, You sent me to China. I have only begun to know the language and have accomplished nothing for my beloved Chinese. Why do you let me die before I have accomplished any work for You?"

He answered me, "It is not My will for you to die, but you will have to cooperate with me in *faith*. Ask the doctor to take the tube out of your mouth. I will enable you to keep down the teaspoon of water every fifteen minutes, but you must cooperate with Me and work."

Again this was a lifelong lesson. Although the battle is in the heavenlies, God does not intend us to acquiesce unless it is His will. To dare to believe Him, to work with Him, often accomplishes miracles which for all time are meant to be a pattern of life in many situations. I was learning eternal lessons. Of course, not only my mother and English friends were praying, but all the mission. God gave me the needed strength and confidence.

When Dr. Ranson came in, I said, through my mouthful of tubes, "Doctor, if you will take these tubes out, I promise you I will drink the water." Either he thought, "What difference can it make?" or something of urgency in my eyes convinced him. He pulled out the tubes. I will never forget Nurse Woosely's return. She had spent a long time amid tears and struggles to get these tubes down, and here was Dr. Ranson undoing all her hard work. She looked at Dr. Ranson, hands on hips, and finally said with exasperation, "Dr. Ranson, if those tubes have to be used again, *you* put them in!"

God worked. I kept down a teaspoonful of water every fifteen minutes. Next day, when Dr. Ranson came, he made a remark which I put in my Bible. "'I think you ought to consider yourself snatched from the jaws of death. Most patients with post-operation obstructions die, you know.' Dr. Ranson—August 3, 1937." Years later, during the war, Dr. Ranson and I were imprisoned in the same Japanese internment camp. I will always remember him for his integrity and great sympathy.

As I trusted in God's promise, He worked His healing. Recovery was slow. I was two months in the hospital. My weight dropped from 140 pounds to 106 pounds in but a few weeks.

One day when I was still convalescing from my illness, I

went downstairs to a large room filled with Chinese students. The message was on I Peter 1:23-25: "Being born again, not of corruptible seed, but of incorruptible, by the Word of God which liveth and abideth for ever. For all flesh is as grass, and all the glory of man as the flower of grass. The grass withereth, and the flower thereof falleth away: But the word of the Lord endureth for ever."

As I sat listening to the Word of God, a strange thing occurred which I will never forget. Suddenly the material, solid blackboard was no longer facing me; the chairs, table, walls were not there. They appeared so *real*, but, like everything else of this world, would disappear. . . . Only the eternal Word of God, and those born of the Word of God will always be real, active, eternal.

At that time the Japanese War was spreading from the north down to Shanghai. The C.I.M. hospital was on the top floor, just below the roof. Now and again several venturesome souls would go up on the roof "to direct the Japanese airplanes so that they would not drop bombs on us." We got to distinguish the Japanese planes by their sound. The continuous noise of firing and bombs filled our ears. Even the windows in my room shook, and we could watch all the flames against the black sky at night.

The streets of Shanghai were terrible to see. Countless families escaped from burning houses into "foreign settlements," and now literally lived on the streets. A cholera epidemic raged. In the span of just three days, within the isolation hospital near us, 400 cholera cases were admitted, and forty died. All our missionaries evacuated to Shanghai were out helping the homeless and needy. Miss Woosely went out as matron to a hospital for wounded soldiers.

At the same time Communist guerrillas again attacked Yu-Kiang. All missionaries were evacuated, and all our belongings were lost.

Miss McQueen and I traveled from Kiangsi to Shanghai in the flimsiest of clothing. By this time, November 1937, it was really cold in Shanghai. We yearned for our nice warm woolies we had left at our station with everything we possessed, including my precious books that now had been lost for the second time. Kiangsi was soon to be looted again by another Communist band. However it was great to belong to such a warm, loving missionary family as the C.I.M. where missionaries literally "have all things in common." I was given a coat and lovely clothes from headquarters' missionaries.

God graciously gave me the delight of meeting missionaries who had been evacuated from their stations during this unsettled period of guerrilla warfare and invasion by the Japanese.

I marveled at the heavy burden the directors of the mission carried. Missionaries and children were attacked by either Communists or Japanese. We had 1,368 missionaries (not to speak of children), and thus great financial needs, yet that year the *unsolicited* funds rose to the highest total since 1929.

Every morning we had a prayer meeting concerning the whole Japanese and Communist situation. Here we were, in the midst of a war for the possession of Shanghai. Shrapnel was dropping everywhere, a cholera epidemic was at our gates, the sound of firing and menace of bombs overhead never ceased. Yet not a hair of our heads was hurt. No plague touched even the experienced missionaries ministering outside of our headquarters. Our minds were kept in perfect peace.

At this time it was a great inspiration to receive a four-page letter written in pencil (while in bed with bone cancer) by Miss Amy Wilson Carmichael of Dohnavur Fellowship in India. She had received a letter from me on one of her "bad days," yet she began her reply, "Your letter has been in my heart ever since it came. Do you know what it is to have a letter you cannot immediately answer, but cannot ever forget? That is the kind yours was." Coming from such an esteemed spiritual missionary to an absolute novice, this encouraged me greatly, and a fairly close and enriching correspondence followed.

When the war in the Shanghai area erupted, it happened

that the final strategic point of the fighting area was situated on the grounds of the China Bible Seminary, for the seminary was very near the railway.

Previously, in 1927, the buildings had been burned to the ground. They had been rebuilt, but many persons believed that the same catastrophe would happen again. At first they were occupied by Chinese soldiers who were fighting against the Japanese. They fortified the buildings and dug underground trenches. Had the Chinese not been forced to retreat, these buildings, although already badly damaged, would be in complete ruins.

While Miss Brittain was a refugee at the China Inland Mission headquarters, she did not know whether her seminary would survive. Most persons regretfully presumed that these buildings would again be razed to the ground. When news came in of the final skirmish in that area, she saw in her mind's eye the buildings in a mass of ruins. However, she testified that this was a wonderful experience, for while others had their hearts full of sympathy, she said she believed she saw a cross rising up out of the ruins. She recognized that after the Cross comes the Resurrection, and believed that if Satanic forces temporarily prevailed, God had *some better thing* for the seminary.

God confirmed her faith, for later other new buildings ideal for the work were built.

It was during this time that Miss Brittain became even more of a friend and something of a spiritual mentor to me. I remember going into her room once feeling very despondent and like an unworthy Christian. I said, "I need a fresh touch from God, perhaps an outstanding work of the Holy Spirit." She replied, "What you need is to saturate yourself in the Bible. Why don't you leave your study, and lie on an enclosed private porch, and meet God through saturating yourself in one of the books of the Bible?" This was a shock. I had just come out of the Bible Institute, under Mr. Hogben no less, and thought I knew the Bible.

I thought, *She has no idea how well I know the Bible!* Surely there is no person so sure of herself in Bible knowledge as someone just out of seminary or Bible school, and especially one who has just come to the mission field! I had given many testimonies and led many meetings. I really considered I knew the Bible, I knew all the answers! So I thought, *Isn't it too bad that she does not know how much I have read the Bible?* I left disappointed, like Naaman, the captain of the king's guard, who went to Elisha for a cure for leprosy. Elisha offered a simple remedy which disappointed the captain. Naaman expected no less than for Elisha to call on the name of God Himself, at least for some outstanding miracle to be worked. Instead the prescription was a humble one: "Wash in the Jordan seven times."

However, in the mercy of God, I went upstairs and did what Miss Brittain advised. I went onto the balcony and opened my Bible to the book of Hebrews. I started reading the first chapter in the way I always had, analyzing and studying the text as I read.

But something was wrong. I said to myself, "I'm not receiving a thing." Then I looked right up to God and said aloud, "Father, You said that 'man doth not live by bread only, but by every word that proceedeth out of the mouth of the Lord' (Deut. 8:3). Now, Lord, I am a missionary, and I am supposed to tell others that they can live by the Word of God. If I myself do not live there, I'm a phony. Now please prove that I can do this. Lord, I am serious, I am asking You. You promise that You will reward a person who truly seeks You. Lord, it is up to You! I am going to begin reading again. Lord, please make Hebrews come alive to me." I began to read Hebrews again, starting from the beginning.

The next time I looked up, I had finished the whole book. Almost four hours had gone by. Looking back I cannot explain any particular truth the Lord gave me or remember any particular verse that shone with special meaning. But what happened was this. Through reading God's Word in the power of the Holy Spirit and depending upon God to give life through it, it was as though God had picked me up and taken me into Heaven where He dwells. I had been with Him! My entire spiritual being was renewed. Leaving the balcony, feelings of lassitude disappeared, depression was gone—I had received God's words and was rejuvenated in every part of my being.

I write this because it has been one of the secrets of my life. Again and again in China it was impossible to avoid acute loneliness. Sometimes there were acute problems and I suffered from depression. Then I would remember the solution— to saturate myself in God's Word, in other words, God Himself.

(There was another time, much later, in America in the early fifties, and I was reading the Bible one day in Samuel. I was so thrilled over it and I thought, "Oh, what an intellectual treat this is; apart from the spiritual angle, it's such a delight to my mind. There are such rich verses and thoughts in this. It's so marvelous. What do people do who don't have a Bible?" Then I began to reproach myself and say, "Now wait a minute. Don't get to worshiping a book like the Mohammedans worship their Koran. You worship the Lord, not a book. Let's not get to worshiping the Bible!" And it was as though God said back to me, "Yes, but the Bible is different from everything else, because the Bible is the revelation of Me! How I deal with people, what My character is like, what My life is like. I reveal Myself in the Word, and you can love the Bible as much as you like because through it you are loving Me!" And I found that I could love the Bible because I really wasn't loving a book—I was loving the *Lord* who reveals Himself in this book.)

It happened that Dr. Reese, one of our missionaries, examined me. He said I had started into Chinese study too soon after my operation. He ordered from three to six months of complete break from it. As you may imagine, I could not keep staying at the C.I.M. headquarters doing nothing.

Miss Brittain had just managed to rent a building on Yu-Yuen-Lu (a street in Shanghai) and was reopening the China Bible Seminary, which at that time took in fifty-six students, including several young Chinese men who were studying for the ministry. They asked to be allowed to attend classes, since because of the war there was nowhere else they could go. This ultimately led to a new venture for the seminary.

Miss Brittain asked the general director of the C.I.M. if they would be willing to loan me temporarily to the China Bible Seminary to help with secretarial work and bookkeeping. She also hoped that I would be available to teach. How I thanked God for my father's strong insistence on business training. What a joy it was to teach! I deeply enjoyed the family life of the Chinese professors, who occupied the highest positions, as well as getting to know the students. This change brought a real exhilaration. My experience in the Word and these later events made me recall the words of David: "Delight thyself also in the Lord; and he shall give thee the desires of thine heart" (Psa. 37:4).

THIRTEEN

MINISTRY AND CRISES AT MY SECOND INLAND STATION

God of the Heights, austere, inspiring
  Thy Word hath come to me.
  Oh, let no selfish aims, conspiring,
  Distract my soul from Thee.
    Loosen me from Things of Time;
    Strengthen me for steadfast climb.

The Temporal would bind my spirit
  Father, be Thou my stay
Show me what flesh cannot inherit,
  Stored for another day.
    Be transparent, Things of Time
    Looking through you, I would climb.

Now by Thy grace my spirit chooseth
  Treasure that shall abide.
The great Unseen, I know, endureth,
  My footsteps shall not slide.
    Not for me the Things of Time;
    God of mountains, I will climb.

Amy Wilson Carmichael

It was eighteen months after leaving my first station in Kiangsi that I was sent to Lin Ming Kwan, the inland station in north China in the province of Hopeh, arriving toward the end of March 1939. For two days the little train, crammed with Japanese soldiers, officials, and Chinese farmers, had wended its way from Peking through the wide stretches of sandy plain with a stunted tree at intervals to relieve the monotony. Suddenly there would be a gust of wind, and in a moment the whole wilderness would be enveloped in a grey mist with human shadows fighting in the midst of it. That, they told me, was a bit of a windstorm—an everyday affair in Hopeh in this season.

A warm welcome awaited me at the station platform, from Miss Mower, senior missionary, and Miss Onions. We walked along in the biting wind through the yellow desert-like land toward the city. Gradually there loomed before us a grey brick barrier partly in ruin with sand encroaching upon it and a large hole in the middle. This was our city wall! From there we walked along a dilapidated alley, with hundreds of ramshackle mud huts huddled together on each side. This was the main street, one mile long!

However, as one continued walking, it improved upon further acquaintance. Later we walked underneath a beautiful archway over which an idol temple had been built. The colors delighted the eye, for it was set with tiles of blue, yellow, and vivid green. There were two stories with balconies on every side, and the whole was covered with the typical Chinese roof that curls upward at its four corners. One gazed, however, with loathing on the huge, hideous idols outside, which portrayed the heart of the god of this world and represented his power over the minds of the fear-bound people of this little town.

It was a relief to pass under the bell tower at the top of the hill and into the C.I.M. compound, feeling and seeing dust everywhere. The real welcome began when the warm-hearted Chinese Christians gathered around, and I was made to feel at home and wanted from the very beginning by my two dear fellow missionaries.

The compound was really quite celebrated, for the Empress Dowager of China once made a stop there and ate in our dining room. However, since that time several businesses on the premises had failed, and because of this the house gradually became known as "haunted." Finally an independent missionary dared to buy it for a mere song and lived in it. The compound was given into the hands of the C.I.M. about twelve years before my arrival. It was a rambling old place. Every room had a ceiling as high as a barn, many windows, and plain white walls. There were two large courtyards, with the main building making a wall of partition between them. The first one was entered from the bell tower, and was known as the missionaries' courtyard. Several rooms opened on to it. At the back was the women's courtyard, and my room opened on to this, giving me the privilege of living at close quarters with the Chinese. One went out of the back gate and across the street to quite a nice chapel, large enough to seat some 600 people, with little rooms for Chinese Christian workers all around.

My own room was not connected to the house, but was a little shack in the compound. It had a little wooden partition that shut it off from the corner where I slept. There were two cupboards and a writing desk which were set into the wall. Otherwise the only furniture consisted of a camp cot, two tables, and two hard chairs. (The soldiers had used most of the old furniture for firewood when they were in occupation there.) Still, it was surprising what pretty curtains, calendars, and cretonne covers over the wood-covered tin boxes (which were used for chairs) did toward making a room look attractive. For my part, when I knew that so many of the people who came and looked around had recently lost all that they had, I was thankful that I did not have those pieces of furniture which seem so necessary in Western countries, but which would look grand and costly in the eyes of my Chinese sisters.

There was a sameness about every day which might suggest a monotonous life were it not for the odd happenings which distinguished one day from another. All the time I spent at Lin Ming Kwan I was concentrating hard on Chinese study. It was all very different from the eventful days in Shanghai when there was always something special going on at the seminary, and students and teachers were coming back and forth to the home.

Most of my time at Lin Ming Kwan was spent alone with Miss Mower. She was nearly seventy, and I was not quite thirty. Miss Mower was a very earnest Christian. But our general background and personal lifestyles were totally different. Never once did a wrong word pass between us, and we were closest in prayer and in talking about the Lord.

I always remember one funny incident that happened when Miss Alison Ballantyne was still with us. At that time I was an avid reader of John Buchan's books (this was the nom de plume of Lord Tweedsmuir who was then prime minister of Canada). He wrote books of "intelligence intrigue," mysteries which were so well written as to include many enriching thoughts. Of course, any book of that description had to be sent by friends from England. I had just received such a good book by John Buchan, which, after reading, I loaned to Alison Ballantyne. The next morning she appeared at breakfast a little bleary-eyed but purred with delight over the book which she had not been able to put down that night until it was finished.

This was too much for Miss Mower; she said, "I don't know how you two can enjoy these books, which after all, are only stories."

We left the book on the table. It disappeared. Some time later Miss Mower returned the book. We asked, "What do you think of it, Miss Mower?" She replied with great heat, "Thank God, Scotland is rid of that awful villain!" We answered, "But, Miss Mower, it's only a story. It did not really happen." She was nonplussed.

Meetings at the station were held all day Saturday and all day Sunday. One drippingly hot Saturday morning was typical. The preacher was fanning himself desperately. Alas, for the many dear Chinese who had risen at 4:00 A.M. to get there! Mrs. Chang (an ardent worker) went around in between all the sleeping saints, prodding them awake. I myself was terrified I would be caught napping one day! From the seat immediately behind me came rhythmical guzzling noises from an infant of two or three weeks old, who was having a good, comfortable breast-feeding. Periodically, I would draw myself up from the bench to see whether I was as yet stuck to it! (Miss Mower had had a big patch of brown varnish on her dress the day before.) What alarmed me most was the fear that one day I might get up suddenly after a long meeting, and leave a portion of my Chinese gown on the bench. This would demonstrate to wondering, very interested eyes what village Chinese always wanted to know: namely, do missionary teachers wear any underwear? This for some reason, they had always questioned!

Sunday also was a day full of meetings. There were usually seven (including our own morning prayers). The women came into our compound for the whole day. They thought nothing of walking eight or nine miles to get there, and many of them still had their feet bound, which made walking very painful. They also literally carried their lives in their hands, for robbers abounded. They all wore coarse, blue home-spun smocks and long, dark trousers bound tightly up to the knee.

Prayers were uttered aloud by all. The congregation numbered about 300. After several morning services, we missionaries and Chinese all met in the courtyard to chat. Often I would see some woman in one corner, pouring out aloud her prayer to God. (Many times I witnessed miraculous healings in answer to their simple prayers.) This lunchtime was always spent by the missionary in personal counseling. After lunch, there were services, with singing, all praying their different prayers aloud, and at least three hours of preaching by a

Chinese evangelist. Finally we would say good-bye to all our guests at about 7:00 P.M., after which we nearly keeled over from fatigue.

My family had sent me a small phonograph and complete records of Handel's *Messiah*. Miss Mower and I, utterly exhausted, would sit together and listen to it all, dutifully standing up together for the "Hallelujah Chorus." It was God's message to our souls.

Although those days were not easy, there were delightful breaks. The China Inland Mission always saw to it that their missionaries had times of rest and refreshment periodically. After experiences of illness at Lin Ming Kwan, I went to our nearest beach resort at Pei-teh-ho, where the C.I.M. had a cottage for missionaries on holiday. This was the year 1939. While there we heard of the declaration of the Second World War in Europe, after which our world was never the same.

It seems good to record two blessings which still stand out, both belonging to that time at Pei-teh-ho. To begin with, I have a passion for both the sea and mountains. I find God most near when I am alone in such places. It was so beautiful to sit on the rocks, to bathe, to watch the Pacific Ocean as far as the eye could reach. I thought how good it was to be alive for now and eternity, and how good our Creator is to surround us with such beauty. My heart was so filled with joy that God led me to write a thanksgiving letter to my dear mother, as I remembered some of the trials through which she had passed since I was born.

I thanked her for giving me birth, with all the joys of life which the believer inherits. I thanked her for giving me up to the precious work for the Lord among pagan Chinese. Most of all I thanked her for the spiritual heritage she had given to me. Little did I suspect that this letter was the last one she would receive from me. She read it with great joy. However, not long after this she had a stroke and died.

The second experience which left an eternal mark came through companionship with a fellow-worker a little older than I, Miss Lily Snyder. At that time she was engaged in a heavy schedule of teaching the Bible to Chinese in her city. She deeply loved to see the Lord's divine work in the hearts of those she taught. However, her earlier days had had their difficulties. She was placed with a missionary due to retire, who was noted for a very strong will. After Lily arrived at this station, she was surprised that there was not any prayer meeting for Chinese and missionaries together. Very tactfully and rather shyly, she asked whether it would be a good idea to have a combined prayer meeting some day! Her senior missionary made no remark. But, unknown to Lily, she arranged for such a prayer meeting. In fact, Lily heard about it indirectly, and became furious. She thought, "Since I'm not wanted, I won't go to her prayer meeting." Then she realized that it would not be pleasing to God and decided she should make her appearance at the meeting (whether she was invited or not).

Then she recognized that her deeply resentful spirit would hinder any movement of the Holy Spirit at the meeting. In despair, she went down on her knees and pled with her Lord to "prove His power" by delivering her completely from resentment. She went to that meeting filled with the Holy Spirit, completely at rest and happy.

Soon after this she was moved to another station when the older missionary retired. However she made me realize that her acceptance of the Cross *and* the Resurrection was the secret of her most blessed ministry in teaching Bible to the Chinese of her city. How I thanked God for the joy of praying together with her in Pei-teh-ho, and have often thanked Him for our warm relationship ever since.

These were difficult days for me. Cables had arrived stating that both my dear mother and my sister, Marjorie, had died. Marjorie had drowned in a river while rescuing her two little daughters, who had ventured into waters too deep for them. Mr. Roland Hogben, my former C.I.M. Training School professor, was killed in an accident on the Burma Road at the beginning of a tour of China, and I felt as though I had lost a relative.

Once when I was ill I had to travel about one hundred miles to a hospital at Shunteh-fu. There I happened to meet an older missionary, Miss Griffiths, who told me an interesting story, which prepared me for seeing the presence of "demon possession," which is particularly rampant in pagan, idolatrous countries, and is not just a manifestation of psychological trauma.

A demon-possessed woman, a young bride, had been brought to Miss Griffiths. She laid the woman on a big bed in her guest room, when suddenly demons seized this Chinese woman, who then spoke in violent language and sought to destroy herself. The young missionary simply stood and said tremblingly, "This is Jesus' house. Satan cannot come here. Satan, Jesus says you must go out." The woman cried out with a loud cry, and fell back unconscious. When she came to, she was absolutely normal. I never forgot the lesson of the story Miss Griffiths told. Later, I, too, occasionally had to claim God's promises for this purpose, with Chinese helpers who always recognized the difference between demon possession and a simple mental or nervous breakdown.

Those first days in Lin Ming Kwan were very lonely. God allowed that for His purpose and for the future. I was thrown entirely upon Him. I recalled these lines:

> Need'st thou pity, Knight of Jesus?
> Pity for thy glorious hest?
> On, let God and man and angels
> See that thou art blest.

H. Suso

When I returned to Lin Ming Kwan from Pei-teh-ho, I experienced a spiritual crisis. By this time I had passed another examination: I now spoke and understood the language with reasonable facility and enjoyed the Chinese Bible. Although continued study and more examinations were required, I was aching to go to out stations with our Bible woman and to teach. At this time the mission was following a wise policy, that of turning over most of the work to the Chinese, while the missionary "stood in the wings" with counseling and teaching of the evangelists. However Miss Mower had taken the policy farther than was intended. She felt that we should keep ourselves completely in the background and that our primary duty was to pray.

I decided I could not continue under these circumstances. I longed for the teaching days of the China Bible Seminary. I longed to go to the out stations where the Chinese had never heard of Christ and never seen a white woman. I needed a good teacher of Chinese literature to help me prepare for strenuous examinations. There was one good teacher available, but Miss Mower would not allow me to use her because of some church connection which she did not approve of. I decided I would write to the mission asking for a change.

I knelt down by my little cot with my writing pad and pen to ask God how I should write so as not to involve Miss Mower in the problem. While praying, I looked up and saw the large Chinese poster that hung over my bed; it contained the image of the cross as well as a crown of thorns, and there was also a text.

Then it happened! I heard in my mind that record of my commitment again, "Lord, I am willing at any cost that Thy death be worked out in me, in order that Thy resurrection life may be manifested."

In my mind I saw the Lord Jesus, the Lord of Glory, Creator and Sustainer of the universe, in the "sticks" of Nazareth for thirty years. The most brilliant "man" the world has ever known was a common carpenter, because God wanted to show His glory that way. Who was I to think my "talents" or life were wasted? He seemed to say, "You may be able to teach Romans in a Bible school or seminary with good homiletics and clarity, but it will never have any power because you are not willing to live by this. You are here because *you need* this lesson."

Needless to say, the poster, the text, the vision of all that the Lord Jesus endured which was contrary to what He in His humanity would have desired, tore my spirit, bringing tears of repentance. The letter was never written.

Immediately, a brightness seemed to fill the room. There was no darkness at all, just an overwhelming consciousness of His presence. At the same time, re-reading Isaiah 41, I recognized that the "mountains" of difficulty which seemed to block the way to ministry could be swept away by the power of prayer. At that time the following verses were given to me:

ISAIAH 41:15, 16

Fan them with the breath of prayer,
  'Tis God's word to thee,
Thresher of the mountains, Thou
  Take the victory.

Fan them with the breath of prayer,
  Mountains though they be;
And God's wind the heights shall tear
  Scattering them for thee.

Fan them with the breath of prayer,
  E'en the hills shall be
But as chaff, as thou dost dare
  Order them to flee.

Fan them with the breath of prayer,
  Born at Calvary;
Thresh the mountains in His name,
  Claim the victory.

A. Wetherell Johnson

The next day the area superintendent, Mr. R. E. Thompson, came. He talked to Miss Mower, asked about a teacher, asked what Chinese ministry the newest missionary was being given. Without one word from me, he saw to it that I was given a good teacher and recommended that I should be thrust into the Chinese work on my own with the fine Chinese Bible woman we had.

Soon after he left, a Chinese woman about twenty years old knocked at my door and asked how she could be saved. She could not read Chinese; I taught her to do so. Before I left Lin Ming Kwan, I heard her recite from memory the entire book of Matthew. It took about four hours. (The power of His resurrection follows identification with Him in his death [see Rom. 6:5].)

Following this, and through the testimony of this girl, I was asked to lead alone a Chinese Bible class. It almost seemed as though a small revival broke out, for many were saved out of that previously untaught group. It meant teaching them to read first and then explaining the spiritual meaning of the texts. This was followed by singing and a short talk. God gave a special joy in Himself and what He would do, despite inadequacies of the instrument He had chosen at that time.

It is interesting that less than five months elapsed before the C.I.M. headquarters ordered us all out of Lin Ming Kwan because of Japanese invasions and constant fighting. How thankful I am to all eternity that the Lord prevented me from requesting the change. He knew the future and needed to discipline His child to be completely open to His Cross. I wrote this in a letter home:

> For the eternal substance of a thing never lies in the thing itself, but in the quality of our reaction toward it. If in hard times we are kept from resentment held in silence, and filled with inward sweetness, that is what matters. The event that distressed us will pass from memory as a wind that passes and is gone, but what we were while the wind was blowing has eternal consequences.

FOURTEEN

EXTRAORDINARY DEMONSTRATIONS OF GOD'S POWER AMONG PAGANS

But ye shall receive power, after that the Holy Ghost is come upon you: and ye shall be witnesses unto me both in Jerusalem, and in all Judea, and in Samaria, and unto the uttermost part of the earth [Acts 1:8].

Mrs. Wu, our Bible woman, was an outstanding character. Her education was less than that of any reader of this book, but her spiritual walk with God taught me many lessons. Once, when her brother fell downstairs and broke his leg, she said, "Praise the Lord." This was too much for me. It seemed to me a cliché. But when I challenged her, she said, "But Teacher, is not everything that God allows to happen to us intended to bring greater blessing to us?" I was silenced by her obvious spirituality.

Mrs. Wu and I took a two-week trip into an inland village of more than 2,000 untouched souls.

We started early. There was a lovely, clear blue sky. Although it was April, the weather was like an English June. Our bedding (a kind of eiderdown called *pou-kai*) was always with us. It was spread at the bottom of the cart for us to sit on. The cart was a covered, cage-like contraption, three feet by four feet, without springs, and open at the front. I sat in front with my legs dangling over the side, with my back to the carter when he chose to ride (he often walked). The cart was drawn by a donkey, a bull, and a mule (talk about being unequally yoked!).

We lumbered down the smelly lanes of the city, out through the heavy gate, past the temple standing under its sacred tree. Finally we reached open stretches of undulating green wheat about a foot high, making a picture of green with a background of sand. Alas, many mounds were in it which marked the burial of unwanted children, most of them girls. There was a gleam of silver, where water splashed over the old-fashioned irrigation wheel in the shade of a plane tree, and we noticed the scarlet of a child's jacket as he stood to guide it into its appointed channel. Water wheels were turned by a blindfolded donkey or perspiring men and women. There were crowds of magpies, looking like waiters in white dress shirts and black tails. Their calls and the drowsy creak of the water wheels were the only sounds which disturbed the warm stillness.

Then Mrs. Wu got out, and I followed. She saw some men and women working in the fields. After the usual, "Where do you come from? Who are you?" she looked at their beautiful green wheat and pointed to the sky. Using the Chinese term for the God who lives in the sky, she asked, "Doesn't He give you the sun and the water to make things grow? Have you thanked Him?" The answer was "No." Then she spoke of how He sent His Son to save them. Thus we moved on, not knowing whether this seed would fall into "fertile ground" or "stony ground."

We passed through a village of 7,000 souls and later through four even larger ones where they had never seen a white woman nor ever heard the gospel—yet Hopeh province was known as an "evangelized" province of China!

Finally we arrived at a village where there was a nucleus of Christians. We clambered down, and while the Christians were sent for, a crowd of children in motley garments—rags or no garment at all—swarmed around and followed us into the little room prepared for us. They stared and poked holes in the paper windows. They climbed up on anything they could for a better view.

Then the men and women pushed and squeezed in, and a barrage of questions ensued. "How old are you? Are those queer shoes comfortable? Let us see how you walk in them. How many children have you?" They felt our clothes, asked the price, and asked why we had come. A steaming bowl of noodles with pickled greens on the top was brought in with chopsticks, and the imperturbable crowd stayed to watch us eat.

At last three or four believers arrived. What a thrill of joy it gave to hear that Christian greeting, "Peace be to you" in the midst of a heathen rabble! The large market-place outside was now crowded with over 1,000 pagans. I knew I was to speak first, and after that Mrs. Wu would give a long sermon. I used a poster with a text; though I had spent hours preparing the talk, it was short. Once I began to speak, looking over the sea of faces, I became absorbed in the message and desperately longed to convey it fully to those heathen, who had never before heard the gospel.

I was the only white woman there, and at my appearance many of them were astonished. I must have looked to them like some kind of porcelain doll, for when I spoke, they were surprised. "Oh, she can speak!" they said. But the message of Jesus was passed from one mouth to the other—"repent and believe." Gradually Mrs. Wu managed to get to the front and start singing a Chinese tune, and I watched the faces of the crowd as they listened. Again and again came the devil's attack on my mind. These people were pagans, animists, Buddhists. All their life they had never heard the gospel. How could they turn from a life of idolatry to belief in our Lord from one or two messages given by two women—one a Westerner! I answered the devil's words in my mind, quoting over and over Romans 1:16, "I am not ashamed of the gospel of Christ: for it is the power of God unto salvation to every one that believeth. . . ." This attack and my scriptural response to it were repeated I don't know how many times that day.

The next day we sat on the *kang* where we had slept the night before. A *kang* was a raised long brick deck which in winter has fire underneath. To sleep, one curls up in one's *pou-kai*—dressed or undressed—for that is our bed. During the day the *kang* became our receiving room; it was at the back of a shop, owned by the Christian leader in this village, who was also our host. Again the inevitable crowd pressed upon us, beginning with morning light.

One of the blessings of life in China was that of seeing the New Testament come alive in the imagination. As I sat there I thought of the words of Mark 2:2, "Straightway many were gathered together, insomuch that there was no room to receive them, no, not so much as about the door, and he preached the word unto them." I knew exactly why and how those four men let down their friend in front of the Lord Jesus. I knew what it looked like when "the whole city was gathered at the door," and how it was that "they had no leisure, no, not so much as to eat." I often wondered at the thoughtful love of the Lord for His disciples, and His self-lessness, so weary at the end of that long day when He constrained the disciples to get into a boat and go off, while He Himself sent the crowds home. When after only one or two days of crushing multitudes the longing came to hide my head in some corner where curious eyes could not penetrate, I remembered the Son of God Who lived continually in the midst of such crowds. Whenever He saw these multitudes pressing upon Him, His great heart of love was moved with compassion for them, "Because they [also] were as sheep not having a shepherd."

When I was answering questions in my group, a young girl of about eighteen suddenly said to me, "Can I believe if my mother does not?" There was a great wistfulness in her eyes. Of course I told her "Yes," and talked further with her of the Lord's love for her and His power. I urged her to come to the evening meeting to hear more, but at this juncture her big sister appeared from the back and marched her off. We never saw her again. These things break your heart.

The evening meeting began each night after 9:00 P.M., when the men had returned from the fields. Even though my Chinese was still weak and speaking to crowds was difficult for me, I always thanked God for the privilege of this wonderful experience to give out God's living eternal message to a heathen crowd. One was nervous until the moment of standing up, for the atmosphere of unbelief was like Satan's poison trying to seep its way into one's mind. However as soon as I was on my feet and could get my mouth open, the consciousness of the living reality of God's power in the message and the thrill of declaring it overcame any other sensation until I finished. Then Mrs. Wu, on the first night (out of ten) got up and tactfully said, "The foreign teacher has given God's message very clearly," after which she proceeded to tell them what I had said, but more clearly! Words proceeded from her lips swiftly, delivered in the rough country dialect, with many a fitting everyday illustration to prove her point. At least sixty men and women were in the room with many standing outside, listening in the moonlight.

Then someone said, "The teachers are tired, they must go to bed." Again we rolled ourselves up in our bedding and slept together on the brick *kang*.

It was in those days that God gave me visible proof that men and women could be saved even after only one hearing of the gospel. A woman of about fifty came in from an outside village. She had not been heard of before and brought five other women from her region with her. When Mrs. Wu welcomed them she suddenly exclaimed, "You are Mrs. Wu, are you not?" On being assured on that point, she then said, "Surely you are the Mrs. Wu who spoke to me at Ming Shan [a village about three miles from Lin Ming Kwan with over seventy temples at its base]. You had a little baby in your arms then."

"Yes," said Mrs. Wu, "I remember speaking there when

my little girl was a baby. She is nine years old now."

"You remember that I was in the temple bowing down to the idol. You gently touched my arm and said, 'Oh, my dear, you should not worship this idol. The great God of the sky sent His Son, Jesus, because He loves you. You should worship Him.' Then you had me repeat a little prayer. I picked up my basket and went out. Suddenly when I was halfway home something happened here." She then pointed to her heart. "I knew inside me that what you said was true and what I worshiped was not true. I went home and took down my idols."

(I personally trembled as I heard her say this for I had once attended a ceremony of burning idols in a house and have never felt so deeply the power of Satan. This power is fact and not superstition. His power and demon possession is recognized by experienced missionaries in pagan lands. Satan has been known to set fire in revenge when people destroy idols which are from him. On that former occasion, I remember trembling, lest the householder's belief was in us and not in the Lord Himself. I pled the power of the blood of God's protection for that family and actually felt I touched the Lord. I realized what these peasants were up against, but our Lord protects His own when they truly believe in Him.)

The woman continued, "I have never worshiped idols since. I found another woman who knew about Jesus and told me how to pray to Him and I have brought these other five ladies to learn about Him."

This was a joy to Mrs. Wu, and she gave the glory to God. This true story seems almost unbelievable when one knows a pagan land. It thrilled my own heart with unspeakable joy and faith in the power of Christ as I remembered the constant attacks of Satan. To think that this woman had heard the gospel only once and believed is a miracle which has to be seen.

The Japanese-Chinese War made it impossible to carry on a ministry. The C.I.M. ordered all missionaries in our area to return to the Shanghai headquarters until the hostilities had died down. As it happened, we were never able to return to this part of China.

I shall never forget Mrs. Wu coming into my room very early in the morning, kneeling by my bed, and sobbing her heart out, for we had become very close.

There was one other Chinese who had become very special to me. It was Mr. Ren of the village of Wu-Chuang. He was a very simple-minded Christian who never could make much of reading, though he tried his best with his Bible. His was the only Christian home in the village, but he had lived an earnest, God-fearing life, and his wife had believed with him. He had been slowly dying of cancer of the throat for several months; the last month had been one of slow starvation and much pain. He arranged his affairs, did his best for his wife, and got his daughter promised to a Christian boy.

With everything settled, he said, "I'm ready, Lord Jesus, any time now." On Tuesday morning we knew he had not long to live, but at 9:00 A.M. as he lay quietly, fully conscious, his face suddenly lit up with joy and he said, "The door is open, I can see hundreds of them all waiting for me."

"Who?" asked the Bible woman.

"Why the angels, of course, they are all in white, and they are smiling and beckoning. Be quick and put on my shroud, for my soul is on its way." He was perfectly conscious all the time and spoke to people who came in, calling them by their names, and said, "Amen," to prayers offered up for him. Then after about half an hour, his eyes had a far-away look in them, and he said, "I'm going," and just as gently the breath stopped. The heathen were awed: they had never seen a death like that, and he had been so obviously conscious. There were no tears, for his joy was infectious. It seemed as though the doors had opened right into the sunshine of Heaven, and we felt the darkness and weariness of this sin-stricken world all the more, for our hearts were sick with longing to be there.

FIFTEEN
PREPARATION FOR ENEMY OCCUPATION

When the enemy shall come in like a flood, the Spirit of the Lord shall lift up a standard against him [Isaiah 59:19].

Upon arriving in Shanghai, we found our mission directors making plans for future eventualities of war. So severe was the fighting in the city that the C.I.M. set up a second headquarters in western China, in Chungking. World War II was being waged furiously in Europe. Even there the C.I.M. was under fire: in a particularly terrifying German blitz, the London headquarters was damaged. However, in spite of the bombings, 800 persons dared to attend the C.I.M. annual meeting in Queen's Hall.

Miss Mower and I, as well as many other evacuees, were warmly welcomed at the Shanghai headquarters. It was a delight to get to know the missionaries for whom we had prayed, all arriving from different stations.

Life goes on even in the midst of war. Some parts of nearby Shanghai were safe, and I was able to take advantage of some free time to do some shopping for dresses. Shanghai had a good tailor whose unintentionally humorous advertisement, splashed on his window in big English letters, we all enjoyed: LADIES HAVE FITS UPSTAIRS.

I was asked to fill in for a missionary schoolteacher at a C.I.M. organized high school for girls in Yangchow, which is some distance from Shanghai. I was to be the teacher companion to the senior missionary Miss Lena Sellon. The high school was at the far end of the compound where we missionaries had received our language training and overlooked a large, beautiful garden. This was where I had had some precious meetings with the Lord in the early days in China. It turned out that my bedroom also overlooked the garden, and I would push my bedding out onto the balcony, cover it with waterproofing, and fashion an umbrella over my head. I reveled in the thunderstorms, remembering what the Bible says in Psalm 29 and again in Job, that the thunder is His voice. This will ever remain a precious memory with me. Unfortunately it was shortlived. Dear Miss Sellon came to me one day and said in those familiar words, "For the sake of the Chinese. . . ." So, in an effort to uphold Chinese etiquette, back into the bedroom went my bedding!

My work was to teach Bible to the Chinese students in Chinese. One afternoon I taught the story of Moses and the Israelites when they were chased by Pharaoh's great host and stood before the Red Sea with apparently no escape. Moses stood alone in an impossible situation (Ex. 14:10–12). But Moses believed in God's deliverance, and the outcome was miraculous. At that time, as always, I emphasized that the Egyptians of that day worshiped idols but the Israelites worshiped God, and God delivered them.

The next morning one of the students came to see me long before school started. She said, "After yesterday afternoon I decided I would never again worship idols." Now Chinese custom was that before leaving home for work or school every member of the household would go before the house idol and kneel down, with the head touching the ground in worship for that day.

When this girl (the youngest of twelve children) came to her turn, she stood straight and said, "I worship Jesus and I cannot bow down to the idol." At first her mother and father tried persuasion, but she was adamant. Finally, her father had had enough; he took her and beat her unmercifully with rods all over her body. Yet still she refused to worship the idol. As I looked at her bruised body and heard this story I began to weep. She then said, "Don't cry, Teacher. The Lord was with me just as He was with the three Israelites in the fire, and *He has taken the sting away.*" Little did she realize what her words meant to me. Many a time I have been wounded by some situation or an injustice since then, and again and again the words come back, *"He has taken the sting away."*

It wasn't long before the war situation forced Miss Sellon and me out of Yangchow back to Shanghai. C.I.M. "loaned" me (at Miss Brittain's request) to the China Bible Seminary in Kiangwan (the seminary was also sometimes called Kiangwan Bible Seminary) about ten miles outside of Shanghai.

When I returned to the seminary, where Miss Brittain was still principal, there were some 110 students enrolled from nearly every part of China as well as Singapore, the Philippines, and Taiwan.

I taught Romans and Leviticus, this time in Chinese. I gave the students questions to prepare for class before any lecture was given (a la Mr. Roland Hogben!). I also made a point of counseling with each student, hearing each one's story and by God's help answering any personal questions he or she might have.

One man had been since college days a key liaison for colleges on behalf of the Communists. He completely accepted Marxist doctrine (although he came from a family who were deeply loyal to General Chiang Kai-shek and others in high places). Later he worked closely with Communist Mao Tse-tung. One day during the internecine fighting, he was captured by Chiang Kai-shek's army and put in prison under sentence of execution with six others the following day. He concluded that his end had come. However, because of his father's influence, while the other prisoners were executed, he was set free. Soon after, he contacted one of the seminary's woman graduates working on the

Burma border, who spoke to him of our Lord and urged him to come to the seminary. She nonchalantly wrote to Miss Brittain and the dean of women recommending him but not giving any of his history! Had she done so, he would not have been accepted, for screening was strict during those tumultuous days.

He was placed in my class during our study in Leviticus! We had reached Chapter 25 on the theme of the "Year of Jubilee." One day, after he had been with me about three weeks, he came to my office and told his whole story. He began by saying that the Marxist ideals had been in the center of his heart since he was sixteen years of age; he demonstrated with his hands as though acting a charade. By this time I was gasping! Just how had he slipped through admission? Then with the same vivid gestures, he pointed to his heart and said, "This is all gone . . . the Lord Jesus is here now."

When asked what had made this change of attitude, he said, "I joined the Communist party because of their ideals of comradeship. However, I slowly discovered that the 'comrade,' like every other natural human being, sought first his own welfare. I concluded that this was life and accepted what I presumed was the realistic situation. But when I came to this seminary in the middle of the school term, to my amazement the men students came to welcome me at the gate and insisted on carrying my baggage [which was counted as coolie work in China]. Then a student gave up his best bunk [the lower one] to me, while he occupied the top bunk. This was truly comradeship of a high order." Mr. "X" was impressed by the hour of earnest prayer, Pastor David Yang's messages, and of course, the loving Christian atmosphere.

What intrigued me was when he talked about the Year of Jubilee and God's command that every slave be freed and every man's land that had been taken from him, be returned. He said, "But this is absolutely contrary to what the Communists believe about the 'caring' Christian's God."

A literary man whose experience had been as a brilliant journalist, Mr. X had an interview with Miss Brittain.

As a result, he was appointed to assist me with Chinese writing and speaking, and we became close friends in our work. Eventually he married the girl who had recommended him to the seminary! Later he continued to work strenuously for the Lord in far west China.

At communion service, we always invited Christian believers from Kiangwan village (mostly brought to Christ by students) to join us as Pastor David Yang took charge. Once a student unobtrusively came to me in the middle of communion and whispered, "Teacher, there is a village woman outside sobbing her heart out." I quietly slipped out and found her in floods of tears. I asked what was her trouble and she said, "I want to take communion so much, I cannot bear it. But I cannot come in, I am too unworthy." I explained to her that the blood of our Lord Jesus was shed for her, and that God counted her completely worthy and even wanted her to eat with Him. I brought her in to sit next to me. Never will I forget the ecstatic look of unimagined joy on that face as she took of the bread and wine and joined in our praise! I often wonder if the Western Christian world has not become so casual about communion that we are in danger of losing the joy and love of the early Christians.

I was truly in my element, realizing that this was what God had foreordained for me, before the foundation of the world (Eph. 2:10; Ps. 139:13–16).

Although at the beginning of 1941 the seminary ministry seemed to be reaching a new peak, the Japanese invasion tactics were increasing. I vividly remember one day standing quite near the largest hotel in Shanghai with a young missionary, when suddenly a bomb fell in a direct hit on the hotel and planes flew above us. The young missionary clutched my arm saying, "Audrey, what shall we do?" The only answer which came to my mind was a sentence by Tennyson, "Man is immortal 'til his work is done."

While going back and forth to the C.I.M. headquarters, we British and Americans and other nationalities would be glued to our radios. Nonetheless, we would come to our mealtime tables to sit opposite German missionaries (who often knew little enough of the real story of their country's Hitler), and carefully no one, but no one, made mention of the Second World War. We knew that should America be brought into the East, our work in China would be at an end. At that time the following words came to mind:

February 1941

'Though China's torn
And Europe ravaged
By enemies fierce and lawless
And America's threat
To come into the war
Full soon may be upon us,
'Though all the world's chaotic
And nothing stable is
Our God who controlleth the stars in their courses
And biddeth the wind to cease
Sees nations as drops in a bucket
And where He dwelleth is Peace.

'Though friends depart
And home ties break
And work is interrupted,
'Though plans of years
Built up with prayers
Be suddenly disrupted,
If those we love
Must suffer pain
Which we would fain remove
Or tread a way
Not understood
That God their faith may prove
He who after the counsel of His perfect will
Aye worketh His purpose of grace
Hath promised our Spirit-born hope to fulfil
In acceptance lieth Peace.

'Though the minions of hell
My spirit assail
With doubts, dismay, or anxious fear
Or subtle panic guidance,
If ills befall
When bereft by all
In whom I've placed reliance
And alone I fight
'Gainst Satan's might
Whose time's too short for dalliance,
Then I'll take my stand in Christ's triumph train
Led forth from place to place
So that incense fragrant—knowledge of Him
Is sent to every race.
The victory's been won
On the Cross by God's Son;
He Who stands in that triumph has Peace.

A. Wetherell Johnson

Later in the year fighting intensified, and American intervention seemed inevitable. At that time the American consul ordered all Americans to leave, if possible. The English consul advised leaving China if one had children or was in a lonely position, although he did not insist on this as strongly as the American consul, who knew that American aliens would be the number-one enemy. Consequently, many C.I.M. missionaries had to leave the country.

Although I missed my fellow missionaries very much, it was a thrill to be working alone with the Chinese. Now, for the first time at the seminary I was teaching a theology class.

I had promised the C.I.M. that if there was any kind of suspected danger I would immediately return to the C.I.M. headquarters in Shanghai. Then came Pearl Harbor. The little English gun boats in the Wangpu River at Shanghai sank with all their guns blazing until the end. At that moment I was

141

speaking at morning prayers. I heard the guns but said hopefully, "It's just thunder."

Classes continued that morning. However, unknown to me a foreign school near us had been burned to the ground, and aliens, not far from us on the other side, had suffered a bad instance of several rapes.

At about 11:00 A.M., as I was teaching theology, Miss Caroline Ho (our dean) came to me. She said, "Teacher, we have tried to hide you from them, but they know you are here and insist on seeing you." I replied, "You should not worry. Thank you. I will certainly return to the residence and meet the Japanese soldiers." I'll always remember that walk edged with weeping willow trees from the administration building to the residence. Knowing all the students were praying for me, I stopped a moment under a willow tree to pray for courage. The Lord said to me, "You are in Me; no one can touch you unless he touches Me first." I walked into our living room to meet six Japanese soldiers with bayonets drawn. They put them against my neck, saying, "This is what we will do to you if you move from here." Then they left.

Of course all telephone communication was cut, but the Chinese had ways of seeing that a message could be delivered the ten miles to the C.I.M. compound. The next thing I knew German missionaries (allies with the Japanese) had arrived by car to rescue me, an enemy alien.

The China Inland Mission received me with open arms. Presuming I was in shock, they offered me tea and rest, and gave me much love. I delighted in the love of the missionaries, but thanks to God was not even remotely in shock. That which impressed me most was the fact that England and Germany were violently at war, yet the Christian fellowship and kindness of those German missionaries surmounted all tensions.

By this time the Japanese had taken over Shanghai completely. We missionaries were all given numbered arm bands which had to be worn whenever we went out, boarded a vehicle, went shopping, or walked in the park. Someone must have informed the Japanese that 666 would not be an acceptable arm band for missionaries, for with the hundreds of arm bands no one had that number! Mine was a bright red 15421, a number I was to become quite familiar with.

It was hard to leave the delightful work of teaching at Kiangwan. However, missionaries began to recognize that the less contact we had with the Chinese, the safer it was for them.

Soon we heard that all enemy aliens were to be interned in Japanese camps. This possibility brought us to our knees for an extra day of prayer and fasting. We prayed alone in our rooms. Outside in the corridor was a table with water and dry bread. No one knew who decided to fast completely or who felt led to take nourishment.

Later we met in the conference room. It was interesting. The expectations of our prayers and faith ran along two lines. Some prayed that God would make a difference between believers and the purely secular groups as He did at the time of the Exodus. Others prayed that we might be spiritually fortified and be a blessing to non-Christians if God willed for us to undergo internment. Such was the working of the Holy Spirit in our midst that when evening came all the prayers were along the same lines. God Himself revealed to us gradually that He was going to allow us to be interned for His purpose.

Soon after this prayer meeting the Japanese news came as a final order. We were to prepare to go into camp, each person with one bed and bedding and one suitcase. We all expected that the war would end soon. Perhaps we would be interned for six months, at most. Little did we anticipate that it would be almost three years.

> Gently loosens He thy hold
> Of the treasured former things
> Loves and joys that were of old
> Shapes to which the spirit clings
> And alone, alone He stands
> Stretching forth beseeching Hands.

G.T.S.

S I X T E E N
INTERNMENT

*How excellent is Thy loving-kindness, O God! therefore the
children of men put their trust under the shadow of thy wings*
[Psalm 36:7].

On a boiling hot day in August, the Japanese came to the
C.I.M. headquarters, and all of us there were herded into
buses. There were two internment camps in the area, one in
the heart of Shanghai and another about fifteen miles out called
the "Longhua camp" to which I was designated with nearly
2,000 other aliens. There were Russians (married to British or
Americans), English, Belgians, Americans, Scandinavians, and
other nationalities.

My Chinese friends came to help me. I had just a single bed
and bedding, but it was amazing to see all they hid inside—a
sack of charcoal and a little stove which later made me very
popular! Since this was all that each person could take, I had
my worldly possessions, precious mementos of Mother and
family, prized books, and everything which I valued most
packed into three tin-lined "tea boxes" (wooden boxes of
about two cubic feet). I left these with my Chinese friends to
store until we were released.

Just as I was leaving the empty headquarters building I saw

a fat book with the cover torn off lying with the garbage on the floor. Realizing I would have no books except a Bible, I tucked it under my arm. At that time, although I dearly loved all Americans I had met, I had never been in the United States. Miss Brittain came from Birmingham, Alabama—the book was *Gone with the Wind!* Although I had some reservations as I read this book, it gave me an insight into the American south which I never forgot.

After we alighted from the buses, we found ourselves in a large compound which had once been a high school. The Japanese guards had already taken the best buildings. But many of us were put into the former horse stables, slightly adapted for human use. My hut was about 100 feet by 50 feet, and when we arrived, it held eighty-nine persons. The men internees were ordered to help with the beds. Beds, with not more than two to three feet between, were all lined against the right and left walls. In the middle of the hut was another row of beds. At one end there were two small wash basins. Also there were what we called "the horse boxes" because the top half was open to the world! These were the six toilets for eighty-nine persons.

Eventually the Japanese put the married women and children in one hut, the men in another, and what they called the "loose women" in huts like mine.

I shall always remember the tumultuous arrival of that first day. The heat was stifling. We were all waiting our turn for beds to be unpacked, and of course there were no chairs. One lady nearby had her little girl and husband. Her husband was bitter. The small child began to cry, "Let's go home now, Mummy. I don't like this place." Then the mother cried, and finally the father cried too. The company was very mixed. My bed touched the bed of an infamous madam from Shanghai. Further down the room was the principal of the finest girls school in Shanghai. One woman was the loudest snorer I have ever heard. Some of the eighty-nine inmates would surround her bed to wake her up in order that they might get some sleep. Near me was an elderly C.I.M. missionary, Miss Smith, who later died of ptomaine poisoning. She was taken out in a coal-cart with soiled canvas for a cover. How good that she was in Heaven, for she was a Scottish woman who had often spoken about the dignity of funeral services.

Our meals were somewhat special. Each internee had been ordered to bring one thermos bottle, one enamel basin (in which to wash, usually placed on the bed!), one enamel plate for all food, and an enamel mug.

I do not remember the first night's meal, when the 2,000 lined up for their food, sat on backless benches, and later washed their own plates, but I vividly remember the first breakfast. Every morning it was rice. There was no milk, and we never saw an egg! At first I was particular and took quite a long time removing the worms from the rice, but later I ate everything. After all, it was meat! At midday we ate rice again. At night there was rice and a one-inch cube of meat for each person. However, some gardening people in our camp had the sense to bring seeds in their pockets and suitcases. In our spare time they organized other internees to help plant these in empty places on the compound. Gradually, plants of spinach, cabbage, tomatoes, and beans came up. Internees were supervised by Japanese to prepare the meals. Therefore, now and again our evening meal included half a spoonful of *our* vegetables.

We stood in line twice a day for water. Longhua water was undrinkable, so all our drinking water was brought in from the city by water-cart. Also, it had to be boiled.

As time went on we got more hungry, especially at night. When I entered camp I weighed about 145 pounds; three years later I was less than 106 pounds. No trouble about losing weight in those days!

At night when the war was at its fiercest, the Japanese would not allow us any light. We all went to bed at 7:00 P.M.—all eighty-nine of us! We would get into bed and strap ourselves with a tight belt which helped diminish our hunger pains. Then one woman would start, "Girls, wouldn't you like a beef

147

steak?" "Yes!" "With potatoes?" "Yes!" "And strawberries, with cream?" "Yes!" And so the suggestions would continue. We would dream we were eating this wonderful food and wake up in the morning to *rice!*

Every morning there was a Japanese inspection. Beds were made. It was insisted that we stand at attention as the guards might come in at any time. This meant standing by our bed, hands at our sides, feet together, all at strict attention. I saw a woman of about seventy just opposite me who chose to stand at ease; she received a bayonet jab in her thigh. We learned that it never paid to relax. Internees invented names for the different guards. One was called, "Mussolini," another, "The Face Only a Mother Could Love," and we gave each guard a similar appellation.

In the winter when it was very cold, sometimes fifteen below zero (of course, with no heating in that uninsulated wooden hut), we all went to bed fully dressed wearing coat and all! Doctors told us not to wash except just around our face to avoid losing necessary body oil. It was just too bad if one had false teeth and put them in a mug of water. They would have to wait until midday for the ice to thaw! Once I decided to save my evening thermos water for washing in the morning. I put my enamel basin on the bed, poured out the warm water, washed and dried my face, then found a layer of ice had already formed in the enamel basin. And my face cloth was frozen solid.

In summer we suffered intense heat and sickness. The Japanese did not spray the rice paddies which lay behind our electric fence around the camp. Therefore, 90 percent of the internees suffered from malaria. I once took the temperature of a woman next to me who had a high fever, and discovered to my horror it was 108 degrees. Yet she was not considered ill enough to go to the twenty-bed hospital because it was "just malaria."

Because of the extreme crowding, it was difficult to get into serious conversation. In addition, we all spent each day in various occupations. However, there were some opportunities to speak of Christ. I remember one girl, twenty years old, who came to know the Lord. After this, she attended a teaching session with a noted liberal professor. She came back to me asking about the authenticity of Genesis. As I looked at her, suddenly I remembered I John 2:27, "But the anointing which ye have received of him abideth in you, and ye need not that any man teach you; but as the same anointing teacheth you of all things and is truth, and is no lie, and even as it hath taught you, ye shall abide in him." I had plenty of explanations of faithful interpretations of the creation but I was led to turn to this verse. I said, "The Holy Spirit Who inspired Genesis is *in* you. Actually, Doris, you know now what is fact and what is theory. Think and pray about this text, and then tell me your impression." I looked hard into her eyes and prayed with her for God's revelation. She not long afterward came back and said, "Miss Johnson, I believe that all the time I knew the answers, but now I have no question at all. God has shown me His Bible is authoritative."

Later, while ill in the hospital, I shared a room with a Jewish girl, Sheila Abraham. We had long talks about what Jewish animal sacrifices represented. Her Jewish father began to be anxious about her and started talking with me. One day he came in and we had a discussion. I asked him what he thought God intended the animal sacrifices to represent and what he understood concerning the Prophet about whom Moses wrote in Deuteronomy. His reply startled me. He said, "Moses said that if a prophet prophesied *not* in God's name that prophet should die. And this is what happened to Jesus." I was quick to respond, "But He arose and ascended into Heaven, seen by many witnesses." Mr. Abraham shook his head and we left without further discussion.

Mr. Abraham had twelve children, the youngest of whom was a son, Ezekiel. He was a noble man and a real believer in Jehovah. When internment was over and internees were being dispersed, I overheard in passing an interesting conversation. An English policeman said sneeringly, "You won't have any trouble finding a place to live; you will have money tucked away." Mr. Abraham replied seriously, "My God always provides for the needs of His children." I thought: *what a complex of belief—so near, yet so far!*

Perhaps the most difficult part of the internment for me was the total lack of privacy. I would feel the person in the next bed move during the night and would pull my bed out, only to find she had pushed hers further toward mine in order to give herself more space on her other side. I have seen women tear each other's hair out over space between beds, or whether windows were to be open or shut. The atmosphere was often very tense as the months dragged on, and even the smallest things would develop into minor crises.

At one time we had a situation which reminded me of Paul at Ephesus. In our camp there had already been a disturbance over an escape. It involved a broken marriage relationship, and the Japanese decided just to wink at it.

Later, in mid-August, somehow six men succeeded in getting away in spite of the electric fence around the compound. There was pandemonium in the camp. All of us, including 500 children, were not allowed out of our huts and were kept without drinking water or food. The Japanese severely interrogated the "captains" of the rooms where each of the escapees had been located. One of these young captains did the worst thing possible. He dashed through the door and fled across the green patch close to our hut. The guards pursued him, knocked him down, and began beating him without mercy. This was too much for our eighty-nine women. They flew out of the hut and laid onto the guards like hornets! This incited the rest of the inmates who also joined in the fray. At this the guards were naturally frightened and fled.

By now, the entire camp of internees were gathered outside the balcony of the stonehouse used by the guards, shouting all their pent-up venom. "You little yellow devils," "You monkeys, we hate you," and on and on for two whole hours. (I love the Japanese. Let the reader remember this was war, when the worst of humanity is seen.) I was in the mob, not shouting but watching the large number of guards with guns trained on the mob. They were longing for the order from their commandant to shoot us. But he realized that if one of us was shot, the 2,000 internees would, in their insane fury, probably kill them all. After that we would all have been massacred. It was a most dangerous moment.

Finally, the Bishop of Shanghai and the Belgian consul asked to be allowed to speak to the mob. We were ordered back into our huts by them. Meanwhile these two officials tried to effect a compromise with the Japanese commandant. They asked first that the "room captains" be released without punishment. Second, they requested that food and drinking water be provided, and that the children, at least, be allowed out of their huts. In return these two gentlemen promised that they would see that there were no more "mob scenes," and that we would obey the rules of the Japanese. Following this conference they sent word to all of us to submit if we wished to live—and we did!

What a mercy of God's protection was here! I knew enough of the history of Japanese invasions and punishments in time of war to realize how wonderfully God had delivered us from total disaster.

The next morning we opened our eyes to find the whole camp filled with armored tanks. The "room captains" were never seen again.

Unknown to the majority of the internees, a group of six men had made and operated a radio, having hidden it in a wall. They were brave men, for the same thing had been done in a Hong Kong camp, and twenty-seven men had been executed when discovered, although none of the men would have betrayed another. Therefore, our men were very cautious. There would be rumors among the internees who imagined that news was carried by the Chinese drivers of the drinking water carts. Watch though I did, I could never detect any conversations that would account for these rumors.

At those times I would recall these lines:

151

When hosts of hell encompass me
And fears upon the soul advance,
Open my eyes, dear Lord, to see
Thine armies of deliverance.

The heavenly hosts the mountains fill,
O Leader unto victory,
Lead through the long day's journey fight, until
This land shall know thy liberty.

One amazing triumph during our internment was the education of 500 children of all ages in one room, mostly without the aid of books, but with teachers of excellent experience. In one corner children were learning to read from a blackboard; in another part of the room a senior mathematics class was going on; and somewhere, in the middle of the room, physics and general science was taught to seniors preparing for matriculation. I taught a group who needed study in French, and someone else taught Latin.

I will never understand how so many different and important educational groups managed to be carried on in one room. And the true concentration of these many children! The greatest reward of the teachers was that when matriculation examinations were held for English schools, students from these classes were accepted without question when the war was over.

During these days I made a bad blunder. I realized the monotony in our huts needed to be broken by some fun. I had in my possession a really funny mix-up of Scriptures, which I read aloud, resulting in peals of laughter. But nearly as soon as I had done this, the Lord convicted me deeply for using His most precious Word in jest. When one constantly studies any book, words and phrases from that book are apt to be thought of more lightly and likely to pop into one's mind at inappropriate situations, rendering them comical. But I was convicted that it was blasphemy to use God's Word in such a way, so frivolously. I was disturbed to realize that despite all the spiritual light God had been so gracious to grant to me, that I could have been so blind to have done this.

Periodically, a little group gathered for prayer. I will never forget the recitation of the Lord's Prayer in that group. The word "Father"—His love, forgiveness and grace so filled me that even my sin of misusing Scripture was put to a good purpose—led me to a new realization of relationship with my heavenly Father in his forgiveness.

There *were* fun times, though. One evening the Japanese allowed us to get together for an operetta by Gilbert and Sullivan, which we had to perform from memory.

Following this, knowing the guard would not understand what we were singing, we sang to a catchy music hall tune:

> *Picadilly, Leicester Square,*
> *We don't mind how soon we're there.*
> *How much longer must we wait?*
> *Come on, Winnie, don't be late;*
> *Open up that Longhua gate.*
> *Picadilly, here we come. . . .*

Allied planes appeared from time to time, but we were told that if we went to the windows or showed any excitement about these planes, we would be punished. The reader should realize that we had *no* news of the progress of the war, yet now it was actually nearing the end.

Under such circumstances verses came easily to mind.

In Autumn: HOMESICK FOR ENGLAND

> *Oh England! Nature's England*
> *How far thou art away*
> *The longing for my countryside*
> *Is with me all the day.*
>
> *Those lovely lands all filled with mist*
> *Mysterious, white, enfolding*

The keen fresh air, all fragrant with
Wet earth and leaves a'moulding.

That rustle underneath one's feet
A carpet russet brown,
While overhead some scarlet haws
A wild rose hedge doth crown.

Through beeches tall, close fitted, grey
The uphill road doth wind
Their flaming branches red and gold
Do steal 'way my mind.

Till I forget this ugly camp
And cease to smell this fetid air
For I'm lost in glorious English woods
Now that Autumn's there.

A. Wetherell Johnson

DELIVERANCE

*Thou hast caused men to ride over our heads; we went through
fire and through water: but thou broughtest us out into a
wealthy place* [Psalm 66:12].

Once, when we were standing at attention waiting for inspection, my friend muttered to me, "They say the Allies have dropped some kind of bomb. Do you believe it?" I said, "No, I don't."

We were again standing waiting for inspection one day in August when one of our internee men, already inspected, put his head in the doorway of our hut and said, "Cheer up, girls; war's over!" We all looked at each other and wondered. There had been so many rumors, yet "hope springs eternal in the human breast." But this time confirmation was not long in coming.

The Belgian consul, like most of the men, went around in the summer heat in shorts minus a top. That morning we saw him nobly attired in full regalia, coattails, pin-striped trousers, and spats! We saw him walk toward a car, and, wonder of wonders, the Japanese commandant, whom we greatly feared, was opening the car door for him and bowing to him as he went out through those gates en route to the Swiss consulate!

Only then did we know that the rumors were true: the war had ended. The whole camp went crazy with delight! Somehow thoughts of the Lord's coming came to my mind!

The Japanese guards, who had toward the end of the war acted cruelly toward the men, feared reprisals. They were now in the position of defeat. Therefore, they shut themselves in cabins, barricading the doors, and we did not see them anymore.

Meanwhile, we were rejoicing in victory and gazing up into the sky. It was full of planes with parachutes of every brilliant color—yellow, red, green, blue. I still have a part of a red parachute among my mementos. Each parachute carried cartons full of cans of food which were collected in the kitchen quarters. As the internees lined up for the distribution, I met one girl coming out of the building, carrying a large carton. I asked, "How many cans of food are we allowed?" She replied, "We each receive a whole carton." I was stupified—"a whole carton?"

Great was the excitement as the cartons were opened. There was a tin of powdered milk, called "Klim"; there was tea, powdered egg, cans of bacon and pork. The Jews of course did not want the pork! I always remember a somewhat embarrassed Jew coming to me, holding in his hand a can of pork which he wanted to exchange for toilet paper. All the time we were in camp we only once received toilet paper. That was one Easter when we heard that the Japanese emperor was to give a gift to each of us. This turned out to be the only roll we received. It was always called, "emperor's gift." The Jewish man asked me if I would exchange his tin of pork for an "emperor's gift," some of which had been included in each carton.

Almost immediately an outstanding American liaison officer arrived at the camp. I call him outstanding, for I have never met anyone who had such a thorough knowledge of all areas of World War II fighting, and who could articulate his knowledge in such an interesting manner.

We had not had any magazines or newspapers. We all sat

on backless benches, awaiting his remarks. He looked around and said, "Tell me, what do you know about the war?" The English replied that their last news was the crisis at Dunkirk! Then this American kept us spellbound for two hours as he described the war in Burma, on the sea, the General Mac-Arthur drive, the campaigns in Italy, and the invasion of France and Germany. After that the Americans passed out every kind of journal and newspaper they had brought.

About this time, having lived with only the Japanese flag in sight (which they called the "Rising Sun" but which we impertinently called the "Poached Egg") we wished to unfurl all the flags represented by the different nationalities among us. The women went to work to produce material from their clothes in order to make this into flags. We decided to unfurl them on the same balcony where guards had stood with revolvers drawn at the mob scene of previous days. Just then the religious group in our midst decided that the unfurling of the flags should be embodied in a religious service.

Never will I forget that dramatic scene. Two thousand newly released internees stood before that balcony where the flags were now mounted but still unfurled! Someone had managed to procure from the Chinese a small harmonium. We sang, "O God Our Help in Ages Past," and also "Praise My Soul the King of Heaven." Then the master of ceremonies read two very meaningful passages of Scripture from the Old Testament, chosen partly in deference to the Jewish friends present. He read the whole of Deuteronomy 8, which remarkably fitted our situation and was a warning to the nations, "lest ye perish." Following this, he read the beautiful Psalm 23. There were steps in front of the building on which sat Mr. Abraham with his twelve children. I watched him tracing the Hebrew characters of both passages in his Hebrew Bible with his little boy Ezekiel's fat finger, and I was very moved.

Following the singing and reading, the leader led us in prayer, and all the flags on the balcony—about ten of them—were unfurled. We were asked to keep a deep silence as we remembered the lives laid down for this victory. The sun was

157

setting, the sky was red, the only sound we heard was the flap, flap, flapping of the treasured unfurled flags that represented our new freedom!

At the end of the silent prayer someone sat down at the harmonium and played the national anthems of all the nations represented. There was not a dry eye among us as we sang.

After this, we crowded through the opened gates and streamed through the malaria-ridden paddies to the river not far away, reveling in nature's beauty. Later we returned to camp to find many Chinese there. By now, our relationship with them had changed dramatically. Aliens, including missionaries, had suffered with them against a common war enemy, and they could not do enough for us. Bakers sent bread, butchers brought meat, and a general came to ask what he too could do for us.

Most people reading this history would imagine that everyone would want to return to his own country as soon as possible, but this was not so for me. I wanted first to enjoy my freedom in China: to visit Chinese friends, to see the C.I.M. headquarters (occupied until this time by Japanese) and to meet again my friends among the directors, people such as Mr. and Mrs. Cyril Weller.

Notwithstanding, our governments were concerned to get their nationals back. To my dismay my name was on the list of the first batch scheduled to return to England by ship. None of my friends or any other missionary was included in that list of 300 or 400. Someone said, "Why don't you go and ask to be changed?" But missionaries are not supposed to fuss, so I stayed on the list and said good-bye to many internee friends. Our precious Chinese saw to it that my three tin-lined boxes, which held all I now possessed, were sent to the camp to be put on the boat. There were no labels to be had. The three boxes were simply marked—JOHNSON 15421. As I stood at the rail, I saw the three boxes being loaded safely onto the boat.

We were assigned to an L.S.T. boat. I am sometimes inclined to call it L.S.D., for it turned out to be quite "a trip."

It was flat and we had camp cots lined all along the deck. When the boat lurched, the cots all slid to one side. It wasn't long before I had to be carried down to sick bay by British sailors. We were just out of Shanghai, yet I was not allowed out until we reached Ceylon, Colombo. The sailors were wonderfully kind and treated me like royalty. Having lived for over three years terrified of any soldier or sailor in uniform, I said one day to one of my "nurses," "What makes you so good to us?" He replied in Cockney slang, "Well, you're our'n ain't cha?" (Translated, "You're one of our own, aren't you?") I thought it was the sweetest thing I had heard!

We were all given what we thought was wonderful food: eggs, good tea, peaches, and just about anything we craved. The boat docked at Hong Kong to let off some Australians while I was still in sick bay. Unknown to me, a Captain and Mrs. Johnson were among those who disembarked with their baggage at this port. It was only after we had sailed on to Colombo that I discovered that my three boxes had been unloaded with the baggage of Captain and Mrs. Johnson, bound for Australia. I did not see any hope of ever retrieving them.

To me, everything came to a climax right then. Everyone else aboard the L.S.T. boat was ecstatic. They were so thrilled, they felt they were walking on air. We were then taken to a beautiful estate, covered with velvety green lawns, beautiful, tall spreading trees, and the Indian Ocean splashing at the edge of the grounds. We were housed in a large empty hospital with nurses and maids. The beds were *far apart*, and all had white sheets! We were treated regally. There was every kind of food, including chocolates for all. There was everything one could desire for a ten-day stay. Everyone seemed overcome with joy except me!

My mother had died while I was in China, and also one of my sisters and my closest friend. There had been other painful bereavements. I had been ten years without a furlough, and all I now possessed was in those three lost boxes! I am ashamed to say I thought to myself, "I have been in China ten years and nearly three years in internment camp. I was unconscious and in sick-bay on that last boat, so could not look after my possessions. Really God, You might have looked after my precious boxes!" Those who have read *Winnie the Pooh* by A. A. Milne may remember Eeyore, the donkey who used to look for a bed of thorns to sit on and then complain because they hurt! I was now Eeyore! I was sore and bitter, resentful and weary. While everyone else was exclaiming in joy, I was wondering how I would manage when we reached England on November 11! I knew it would be bitterly cold. All I had was a tiny suitcase of tropical underwear, given to each of us by the Red Cross, and the clothes which I was wearing. I could easily imagine what would happen. England had been rationed with clothes for years. I would have no winter clothes. My dear sister Kitty would deprive herself of her precious war stamps to give to me, and I would be a "charity case." This was not how I had wanted to return home! I sulked before the Lord.

We all turned in to our beds, "purring" over the beautiful conditions of the hospital and kindness of the matron. Early next morning about 6:00 A.M. I got up to walk across the wards through the large front door, out across the lovely lawns with their beautiful trees, and down to the ocean edge. For almost three years I had not been alone nor been able to pray aloud. I always felt nearest to God in the high mountains or by the sea. I reached the edge of these grounds and sat down by the ocean, thrilled to watch the roaring waves. Today I can never go to the sea nor listen to waves without experiencing again that traumatic hour in Colombo. How good to be alone, to pour out my heart aloud to God in the midst of His exquisite creation. There was no one to hear except the ocean— and God! As I looked up to my Father, I remembered all His tender lovingkindness to me every day of the internment camp.

It had been rugged! Just before I left camp a German missionary had come into my little corner where my bed was squeezed in a three-by-six-foot space I shared with the next person and her adjoining bed. Suddenly this missionary began to cry. When I asked, "Gretchen, why are you weeping?" she sobbed, "Oh, I knew it was bad but never thought it was this bad. Audrey, how did you stand it?" Yet God's lovingkindness was in everything.

Sitting before the ocean, I thought of all the tenderness of God in so many little things as He smoothed over the hard places. I cried with sorrow that I could grieve my Father with resentment over just "things," when He had been so good to me! All my years in China I had lived by faith in Him, not knowing how the next need would be fulfilled but knowing the complete faithfulness of God. How could I doubt Him now? I confessed it all aloud to Him and knew the wonderful comfort of the precious blood that cleansed me so perfectly that there remained nothing between us. All that sweetness of fellowship flooded my whole being. I looked up to the sky and said, "Father, all these years You have been my own Father. I am your beloved daughter. You will not let Your daughter be ashamed when I reach England. Therefore, I shall now stand on tip-toe with expectancy to see what You are going to do." I returned back to the hospital a different person. Later that day God gave me a contact with a nurse which led to her conversion. As we were talking together later on, she said, "I think our matron [the superintendent of nurses] is a Christian, although she does not say much."

Immediately I asked to be introduced to her. When we met, it was obvious that she was a believer. She had been led to the Lord by the father of Phyllis Thompson, a colleague of missionary training days. In the rugged atmosphere of the Army Nursing Services in Ceylon she had found Christian life difficult and, being alone, was having a hard time keeping her faith. She was thrilled to meet a fellow Christian, and we had precious times together talking about the Lord. More than that, while the other L.S.T. boat evacuees spent their time on the beach or on the hospital grounds, the matron took me to some of the best Army resorts as well as to Navy bases where I shared my testimony about the Lord. I had a marvelous ten days.

In Colombo the British government gave us each a gift of money. I think it was about thirty shillings. I wonder what you would choose to buy if you possessed nothing in the line of outer clothing except what you were wearing. I decided that at the very least I would arrive in England well shod. I bought myself a pair of brown pumps (the English called these "court shoes"). So now I had tropical underwear and shoes!

When the day came for us to embark on the large ship already carrying some 600 prisoners of war returning to England, the Indian coolies picked up our baggage and conveyed it to the ship. Later, opening my suitcase, I discovered something missing—my brand new pumps! Yet, my Father was so real that this did not trouble me: I knew that He in some unexpected way would undertake for His daughter.

The ship took its journey through the hot, steamy Red Sea. Suddenly there was an unexpected stop. We looked out to see an empty, sandy region where a marquee had been erected. On it we saw a large banner on which was printed, "ENGLAND WAITS TO WELCOME YOU HOME."

We all disembarked. The children were led to a place provided for them with swings and other delights. The adults were taken to rows of cubicles where Red Cross personnel provided for each of us: shoes, clothes, a patchwork quilt, a coat and last of all an attractive "hold all" in which to carry all our things. This was totally unexpected by everyone. No one had asked, "What do you need?" Everyone was given what the Red Cross personnel considered fitting. We were all grateful, yet recognized that usually Red Cross clothing was mainly issued for "getting by" in emergencies. We were content and no one expected anything especially fashionable: I was given ordinary shoes and a green blouse and skirt, but when it came to finding a coat, the Red Cross helper looked at me and said, "You are rather tall. I have a nice coat which I think will fit you perfectly." I gasped when I saw it. It was made of rich broadcloth—a coat which I would be pleased to wear even today! No one else was given anything like it. Was this coincidental? *No!* My Father arranged it, unknown to anyone but myself. Then when the patchwork quilts were given out, I was given an exquisite Indian woven warm "throw," for which I received many offers of a "trade" by fellow internees. (I still have it.) How much more abundantly does our Father provide for us than we ever expect!

After we all re-embarked, our ship eventually arrived at Southhampton, England. It was November 11, 1945. We saw large crowds gathered on the shore and bands ready to play a welcome. Dramatically, the ship docked in dead silence. Then the bands played the national anthem. We all stood at the rails, and tears rolled down our cheeks because the scene was so moving. After this, a particular prisoner of war who had suffered more than most at the hands of the enemy was the first to walk slowly down the gangplank. When he reached the dock, he knelt and kissed the shores of England. We were then all taken to Waterloo Station, London. I remember the excitement of seeing cows, fields, and hedges, noticed most when one has been deprived of them.

My family was there and so were representatives from C.I.M. I was the first missionary internee to return. The Hopeh province superintendent, Mr. R. E. Thompson, was there. I greeted him with a hug, remembering that his son had died in internment camp. Almost the first thing he said after greeting me was, "We are to have a large meeting of thanksgiving tonight for the release of all our interned missionaries: you are the only returnee as yet. Would you be willing to speak tonight at the meeting? So many persons have been praying for you."

As I mounted the platform that evening, I was conscious of my Red Cross shoes and my green blouse and skirt, completely covered by the broadcloth coat—and I was thankful!

Needless to say I needed to be honest and fair to all fellow internees. Therefore, Longhua camp had to be described as it truly was. It would not be right to water things down. I reported then many things now forgotten. However, the audience needed to know how wonderfully God had answered their faithful prayers, and the record of His faithfulness was all important. The main theme was that of the realization of God's tenderness and lovingkindness. I also emphasized the fact that when England was bitterly at war with Germany, it was the German missionaries who struggled to get items of food to us and tried to do everything allowed to help us.

I was speaking to an English crowd only about two weeks after the war had ended. My audience had experienced intense German bombing; many had lost sons and relatives. Increasingly toward the end of the war hate propaganda was at its peak. How wonderful it was to prove that the love of believers for one another transcends the barriers of war. How marvelous to show the real fellowship of the family of God.

Another point needed to be emphasized. We had all *feared* the suffering of internment, even when we expected it to last for only six months. Also the circumstances were worse than anticipated. There is a certain advantage in going through calamity and proving that God's compassion is sufficient. I spoke to an audience that had weathered terrible calamities in England, and I wished to end on a positive note. Even today as one recognizes the possible calamity of nuclear war and other catastrophes, to those who have weathered calamity and proved God's compassion something of the fear of the future is gone. In every calamity God has ways of caring for His own.

In that huge hall somewhere at the back was a former roommate of my missionary training, a friend who had worked in China and later married a missionary to Nepal. Therefore she was thoroughly conversant with missionary situations. As I was speaking, she looked at me and said to herself, "Hmmmm, ten years in China, no furlough, three years in internment camp—she only arrived this morning in England. Just where did she get that coat?"

The welcome home seemed complete when we who had been interned received a personal letter from King George VI. I treasure it today as a precious memento, an example of the King's concern for his subjects.

E I G H T E E N
FURLOUGH

The Spirit helpeth our infirmities [Romans 8:26].

The Reverend Fred Mitchell, now home director of C.I.M. in England, warned me not to accept many speaking engagements for at least two or three months. I tried to hold to his warning, but it was difficult. God, however, saw to it Himself. I was at my sister Kitty's home on a very snowy, slippery day, rushing for a train in order to keep a speaking engagement, when I slipped and broke an ankle. I was immediately taken to a hospital, but had to wait a long time to be attended to—the train on which I had intended to travel had crashed, and the dying and injured passengers were being rushed into the hospital ahead of me. I thanked God not only for His keeping me from doing too much speaking, but also for His protection from serious tragedy.

My broken ankle kept me on a large, comfortable couch in my sister Kitty's home with all the delights of reuniting with her grown children. My niece Margaret was getting her medical doctor's degree, Ruth was preparing for teaching, and David was absorbed with his motorcycle, giving some anxiety to his mother. My sister's husband, Mr. Herman Newmark, was then director of the Society of the Hebrew Christian Testimony to Israel, and we were always hearing interesting Jewish news.

I enjoyed knitting for recreation but reading especially. I told Mr. Fred Mitchell that I was starved for solid thinking. He advised me to read all the books of Karl Barth (with reservations). As he stated, I needed to know where the trend of the New Theology was moving. These I enjoyed, but realized that if the inerrancy of the autographs of Scripture were somewhat discredited, there would be a theological slide in this new era. I also read Emil Brunner and most of C. S. Lewis. It was refreshing to stimulate one's brain to appreciate these books as well as to exercise good discernment.

After my broken ankle was healed, there were delightful times of visiting friends. Then it was convenient to move into the mission headquarters where I stayed until leaving to go back to China. I was impressed by the atmosphere of prayer and the quality of godly character of both directors and returned missionaries.

One conference at which the mission asked me to give a Bible address was interesting. As I got to my feet, I suddenly saw Mr. St. John, the head of the Plymouth Brethren movement, with whom at periods of my life I had had such close contact that I thought I knew what he must be thinking about a woman speaking.

Since the main aim of this address was to inspire young people to hear God's call to teach the Bible on the mission field or at home, I dwelt on the supreme delight of earning one's living by studying and teaching the Bible all the day.

Suddenly a scene of my youth came to mind. Long before I was called to China I was studying piano on the upper floor of the Birmingham Institute. After the lesson was concluded, I walked along the corridor, past an open door from where I could look down on a large auditorium. Mr. St. John was speaking to a sizable group of young people. His words etched themselves permanently on my mind as I walked on. "If you read Shakespeare you will have a Shakespearean mind, if you read Paul you will have a Pauline mind; if you read 'penny horribles' [dime novels] you will have a 'penny horrible' mind." At that moment I determined to aim toward a Pauline mind. This incentive has never left me. I told this story at the conference.

After the conference was over and we were having coffee and fellowship, Mr. St. John came to me and was very gracious. I looked up at him and said, "But, Mr. St. John, I am a woman teaching the Bible." He patted my shoulder and said, "Never mind, my dear, God has plenty of need for prophetesses these days. Keep it up."

Toward midsummer I was invited by Dr. and Mrs. Wasserzug to visit Beatenberg, Switzerland, and to speak in several cities where Dr. Gertrude Wasserzug held large Bible classes. She would interpret for me in German, and in French I would have no problem. Dr. Gertrude Wasserzug was a close friend of the American, Miss Ruth Paxson, who was on the China Bible Seminary board and had therefore possibly heard of me through her.

When I was discussing the invitation with Mr. Bentley Taylor of our mission, who had previously visited Beatenberg, he said, "Don't turn this down. That is the most spiritual movement on the Continent. You will never be the same afterward." Therefore I accepted the invitation.

In all, I spoke at twenty-six meetings in one month of midsummer. They consisted mainly of Dr. Gertrude Wasserzug's own Bible classes. She was an excellent Bible teacher. The smallest attendance was not less than 500 people. In Bern, where I spoke from the stage of a theater, there were over 2,000 gathered. Before the meeting began, the believers often organized a procession through the city, singing German songs and inviting listeners to the meetings.

We spoke in Zurich, Basel, Wintertour, Romanshorn (near Lake Constance where John Huss was burned at the stake), Locano, Geneva, Bern, Lausanne, Shaffenhausen, and many other cities. In fact we traveled together to the four corners of Switzerland from the headquarters at Dr. and Mrs. Wasserzug's Bible school at Beatenberg, looking over Lake Thun and the high mountains beyond.

All these meetings were the outcome of a Bible class of twenty people started as the result of a visit of Miss Ruth Paxson in 1936. Although on most occasions I was the main speaker, I asked to see one of Dr. Gertrude's meetings. Every weekend, Bible classes were held for 500 to 700 persons in all the large cities of German-speaking Switzerland. Often the interest would be so widespread that there had to be two sessions to accommodate all who wished to attend.

I listened to one meeting led by Dr. Gertrude Wasserzug; she had questions previously given out to everyone in the packed church. Answers were given by men and women of all classes. I remember watching Dr. Hirs, whose signature was on all the paper currency notes for Switzerland, stand to answer one question.

After a simple but powerful summary of the passage, an appeal for decisions would be made. I watched, even before the appeal was finished, at least thirty people stand to their feet. Until then I had never been so aware of the power of the Holy Spirit in our midst. Every convert was encouraged to start a prayer cell and to find two or three friends at least for prayer once a week in a home. In this way the whole movement of Bible classes was backed by an innumerable number of praying people. As she spoke I sometimes felt I could not continue to sit down. I needed to kneel in God's awesome presence.

There was a very real interest in China. About forty group leaders came to me, having decided to start a regular C.I.M. prayer meeting in their home or church. I also interviewed some fine young men and women who felt called to China and wished to apply to the C.I.M. This was a revival movement such as I have never seen before nor since. It made, as Mr. Bentley Taylor had predicted, a tremendous impression and longing in my soul.

As we traveled together and as I lived at the Bibelheim (Dr. and Mrs. Wasserzug's Bible school), I was so aware of the Holy Spirit filling her that I wondered where the human spirit ended and the Holy Spirit took charge. In her youth (she was about fifty-five years of age when I was with her) she had taken her Ph.D. in philosophy at a German university, where she was in the same class as Dr. Karl Barth; she knew him well. She and her husband, Dr. Saturnin Wasserzug, had left Germany during the war and together established a little Bible school in Beatenberg, which in my time had about seventy women and men in attendance.

After the schedule of meetings was concluded, Dr. Gertrude Wasserzug asked me to speak to the student body. At that time her husband was very frail, and he died later that year. Since this was to be a Bible study, I spoke on the Cross of Christ for believers, using something of my own experience. At the end of this talk, I asked if any were willing to commit themselves by prayer publicly. I suggested a form of words, "Lord, I am willing at any cost that Thy death be worked out in me, in order that Thy resurrection life may be manifested." There was silence, during which I was deeply conscious of the moving of the Holy Spirit. Then I heard German prayers, mostly with tears. Dr. Gertrude, who was interpreting for me, whispered, "We cannot close this meeting; these prayers are mostly open confessions of sin."

Such was the movement of the Holy Spirit that no one wanted to eat supper. After the meeting and all the next day prayer continued, and there were lines of students waiting at professors' doors to put things right between believers.

And I? What did I experience? A joyous satisfaction? No! I was aware that the Holy Spirit was working apart from me, and that I was spiritually empty and desperately needed help from the Lord.

The next day classes were suspended. I decided to climb up to the end of the tree line of the mountain in order to be alone with the Lord. I had been deeply convicted of the need to be filled with the Holy Spirit. I fell flat against the ground and said, "What shall I do, Lord? I am still *me!*" It seemed that He began at my head; I envisioned spiritually a "stripping off" of the old me from head to toe, through the power of His Cross.

Following this, I poured out my deep hunger for a true filling of the Holy Spirit. I opened the Bible at Paul's prayer in Ephesians 3. I will never forget the glory of the Lake of Thun, the mountains, flowers, and fir trees below, and the consciousness that the Lord would answer my prayer. As I read the last verse, "Far above all you can ask or think," I believed! Being a practical person, I put my finger on that inviolable promise of God and said, "Lord, I take You up on it and believe You will grant to me a new experience of Yourself and power."

Later, I prayed with Dr. Gertrude Wasserzug, deliberately and again confessing my need and also my faith in God's promise. There came a deep sense of serenity. I recognized that the Spirit will only continue to fill our lives as we deal honestly with sin, confessing this and then opening ourselves to the Holy Spirit to fill the entire personality as Lord.

This was a crisis in my life, but always it needs to be followed by a process. One can easily be deceived by Satan and fall away from God's highest. Then there comes a hunger and a realization of a barrier until the situation is handled in His presence, and matters are put right with regard to sin against God.

I have a passion for mountains. Before I left Switzerland, Dr. Gertrude made it possible for me to visit Zermat in order to see the Matterhorn. I had only one day there. People in Zermat said that the Matterhorn had been in a cloud all that year, and the cloud still hid the summit as I walked at its foot. Thinking that this might be the only time I would ever see it, I asked God humbly if it was in His creational and providential purpose to please "move that cloud a little." He did! I then went up in a funicular to Gornergrat, a point from which the Matterhorn is best viewed. The car was full of excited passengers running from window to window as they gazed on the

Matterhorn in all its glory, delighted that it was out of the cloud. I walked all the way down the slopes in a kind of ecstasy.

I had still one other speaking assignment at Emmaus near Lausanne. As I sat in the train I wanted to meditate on the treasured experience I had had and to think about the next meeting ahead. Opposite me sat a Swiss man who wanted to talk in French. I felt provoked and put on dark glasses and looked out the window. Suddenly I wondered, was this of the Lord or of the devil? Therefore I prayed, "Lord, You are sitting here in me. Please will You act now, whether You would be silent or whether You would speak." I took off my glasses and waited. This man really wanted to talk. He asked questions in French and learned I had been in China and internment camp, and was now about to speak at another meeting. He asked whether I went to China because of travel interest, humanitarian impulse, or for "religion." When he heard I was due to speak at a meeting that evening, he said, "I think your mission is very unfair, after all you have been through, to expect you to use up energy in speaking." Without any prethought I replied, "The Lord Jesus is my life; it is a joy to me to do anything for Him." Never had I said anything like that before or since. This was the Lord speaking. The gentleman's eyes filled with tears. He said, "My brother is a minister, yet I have never heard anything like this. Tell me more." We talked and he drank everything in, as a thirsty soul.

When I returned to the mission headquarters in London, friends at the mission came to me, saying, "Audrey, what has happened to you? You are completely different." Then, in private conversations and prayer I told them what had happened and found many were as hungry for the fullness of the Holy Spirit as I was. It was also interesting to compare my new passport photograph with former ones—God even changed my face!

Let no one think, "Well, she has arrived." Far from it. However, whenever one slips back into the old life, there is tugging, as from a kite, pulling one back into God's full purpose and direction.

Before leaving this subject, it seems wise to alert the reader to the danger of depending upon the person God may have used as a spiritual example and help, although that which God has accomplished through a person or a movement is of *eternal* value.

Somehow, for reasons I do not know, that extraordinary spirit of revival and other profound influences had dimmed somewhat when I visited Beatenberg again in the winter of 1947 just before leaving to return to China. Although nothing can ever dim in me what God had done through His servant and the entire spiritual movement, it is always important that one's eyes are never concentrated upon the person or movement alone, but upon God Himself. He gives His special times of refreshing. One lesson we need to learn in our era is that long sessions of prayer and personally drawing near to God are more important than meetings and programs.

When I returned to England from Switzerland I found that my three errant tin-lined boxes, so simply marked JOHNSON 15421, had in some inexplicable way been located by the British government and returned. I have never been able to understand how, with such lack of identification, they could have been returned. It was to me the climax of all God's goodness since release from internment.

NINETEEN

TRANSITION UNDER COMMUNIST CHINA

For I, saith the Lord, will be unto her a wall of fire round about, and will be the glory in the midst of her [Zechariah 2:5].

The time had now come for return to China. The mission had given internees some extra money to make up for the three years in internment. Since I loved Americans so much, I was considering paying the extra cost to travel back to China via the United States instead of taking the cheaper route provided for our missionaries via the Red Sea.

I talked with Mr. Baker, then editor of the magazine, *China's Millions,* who knew America. He strongly advised me to travel through the U.S., saying, "You will never regret the extra expense." He was right!

Therefore I set forth on the *Queen Elizabeth.* Having been so long interned and having lived in war-torn England, I was somewhat startled by the luxury of food presented and the waste on shipboard. But I enjoyed eating it just the same! It was exciting to see iceburgs in the distance, and then what a thrill it was to see at last the Statue of Liberty in the harbor of New York.

I stayed at a small but renowned Christian hotel called Hephzibah House (the name derived from Isa. 62:4). This was run by three Christian ladies. (Strangely enough, it was so well known in the city that once a letter addressed only to the "Hotel of the Three Ladies" arrived safely by post even in that large city!) Mrs. Lucy Sullivan was staying there while working for her M.A. from Columbia University. We became lifelong friends. Later this friendship resulted in opportunities to speak at various colleges where she was a professor.

Mrs. Sullivan was a wonderful guide in New York City. I thoroughly enjoyed the many sights, museums, and famous places we visited together. Being English, I particularly enjoyed the comfort of central heating for the first time. Kind New Yorkers often stopped me when I was about to cross streets, looking the wrong way (left instead of right as I had in England).

I was invited to speak at Nyack Bible College to over 500 students and also had the joy of speaking in Dr. A. W. Tozer's former church. Only later as I read his books and met him personally did I come to recognize and appreciate the privilege this was.

I also visited Philadelphia, Boston, Atlantic City, and Henderson Village in North Carolina, where I stayed with Miss Ruth Paxson. Friends of Miss Brittain had asked me to stay in Memphis and to speak there. This was a thrill. They were so warm-hearted and generous that I realized I had already lost my heart to Memphis! They loved my story about *Gone with the Wind* (my reading it in the internment camp).

From Memphis I was provided with a roomette on the train. It was the month of March, and the moon was full. I thought that since this was the only time I would see America I must not miss anything. Therefore I deliberately stayed awake all night as we traveled through the glorious mountains, their foothills covered with trees and rhododendrons. The wide plains of Arizona and all I had seen overwhelmed my spirit. America was so vast it took my breath away. Then I stopped at the Grand Canyon. Its brilliant, immense, and colorful walls, rising up from the blue river of rapids below, awed me deeply.

How great and how varied was this wonderful land of the U.S.A.!

It was interesting to travel from freezing Boston to Dallas where one sweltered, and then to Los Angeles where I was taken to the summit of Mt. Wilson to escape the heat. While in Southern California I picked oranges and lemons for the first time in my life.

The climax of delight was when the ship to China sailed from San Francisco in the glory of the setting sun under the Golden Gate Bridge. Little did I realize that I would spend a large part of my future living in the San Francisco Bay Area.

The ship to China was an "austerity" ship called the *Marine Lynx*, known to be the worst on the Pacific. It was commonly called by Americans the "Marine Stinks"! However, we had a keen group of missionaries on board; we met for prayer every day at 6:00 A.M. and for Bible study together at 9:30 A.M. One night we held an interesting meeting below deck. About 150 Chinese of all classes stood for two hours, with ship's officers, businessmen, and women listening to and deeply moved by preaching of the gospel, interpreted into Chinese. This continued even against the noisy background of gambling and rioting—all in the same lounge! Hymn singing in English was hearty and effective, accompanied by a well-played piano accordian.

At the end, even without a definitely worded appeal, there were six persons who raised their hand to receive Christ as Savior, and several came to us for private interviews afterwards. Never have I felt more the force of those words, "It pleased God by the foolishness of preaching to save them that believe" and "The weakness of God is stronger than man." Amid all that atmosphere of evil, noise, and discomfort, God proved Himself, His Christ, stronger to accomplish what is often not wrought in the most perfectly organized meeting of Christian civilization. It was a thrill to be a part of it and to experience again the challenge and power of the Holy Spirit.

When I arrived at the mission headquarters in Shanghai,

the directors again wished to loan me and other missionaries to the work of the China Bible Seminary. I received a warm welcome back. The China Bible Seminary buildings looked bare and desolate after the war, having been marred by ruthless soldiers, but they were on the whole in fair condition. Most of the furniture had been looted, but enough remained to temporarily house the sixty women and men who had come from all parts of ravaged China. It was refreshing to find the Chinese faculty triumphant over their hardships. One of them said exultantly, "God knew all along what we would have to go through during this war, therefore it was wonderful of Him to let us have the previous experience of the destructions of 1932, to get our faith deeply rooted in Himself, in preparation for these present trials." Little did she realize His preparation was for the greater trial yet to come in China.

When I returned to China, the Communist takeover was far more widespread and intense than before we went into internment camp. Whole provinces, Manchuria, Shantung, Shansi, and Honan were already in their power. On the other hand, all doors in and near Shanghai were wide open to us.

Although Marxist viewpoints and Communist power were sweeping China, there was a real spiritual awakening. At first missionaries and Chinese Christians were hoping that the political situation might be resolved without too much change. Faith obeys where it cannot see.

At Kiangwan it seemed as though every effort was made to buy up the present opportunity and train more students and university graduates while it was still day. When I arrived, the Lord had already worked in impossible situations to give into the hands of the China Bible Seminary two acres of land for which the seminary had prayed for ten years. A new men's dormitory, capable of housing eighty men, was built as well as an extra women's dormitory. Then we felt the urgent need for university students to have a place to meet, as all meetings on the campus were forbidden in many universities on account of Communist activities. The Lord led the seminary to provide a large wooden hut and dining room for these university students. The first service, held on April 11, 1948, was attended by some 150 students.

As already stated, the seminary's principle was never to ask for money. We prayed to know the Lord's will and knew that in answer to prayer He would lead His people to send what was needed. He did, and it was miraculously timed to meet the need. In regard to the "student hut," someone came with a gift of $300 "for university students." The next day one of the Chinese teachers came back with news that her sister, who had never before sent gifts to the school, had suddenly offered $300. Not only had the erection of the hut cost money, but we needed benches, a platform, and tables. We felt seminary funds should not be used for outside work of this kind.

Just then, Miss Ruth Brittain had a birthday. Our seminary students decided to give sums of money instead of a personal present. Precious gifts of the same type as the widow's mite, wrapped Chinese fashion in red paper, poured in not only from the present students but from the more than 500 graduates all over China, many giving out of necessity until the total amount came to more than $1,200.

In April 1948, 200 men and women from Shanghai universities, representing many regions of China, were gathered on our campus for four days' conference. Mr. David Adeney and Mr. and Mrs. Liberty of the China Inland Mission were helping Pastor David Yang and other Chinese leaders who were the main speakers. One of our graduates led the morning prayer meetings. It was a wonderful inspiration to see our chapel filled with these young people, many of whom had never heard the gospel.

Between sessions, one saw little groups all over the compound, meeting for discussion and prayer, largely led by our own seminary students. In the end, at the testimony meeting more than twenty university students confessed to having accepted the Savior during this conference.

These young people now had their own reading room and meeting place for Bible study as well as for evangelistic meetings in the new land, purchased at a place called "Five Cross Roads."

The fact that at a time of such political unrest God would lead us to expand our operation, to "enlarge the place and lengthen the cords" (Isa. 54:2), led me to wonder if we were being called to be part of a great spiritual awakening in China.

This was rather a strenuous period for us all but also a happy one. God was so obviously in charge. By August, Miss Brittain and I needed to take a break. We had taken vacations together before. One was in the north Korean mountains where we climbed their highest mountain, Bi-ru-ho. Korea is beautiful. At that time it was under Japanese occupation. Many vivid memories come to mind. Once, when climbing the mountain, I had stopped to pick flowers on a narrow trail while energetic Ruth forged ahead. I saw her in the distance and began to run to catch up with her. Suddenly, while running I seemed to feel a hand on my shoulder and I stopped dead, wondering what had happened. In front of me was a huge venomous snake coiled right on my path. I waited until the snake moved and then walked slowly to catch up with Ruth. Was this hand on my shoulder a "guardian angel"?

This year in August, we decided to take advantage of an invitation by my mission to stay in the most beautiful resort in southeastern China, called Kuling. A wealthy Chinese businessman had made a gift of the best hotel in Kuling to the China Inland Mission. Consequently we both stayed in more luxurious quarters than the mission had ever known. The beds were so comfortable! Tired missionaries who came from beleaguered stations were able to sleep—even on the first night! As the China Inland Mission also had a temporary school on the mountain for missionary children, parents could come from as far as Sinkiang (on the Tibetan border) to visit their children.

The way up to Kuling could be hair-raising for people who have trouble with heights, but I loved it. From a point which we reached by river we climbed into "chairs" made of canvas slung onto poles. There was a coolie in front and another at the back. We were taken up tiny trails with precipices on either side. A false step by a coolie and we would be falling down one side or the other. Midway we stopped for a break, standing up to admire the scenery of the covered mountains and rivers and waterfalls. The higher climb was even more wonderful, but the beauty on arrival was indescribable. Miss Brittain and I went for long walks and bathed in the greenest and clearest water pools I have ever seen. We followed streams and explored mountain trails, never seeming to tire of all the beauty around us.

At that time the Generalissimo's wife, Madame Chiang Kai-shek, was also taking a vacation at Kuling; the C.I.M. body of missionaries invited her to tea. There were 150 of us assembled to meet her. She was very gracious and made an impromptu speech when she told us that she and the General prayed together many times every day to know the will of God. We delighted in talking to this earnest Christian lady, realizing the heavy strain under which both the General and she were suffering.

When we returned, political conditions were very serious indeed. However, God was also sending the seminary valuable help for days ahead, as yet unknown to us.

Pastor David Yang was now with us full time, also Mr. and Mrs. Albert Green and Mr. and Mrs. Lyle of C.I.M. together with Mr. and Mrs. Kepler (Mrs. Kay Kepler was a college friend of Miss Hertzler, my later co-worker). These married couples were established in houses opposite the main foreign faculty residence. Mr. Dick Hillis of C.I.M. came weekly as a visiting instructor and was especially helpful in his practical applications. His subject was missions.

In December 1948 the situation greatly worsened. There was a question as to whether the seminary should close. Our position near the railway was dangerous. We were under the airplane route between Shanghai nationalists and Communists. The entire faculty was praying for God's leading. Miss Ruth Brittain was reading Psalm 36 in the Rotherham translation. The main theme of this Psalm is that of God's lovingkindness and faithfulness. Then her reading led on to verse 11, which reads, "Let not the foot of pride reach me, nor the hand of the lawless *scare me away*." To Miss Brittain this was God's confirmation that the seminary should continue a little longer. After all, if missionaries were eventually forced out of China, how necessary it was that the greatest number of students possible should be trained for witness in China.

Perhaps never before in the history of the seminary had there been such a moving of the Holy Spirit, nor such great opportunities to witness to thousands outside our gates during the next two years.

An announcement was made at this time to the student body and faculty that those who came from far distances, such as Formosa or the Philippines, or those who had elderly parents for whom they felt responsible, or those who feared to face the risk of being at the seminary at the time of a complete government overthrow, should feel perfectly free to leave. The following weeks were a wonderful time of testing. Students learned to discover God's will, since each student was made responsible for the personal decision to go or to stay.

Enrollment dropped from 120 to 80. There was no criticism of those who left, most of whom were from faraway places whose parents urgently telegraphed for them to return. But we privately called those who wished to stay the "Gideon's Band" (Judg. 7).

The seminary decided to stay open for as long as God so led. In December 1948 many churches in Shanghai continued in prayer all through the night. On Sunday they went out to preach the gospel to thousands of refugees who had fled to Shanghai for safety! Traffic on the main streets was held up to allow processions of as many as 800 people (holding aloft large banners). Some were dressed in sackcloth and white as a sign of mourning for sin, with the names of specific sins stuck all over their garments. They marched, preaching the need of repentance and belief in Christ, and gave out over a million tracts. The streets echoed with the chorus, "I want Jesus."

During first moments of panic, Christian nationals frantically sought to escape before the Communists might enter Shanghai, but later there was a distinct change of attitude. They said, "Let us humble ourselves before God. Let us not be overcome by trouble, but prove our trust in Christ by being more than conquerors through Him." In view of this awakening, and because of the many prayers of friends at home, we were encouraged to believe that God might even at the last hour, turn back these anti-Christian forces. Perhaps God would miraculously work for the sake of such groups as the Bible Society, Sunday School Union, China Inland Mission, and others whose work touched the whole of China and who had their headquarters in Shanghai. Missionaries and directors questioned if perhaps God would protect this godless city for some purpose revealing His own glory.

The seminary was situated next to a main railway. In 1949 trains arrived with literally thousands of nationalist soldiers en route to Taiwan. They had been fighting and had had nothing to eat or drink. They now camped themselves all around the seminary. Only a little bamboo fence protected our precious girl students from being molested by these tired and desperate soldiers. Yet we wonderfully proved the promise of Zechariah 2:5. Not one soldier broke through our fence, although I went downstairs in the kitchen on one occasion alone, in my dressing gown, and found a hungry soldier helping himself to everything he could find. God was with me. I gave him food and he went quietly away.

Once when the men desperately wanted fuel for a fire, they did begin to break down our fence. Miss Brittain and I went down and asked them to desist. Miraculously, they did so.

All through this time airplanes were dropping bombs between Kiangwan and Shanghai. One night while awake, I thought what a hindrance it would be to the testimony of the seminary if just one of our students were harmed. Surely, but for God's grace the seminary would have been closed. God's answer came so clearly that I will never forget it. Psalm 4, speaking of distress reads, "But know that the Lord hath set apart him that is godly for himself: the Lord will hear when I call unto him" (v. 3). Verse 4 continues, "Stand in awe and sin not: commune with your own heart upon your bed, and be still." Lastly, verse 8: "I will both lay me down in peace, and sleep: for Thou, Lord, only makest me dwell in safety." Not one of our students was harmed either by bombs or soldiers.

Most of these soldiers outside our seminary hoped to get to Formosa (Taiwan) if "worst came to worst." The students moved among thousands with rice and water; they preached to responsive men, hundreds of whom were converted in those days. Meanwhile the glory of the Lord was seen in our midst. Some of us were led to speak of the fullness of the Holy Spirit, and He filled our chapel.

I remember one girl (who was later murdered) who said, "When I came to Christ I thought the gospel meant believe and then do. Now I know it is believe and cooperate with Him. *He* will do!"

We were anxious over another student who came from a very wealthy Buddhist family, living in Shanghai. It was suggested that our dean of women, Miss Caroline Ho, should speak to her concerning going home. We envisioned the uproar if anything should harm her, for her home was so near. Her eyes filled with tears. She said, "If my teacher says I should go, I will obey, but *I am so afraid of missing seeing the glory of God.*" When the end came and the Communists possessed Shanghai, this student's Buddhist home was greatly damaged by a bomb while she was kept safe.

Certainly God was preparing precious Chinese workers by a profound work of the Holy Spirit for the time when the door to the gospel would be closed. (Only time will tell how many of their lives have been spared throughout China, to minister through these long years, even underground to their own people. Now that China has opened a little door to American entry, I hope to hear news of seminary graduates and their ministry amongst thousands of present day Christians.)

Of course the seminary maintained a careful neutral political position. Once, after the takeover, a small group of about thirty nationalist soldiers forced their way through the gatehouse, in spite of strong protest, and fled to the nearest building, the girl's dormitory, where they dropped their nationalist uniforms on the beds. Then while completely naked, they climbed over the back wall to escape! Our very respectable English Mr. Lyle, fearful of any repercussions, urgently helped these naked men over the back wall, and he returned to burn their deserted uniforms. We feared Communists would pursue them, but their escape was completely undetected!

Pressure and trauma for both C.I.M. missionaries and Chinese Christians increased as Mao Tse-tung more specifically applied the basic Marxist policies of his manifesto. In spite of tremendous harassment the inland missionaries of the C.I.M. stuck faithfully to their posts. More and more letters were reaching the Shanghai headquarters of trouble for missionary children, even the possibility of their internment. Also there was news of Christians being arrested and imprisoned, and missionaries being asked not to attend meetings. Then God gave the Shanghai directors a clear confirmation of His will in December 1950.

A church leader from another province came to the C.I.M. headquarters in Shanghai and asked to speak to the China director, Mr. Sinton, and his colleagues. This leader was very embarrassed but felt led of God to explain the worsening situation, and even to make a special request. He dearly loved the mission and the missionaries who were his friends and felt acute pain when he was now forced by circumstances to be blunt, because the governmental pressure on the churches was becoming unbearable. The Communist Manifesto demanded the withdrawal of all foreign "imperialistic" influence. The Communists had asked, "Why have you not eliminated from your churches all imperialists? Why do you allow these missionaries to continue to meet with you? It is your duty to get rid of them." Thus the request which our

Chinese friend had come to ask painfully was blunt: "Will you please go?"

At that time the China Inland Mission director, Bishop Houghton, continued to encourage C.I.M. missionaries to stay in their stations as long as possible. However C.I.M. missionaries who felt led to leave China because of this Communist situation were given permission to leave—but on their own responsibility.

In 1950 Miss Brittain decided to give the China Bible Seminary buildings to be used by a Chinese orphanage. At that time I was living at the C.I.M. headquarters in Shanghai. But I had not yet been appointed to any specific work. I loved China deeply and considered that there was no other mission in the world comparable to the C.I.M., which always had my complete loyalty. I had gone to China "to die there!" How could I leave before *all* C.I.M. missionaries were ordered to evacuate? And yet I was very concerned about the Christian Chinese. They were loyal to the Lord but their relationship to aliens made their Communist government consider them as enemies.

This situation initiated a deep inner struggle for me. It involved an immediate decision as to whether I should stay in China or not. Finally after much prayer, I believed that the Lord was leading me to leave China. Miss Frances Brook (who had greatly influenced my life when I was young) had founded the "Caravan Mission to Canadian Villages." She invited me to Canada to train her teachers if the Communists ever forced me out of China.

With a torn heart I finally gave my resignation to the C.I.M. and prepared to leave for Canada via America with Miss Brittain.

Just as we prepared to board our freighter in Hong Kong, I received news of Miss Frances Brook's sudden death. I left China with tears but knew without doubt that I had obeyed God in my personal decision. I was not alone. Dr. and Mrs. Dick Hillis who later founded "Overseas Crusades" and over eighty other C.I.M. missionaries also felt led to leave China in 1950.

By April in 1951 the number of missionaries in the C.I.M. was reduced to less than 400. The evacuation was a story of tremendous hardship and God's miraculous intervention. The story is written up in detail by Miss Phyllis Thompson in her book, *China: the Reluctant Exodus.*

The C.I.M. directors met together on the slopes of Mt. Dandelong in Australia where, after long sessions of prayer, they realized it was not God's will that seasoned, battle-hardened missionaries should leave the world's needy mission fields. There were many open doors needing to be entered. The directors therefore decided that they would remain in Asia and appoint teams to enter Thailand, Malaya, Indonesia, and the Philippine Islands; an invitation also came from a northern island of Japan.

Unfamiliar languages would have to be learned, and adapting to new cultures would require considerable adjustment as missionaries were re-deployed to new areas. The directors at this time decided to call this new venture, "Overseas Missionary Fellowship," upholding the same proven principles, but which would now become the substitute for the well-known China Inland Mission.

The China Bible Seminary was reopened in Hong Kong where it still continues to train Chinese students for God's work.

Later the Bible Study Fellowship board agreed to contribute to the printing of my Bible Study Fellowship lessons, translated by Miss Caroline Ho. An unusual Bible Study Fellowship class still continues in Hong Kong using the same five-year series (adapted to Chinese culture) as our other Bible Study Fellowship classes.

Miss Brittain lived in Seattle and was taken to be with her Lord April 24, 1981. One can envision her "abundant entrance" and the joy of meeting the uncounted number of martyrs among her former graduates which must have accompanied her welcome into heaven. My own life has been greatly enriched by her godly example and experiences in China while on the faculty of the China Bible Seminary.

Will not the end explain
The crossed endeavor, earnest purpose foiled?
The strange bewilderment of good work spoiled,
The clinging weariness, the inward strain,
Will not the end explain?

Not that He doth explain
The mystery that baffleth; but a sense
Husheth the quiet heart, that far, far hence
Lieth a field set thick with golden grain
Wetted in seedling days of many a rain:
The end—it will explain.

Amy Wilson Carmichael

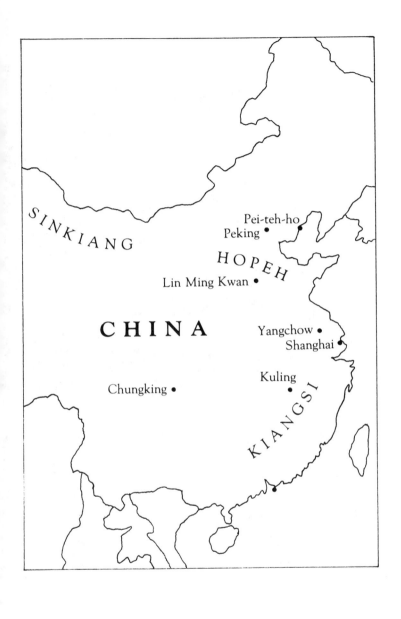

The China Bible Seminary at graduation time.

Top: Miss Ruth Brittain, China Bible Seminary president.
Bottom: Wetherell and Miss Ruth Brittain at their faculty
residence.

中華神學院第十二屆畢業生師合影一九四二冬

Top: The Seminary chapel, where the village woman's sobs
turned to joy!
Bottom: The China Bible Seminary faculty.

GRADUATES *of the* CHINA BIBLE SEMINARY
Serving Christ in China and Southeast Asia

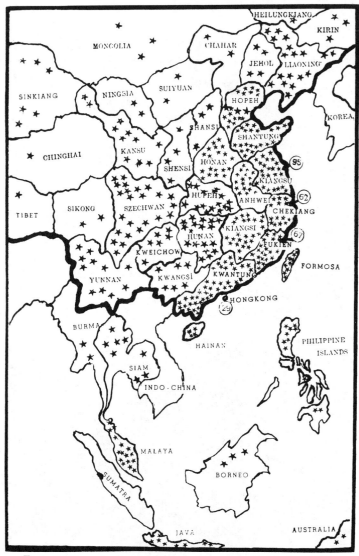

Each star represents a graduate in his or her *field of service.
Numerals in circles indicate the larger numbers.
* Some locations are approximate.

The influence of the China Bible Seminary spreads throughout the Far East.

Left to right:
Alternative village travel.
Our trunks were carried by coolies as we rode up the mountains
in chairs. The waters of the Yangtze River flowed below. Coolies
usually refuse to be photographed; they believe it brings bad luck.
Kuling: The trail of a thousand steps.

Top: Shanghai under Japanese attack, 1941.
Bottom: Rebuilding of the seminary.

Top: Destruction of China Bible Seminary by artillery gunfire in 1927.
Middle: Seminary is damaged in 1937 during Japanese attack.
Bottom: Restored Administration Building. "He hath triumphed gloriously!"

The Bible school in Beatenberg, Switzerland, at which Wetherell Johnson taught.

III

The Years in America

TWENTY
FINAL DEPARTURE

Call unto me, and I will answer thee, and shew thee great and mighty things, which thou knowest not [Jeremiah 33:3].

As I paced the deck of the freighter, alone with God, I realized that what was considered a life work was over. Nothing tangible lay ahead. I would meet Miss Brittain's kind friends; I had a six month's visa for the United States; but what lay in the future? I was already about forty years of age and entering a country where I was not known. Added to this was a constant burden for Chinese Christians left behind.

At this time God reminded me of His great faithfulness, and that He is my Father. He was totally responsible, in love for His own child. Somewhere there would be a future unexpected and more fulfilling than I could ask or think. My heart was filled with His peace.

Our ship sailed under the beautiful Golden Gate Bridge of San Francisco, and we were met by Miss Brittain's friend, Dr. Jean Holt of Altadena, California. She graciously took us into her own home.

The monthly prayer meeting for the work of the China Bible Seminary was held in Dr. Holt's home. Miss Brittain and I both spoke on this occasion in June 1950. Having expe-

189

rienced a special work of the Holy Spirit among the last "Gideon's Band" of Chinese students, this subject was uppermost in my heart.

Miss Alverda Hertzler, whom Dr. Holt had led to an assurance of salvation, was at this meeting. She was then vice principal of a high school of 3,000 students in San Bernardino, some fifty miles away. Immediately after the meeting she needed to return for a baccalaureate service. She told me later that all the way home and during the baccalaureate service, one phrase rang in her ear, "If you are not filled with the Holy Spirit—if not—why not?"

Previously, under the ministry of Dr. Hyman Appleman at her church in San Bernardino, Miss Hertzler had wanted a closer walk with the Lord and to serve Him more definitely. Two weeks after this personal commitment she was asked to teach a Bible class and recognized that the Lord was "taking her up" on her commitment. She said that many in the class knew more about the Bible than she and she longed for further teaching herself.

Shortly after the meeting in Dr. Holt's home, Miss Hertzler invited me to come to speak to her class and to stay overnight in her home. I spoke on the "Glory of God." At the close, looking across the room, I caught a glimpse of Miss Hertzler's face and knew that God had given her a vision of His glory and character! She told me afterward as she left the room that she felt it was as though she was moving in a shining new world.

The next morning as we were washing dishes she told me her life would never be the same, and she praised the Lord. At the same time a premonition seemed to alert my mind. I remember saying to her, "I believe God has brought us together for a special purpose."

Dr. Holt was eager for Miss Hertzler to attend a spiritual conference at "The Firs" at Lake Watcom in Bellingham, Washington. She hesitated about going alone to such a conference, and Dr. Holt then suggested that we should go together. We traveled along the glorious Pacific Northwest coast and all the time talked of Christian doctrines, some of which were new to Miss Hertzler, who had been brought up in what was then known as "the social gospel."

Neither of us will ever forget that conference! For me, there was the joy of meeting missionaries after I had left China only a month before. There we saw a majestic forest of firs stretching their branches toward the blue sky above and surrounding the audience sitting on benches outdoors. Dr. William Culbertson, president of Moody Bible Institute, and Dr. Vance Havner were the main speakers. Other missionaries, including myself, participated in the meetings. Alverda Hertzler remarked that she had never before experienced the impact of such rich teaching from the Word of God. She would return to her room at night, kneeling for long periods in prayer to the Lord for further leading in her life. During free time at the conference, we would both go out into the fields, and I began teaching the book of Genesis to her. I remember how concerned she was about possibly forgetting the truths she was hearing, and I reminded her of the Lord's promise that the Holy Spirit would bring back to her memory all that she received from Him (see John 14:26). She could not help comparing this conference with educational conferences she had attended, and told me, "This is reality."

At the close of the conference, Dr. Grant Whipple (whose father had founded "The Firs") called upon anyone who wished to make a special commitment to the Lord to stand. Alverda Hertzler stood. During the following prayer she became conscious that the Lord was asking her, "Would you be willing to give up your work?" As she considered this later, she found it difficult to believe that the Lord would ask her to give up her educational work. Surely that was her service for Him. How could she earn her living otherwise? Her answer at that time was really no.

On our return from the conference, it looked as though we wouldn't ever see one another again. My plan was to do some deputation work for the mission on the way back to England where I had been tentatively invited to teach in a Bible school, in which I would train future missionaries.

However, I had been through three strenuous years under Communist attack in China. Dr. Holt advised that I should postpone my return to England in order to have a time of rest. After a thorough physical examination, she recommended that I take at least a six-month rest to recuperate before undertaking any new commission from God.

Knowing Miss Hertzler's home would be a quiet haven during the day while she was in school, Dr. Holt asked her if she would be willing to take me as her guest during this rest period. Miss Hertzler had built for herself a delightful white Cape Cod colonial home where she graciously invited me to come as her guest. In later years she told me that her first thought was, "Good, we can go on studying Genesis together in the evenings." Her second, rather disturbing thought was, "Supposing she becomes really ill, what will I do? My work is very taxing, and I myself am not physically strong." However at "The Firs" conference she had also heard the message, "Using Your Home for the Lord." Miss Hertzler then realized that this was God's call to her to trust Him, especially as she had dedicated her home to Him soon after it was built.

I loved San Bernardino. On weekends we would go up to the mountains. Being English, I was amused at the mountain road's name—"Rim of the World"—although it truly looked like it from the summit. We would picnic under the pines and enjoy Arrowhead Lake and Big Bear Lake. Miss Hertzler had a beautiful singing voice and would sing hymns and favorite songs as we descended from the mountain.

I was concerned about paying my board, since I do not believe that "living by faith" means sponging off a generous giver. Dr. Holt had kindly given me a health insurance policy which was a totally unexpected provision. Early in my stay with Miss Hertzler I fell and broke my ankle, and the policy compensation enabled me to meet my obligations! After a very little while I was able to take meetings, especially Inter-Varsity conferences, and college "spiritual emphasis" weeks, as God gave opportunity.

At this time my friendship with Mrs. Lucy Sullivan, which began in New York at the time of my return to China in 1947, was again renewed. Mrs. Sullivan was now a professor at Rockmont College, Denver, and through her I was invited to address the students. Other invitations led me to Westmont College a number of times and to Wheaton College, to Covina Baptist Seminary, and other student bodies. Mostly these were during sessions of spiritual emphasis week.

I was advised on these occasions "to give them deep truths," but discovered that the pagan Chinese who gave their all to the Lord in the exhilaration of finding Him, would receive deeper truths than the more comfortable living American. However, I have always deeply loved such work among students.

As time passed, I met Mr. Robert Young, who was then InterVarsity secretary for the California area. He was a young man in his late twenties at that time, and we became good friends. He now has a Ph.D. and has done missionary service in Tehran, in South America, and in South Africa, prior to settling in San Francisco. He opened doors for me to speak at numbers of InterVarsity conferences.

I shall always be able to recall memories of the first of such conferences, held in San Luis Obispo. We were near a creek which overflowed its banks; no one could enjoy recreational sports. The night before I was to speak, Bob Young said, "Could you be ready for several other messages? It looks as though we will have to hold meetings all tomorrow, as we cannot get out!" It was a cold time of year, and in the middle of the night I came down with an extremely sore throat and croaking voice. I prayed desperately—but there was no improvement. Then God spoke to me, "You are not expecting Me to answer!" The English have a proverb, "Blessed is he that expecteth nothing, for he shall not be disappointed." I then looked into my heart to see if I expected God to work and began to praise Him because my faithful Father would not let me down. I fell off to sleep and in the morning woke feeling well and strong! Meetings and counseling went on all the next day, and we sometimes squeezed into the kitchen for warmth. I spoke during these days on the book of Philippians.

One afternoon, a young student came to me saying, "I sense you and the others have something I don't. But I am a science student and cannot buy these teachings." I replied to him, "You were born with scientific potentialities and can probably understand Einstein. I doubt that I will ever understand the intricacies of Einstein's discoveries. However, I have been 'born again,' and my heavenly Father has given me the ability to understand what you cannot reach. You need that spiritual parentage—'a new birth'—and then you will find that Philippians becomes crystal clear to you. Would you like to receive the Lord Jesus into your heart and be born again?" He said, "Yes!" His prayer was in expectant faith. He came to me later in the evening and said, "You are right. I feel I understand it all now." He has continued to grow in the Lord.

There were many conversions at that rainy, cold conference, and at the same time Robert Young himself received from God a missionary call to South America which was later blessedly fulfilled.

I remember the privilege of sharing in programs with fellow speakers at conferences on beautiful Catalina Island in California, where squirrels are apt to eat the leather binding of one's Bible! My memory draws on many student encounters during those days. I think of one young woman who came to me for counseling. She had an inferiority complex. I was stunned when she told me that the university psychologist had advocated she give herself to the indulgence of sexual relationships. She had followed this advice to an extreme which had resulted in her now feeling utterly debased and beyond redemption. She asked me whether she had any way out. I assured her that our Lord had carried all her guilt, that He loved her and understood her. I told her He would deliver her completely and cleanse her; that He would make her a precious instrument for Himself. God would give her a part in molding other young lives as she let herself become led by

Him. This He did in her newborn life and with amazing results.

On one occasion, I shared a conference program with Mr. Mel Friesen who was then camp director of Campus by the Sea on Catalina Island. One evening we were together at a beach gathering of about 200 students. My sense of humor was aroused when as we sat in the light of a full moon shining brightly on the blue sea where the setting could not have been more romantic, he chose as his subject love and marriage! But I was deeply impressed by the dexterity with which he handled it. First he spoke about the responsibilities of a wife (Eph. 5). Then, while all the men students appeared to be "purring," he suddenly added, "All right—now let's get to the husband's role. Wives may find submission difficult, but you men have an infinitely harder responsibility. You are to love your wife sacrificially as Christ loved the Church and as much as you love your own body!" Never had I heard these two responsibilities so ably characterized. It is unlikely there would be so much feminist aggressiveness in present society if both partners realized our Lord's doctrine of a balanced relationship and the pattern of His own relationship to us His Bride, His Body.

During those first years there were many InterVarsity meetings and conferences. I think of sessions of a week at a time with InterVarsity groups in universities at Stanford, Berkeley, and in the state of Washington as very outstanding. One conference center I particularly loved was in Ontario, Canada, on a wooded lovely lake called "Campus in the Woods." Miss Barbara Boyd and Mr. Charles Hummell, who are still with InterVarsity, were there. It was exhilarating to me that the need to travel to these conferences led me through such grandeur in Canada.

Always there are episodes that indelibly stand out in one's memory and from which lessons are learned. At that time I was led to speak on the Person and Power of the Holy Spirit. At the end of a morning lecture, while I was talking with several students, individually, the lunch bell rang. As I walked into the crowded dining hall, I stood at the door and asked the Lord where He wished me to sit. First, I took a seat by two girls who appeared to be completely absorbed in a conversation they found interesting. Then I was led to act as never before. Before the serving of our meal I moved to an empty space, next to a young medical student. After a moment or two, he said, "Do you believe in prayer?" I said, "Yes! Do you?" He replied, "I was so interested in this morning's meeting, having always thought of the Holy Spirit as a kind of influence in a prayer meeting. I wanted very much to talk to you, but there were too many people around. I prayed that if God wanted this He would bring you to me!" I laughed and said, "Do you still believe God answers prayer?" I then told him of my experience upon entering the dining hall. Following lunch we had a long private talk. Months later he wrote to me of God's continued rich blessing in his life and work. It is quite a lesson to realize how nearly we can miss God's purposeful opportunities.

On another occasion there was—as there is for most speakers—quite a long line waiting for personal interviews. I had a girl with me who seemed evasive and rather flippant in her attitude. My first instinct was to rise and put an end to this interview, but instead while she was talking I lifted my heart to God and said, "Lord Jesus You are sitting within me in this chair, please take over and conduct this interview as You wish." Instantly the entire atmosphere began to change. The girl revealed her deep-seated problem; it was an experience of incest in her earlier days, something she had never told but which made her feel totally unacceptable. How wonderful it was that we could together kneel in prayer and that she received Christ in her heart. She could realize she was perfect in His sight and know the tenderness of her heavenly Father's love as well as the rich fulfillment He had in store for her. I saw how nearly my "flesh" could have blocked His working that day.

Another girl had come one day to talk about opening her life in commitment and receiving the fullness of the Holy

Spirit. We prayed together. As we did so, she committed herself to Him as Lord, with "nothing between." That night during student cabin prayers she refused to pray with the others. The next day, when the students were at recreation, she landed again at my door! "It doesn't work," she said. I replied, "I have given you all I can from the Word of God. You said you received it. I can do no more. God and you must settle the matter. I suggest you take the book of Ephesians to the beach and talk to the Lord alone," which she promptly did. Suddenly—without any warning—the skies poured rain. Students came running back to camp from all directions. In about an hour I saw a radiant, drenched girl landing again at my door. "Oh, Miss Johnson! God spoke to me: I didn't even know it was raining!" She became a valuable worker in Pioneer Girls of Canada. I myself would like to meet God in such a way that I didn't even know it was raining!

These were two years of happy days, but I knew this was not to be my permanent work.

THE RICH YOUNG RULER

He had come running and eager
Just as they do today,
And he was a rich young ruler
Yet poor when he went away.

His life had been clean and moral
As some men's are today,
But Jesus asked for his treasure
And he wouldn't give it away.

Jesus saw him and loved him
Just as He does today—
Had he looked in the eyes of Jesus
Could he ever have gone away?

Were his eyes fixed on the disciples
As men look on them today

197

That bemoaning their lack of culture
He said their Master, "Nay"?

So he made the choice of a lifetime
As students do today:
He could keep his beloved treasure
But he would be sad alway.

A. Wetherell Johnson

TWENTY-ONE

GOD'S CALL
TO A NEW MINISTRY

Thou wilt shew me the path of life: in thy presence is fulness of joy [Psalm 16:11].

With the arrival of summer in 1952, Miss Hertzler looked forward to getting away from the San Bernardino heat. We decided to go to a conference center named Mount Hermon, in California, where we could rent a small cottage located in a quiet place in the midst of fields and large shady oak trees. Here there were conferences we could attend, and at the same time we could rest.

At that time, although several doors of spiritual ministry had been offered in the United States, I did not have that settled peace of mind from God which has always been the final confirmation of His guidance. (See Col. 3:15 which can also read, "Let the peace of God *arbitrate* in your hearts.") I was confused and restless, wondering, but not wanting to pull strings, yet uncertain as to how I should use my previous training in God's work. It was then Miss Hertzler gave me a book I had long loved, Rainsford's *The Lord Prays for His Own*, the subject of which was John's Gospel, chapter 17. As I sat under a giant oak and pored over this most heart-warming chapter, I prayed. It seemed then that the Father was saying to me, "Why do you fret? I am the Employer of all believers who are in My service. Just as an employer decides where an employee will be placed, even so I know your abilities. Trust Me to give you the work for which I will fit you." After this, I had complete peace. At my missionary ordination in 1936 the text had been given to me, "As my Father hath sent me, even so I send you" (John 17:18; 20:21). Thus I became completely willing to wait for His direction.

We returned to San Bernardino where I fulfilled a speaking engagement in a local church. Following the message, five ladies came to Miss Hertzler's home asking to see me. They asked if I would please teach them from the book of Colossians. These were all earnest Christian women, well versed in Bible content. My heart fell! What had I come to? There in San Bernardino was such an abundance of churches where people could hear God's Word, while by contrast in China were millions who had not even heard His name. *Am I to give more to those who already have so much?* I wondered. In reply, I promised to pray about their request, and when they had gone I poured out to God my longing to teach pagans. He reminded me of Jeremiah 45:5, "Seekest thou great things for thyself?" (such as seeking to train teachers for China's millions), "Seek them not!" Again He gave me His message to Zechariah (4:10): "For who hath despised the day of small things?" It seemed that He meant this for me. "You are here, not yet recovered in health; cannot you do this small thing for Me with these dear ladies who desire teaching?"

A few days later, when these ladies returned for my answer, I said, "I will not spoon-feed you. Are you willing for me to dictate a few questions which will help you in your study of each passage? I would then like you to first share with all of us what God has given you, after which I will share with you what He has given me." Readily they were happy to agree to this method of study and teaching.

Soon these five brought other friends. They enjoyed discussing their God-given thoughts after thoroughly studying the passage. As I gave the lecture I saw them taking notes and realized that this could lessen any spiritual impact and concentration on the message. Therefore I decided to type a resumé of each lesson, together with typewritten questions applying to the following lesson. I stipulated that the use of commentaries would not be allowed! Little did I anticipate then that these lesson notes, with questions, would someday develop into the composition of 5,000 words to each set of notes and twenty related questions for the following week's lesson.

As this class grew in Miss Hertzler's home, members would bring others who had problems about which they needed counseling and some who had no assurance of salvation.

One lovely lady came for an interview, in deep distress. She could not understand why everyone else seemed to have "something" she did not have. I inquired about her religious history. She told me that an appeal for church membership was made one Sunday in her church and she responded. The pastor simply shook hands with her in public and accepted her into his church membership as a Christian person. No! She had never been told to "receive Christ through the Holy Spirit into her heart." She did not understand anything of the new birth, nor that Christ had carried all her sins on the Cross. I talked with her along these lines, emphasizing particularly Revelation 3:20, and asked her whether she would like to invite the Lord Jesus into her heart. She said yes. When we got on our knees in prayer I prayed first, then asked her to pray. To my surprise, she began confessing her sins (about which no reference had been made). Especially did she ask God to forgive her for hatred of her mother-in-law. She asked for God's cleansing.

As we rose, I asked her if she now knew Jesus had come into her heart. She seemed doubtful. Therefore I told her to read Revelation 3:20 again. Gradually a light came into her face. She said, "Well, I've done what He said. I suppose He has come in." Then I explained that while I prayed with her it was impossible for her not to be influenced by my presence. I recommended that she return to her home and pray alone to God. He had His way of revealing Himself to her personally. I suggested that if, after this, she felt so inclined, she might telephone me. Within an hour the telephone rang, and an ecstatic woman said, "I did talk to Him, He said He is my own Father." She is now a very old lady, and all through her life her influence, joy, and power to win souls has proved what God will do for those who choose to come believingly to Him.

Another lady was an inveterate gambler, so addicted to gambling she was a slave to it, and could not break the habit which she realized was ruining her home. Miss Hertzler had already led her to the Lord, and she and I prayed together that God would break the power of Satan's possession over her. God delivered her and she too became a leader of others.

As these meetings continued to grow, some of the ladies came to me and asked, "Miss Johnson, if it is not too personal a question, does your mission support you? Do you have private means by which you live?" I laughed and replied no to both questions, adding, "If I do a good day's work for the Lord, He sees that I do not lack." As mentioned before, the settlement from my insurance policy had provided some financial help, and former China prayer partners in England (who knew nothing of my present circumstances) were sending small gifts, providing me with enough to get by!

One day after our class dispersed, I saw to my dismay some money left on the coffee table. I began telephoning to inquire who had misplaced their money. The reply was, "It is for you, for lesson paper and other expenses. It comes from God, through us." After that, members of the class would take a plate from Miss Hertzler's china cabinet and leave their gifts each time we met.

Before long we began to realize Alverda Hertzler's home could no longer hold all the people who seemed so hungry to understand more of God's Word. We first moved to the larger home of a new convert in our class, who took great delight in having us meet there. This was during the era when McCarthyism was a common household word and our regular gathering with cars assembled outside roused the concern of neighbors. One neighbor asked, "What are you doing? Is this the start of a Communist cell?"

Even her home grew too small as more friends of class members felt the need to come. Young mothers with little children wanted to attend our study, and we realized that provision would need to be made for their children. At this point a pastor of a church warmly invited us to hold our class there. Baby-sitters were provided, and almost immediately the class attendance jumped to thirty and then to seventy regular members.

By this time I had taught Colossians, Matthew, and the entire book of Psalms. Our method was that any in the class who wished to answer a question would put up their hand and stand. Later I taught the History of Israel, inserting the twelve minor prophets where they belonged. I was becoming somewhat uneasy, as those who stood to answer questions were usually the same "eager beavers" each time.

I wondered whether the rest of the class was even reading the passage or if, as I was determined not to do, I was spoon-feeding them. It was especially difficult to teach such a book as Zechariah when I knew that many in the class, more recently enrolled, knew nothing of the Bible. It was hard to satisfy Christians and in the same lecture instruct others who were totally unversed in the Bible.

Therefore, I chose seven persons whom I knew well to meet with me at Alverda's home for a morning when we would plead with God for an outpouring of His Holy Spirit and for His direction toward some solution to this problem. This was a morning of spiritual oneness, never to be forgotten. The Lord made us aware of the power of the Holy Spirit. As we talked together the Lord also gave us a unique pattern of something God would later reveal as a key feature in the birth of a wide ministry He alone knew was to come. We decided to give each of these seven persons a group of ten individuals, graded according to their knowledge of the Bible. Those who could not locate Psalms or John's Gospel in their Bibles would be placed in one class together, to avoid embarrassment. Those with Sunday school background would be placed in the medium-range groups; those who "knew it all" would be placed under a special discussion leader who would help them out of "religious clichés" and into a real intimacy with the Lord and an ability to communicate.

My aim had always been to ensure that *every* member of the class *was living by the reading of God's Word.* Eventually we made a ruling that one should not attempt to take part in answering questions unless there was credible proof of genuine previous study. This necessitated each person having answers written out to which she could privately refer. Surely one should not give an opinion on something one had not personally studied! Perhaps the reader can imagine the impact of this new procedure on a group of ten or twelve women. ("Everyone else can share what they believe is the meaning of this passage, but I must remain silent!") What happened was that some women studied just so that they could talk! And then the Word of God captured them! It resulted in abundant conversions and changed lives through a personal understanding from God and personal enjoyment of reading the Bible alone.

God gave me a profound conviction that the way to know Him intimately as a Person related to me was through study of His Word with the help of the Holy Spirit. I knew the Bible to be the unique revelation of God and His will for humanity. I wanted people to know God has revealed His character and His destiny for the human race, that He has committed this in human language to the prophets and confirmed this by our Lord Jesus Christ and the apostles.

Our Lord Jesus referred to Deuteronomy 8:3 when he said, "Man shall not live by bread alone, but by every word which proceedeth out of the mouth of God" (Matt. 4:4). If someone wishes to know the Lord Jesus as a Person divine but human and God as his own Father, I believe he must *alone* make contact with God, both by reading and by prayer.

Surely the chief weakness of Western Christianity in our day is Bible illiteracy. God intends each of His children to know the "whole counsel of God." Only then does one really see His glory exhibited in the many facets of His character and will, individually. God had given me to feel so strongly about this that always I have had this aim in teaching. Little did we realize during these early days of our class meetings that God would use this pattern as a seed which would flourish to bring forth a harvest of conversions far beyond our prayers or remotest anticipation. Such is the power of His Living Word (see Heb. 4:12).

As our class continued to meet each week, we came to realize the need to train discussion leaders so that they would be able to draw out the most from each of the ten members in each group. This led to the formation of a discussion leaders' meeting. One of our class members, Mrs. Edna Voss, invited us to hold this meeting in her large home. Mrs. Voss was class pianist, but when originally invited to come to this class had emphatically replied, "No! I've heard enough missionaries to last a lifetime."

We arranged that our discussion leaders' meeting should be held each Monday morning. This time was basically intended to prepare each leader to help the varying grades of class members with the answers to questions they had previously studied. I taught these leaders never to respond with "That's not right," but simply to thank the individual and ask if someone else might have a different opinion. Discussion leaders were not intended to teach their class, but rather to encourage fellowship and discussion of answers and to have occasional simple discussion class luncheons. The study groups gradually developed a real fellowship with one another and a liberty to phone their discussion leader, whom they learned to know so well. In these Monday morning meetings we prayed together and reviewed our questions so that the leaders would themselves be prepared to relate to difficulties arising in their groups. We enjoyed a wonderful fellowship!

One leader seemed never to pray; when I privately asked her why, she told me of a fear of public speaking or of praying aloud which she said even affected her physically. I then gave her Paul's word to Timothy (II Tim. 1:7) and told her that this fear came from Satan, seeing that God surely did not give it. I prayed with her and later for her. At the next meeting and always thereafter she prayed. It gave me a great joy to see the day when this same woman became the teaching leader of a large class.

At first the class was called "Miss Johnson's class," which I would not stand for! We then tried the name "II Timothy 2:15 class," as indeed we were trying to "rightly divide the word of truth." Finally, while still meeting in Dr. and Mrs. Voss's home, we settled upon the name Bible Study Fellowship, the name by which it continues to be known. The organization was later incorporated and its name registered in all states.

We established the procedure of having lesson notes picked up by each class member at the close of the lecture. Some people would make copies of their lesson to send to a friend, but this soon led to serious difficulty. I had written about the humanity and deity of Christ in His temptation. Unfortunately, in copying the notes the portion about Christ's deity was omitted. This resulted in class members being warned, by an ardent heresy hunter, that I was a person who did not believe in the deity of Christ! But God soon turned this to good. Miss Hertzler and I consulted with a Christian legal advisor. His counsel was that until there were enough lessons to warrant a copyright, we should limit the distribution of lesson notes strictly to class members and require that they not be duplicated.

Dr. Horton Voss now asked for a men's class. We decided that this initial class would be based on the study of homiletics—the art of teaching and preaching. At the first meeting I asked for testimonies in order to become acquainted with the men who gathered. I shall not forget one man who with simple honesty said his time of prayer was each morning while he shaved! Each class member would give a ten-minute talk, after which everyone would contribute encouraging remarks and suggestions. Out of this group of men, all engaged in various occupations, have come many Christian leaders, one of whom is now teaching in a seminary and is a writer of books.

Shortly after this, Dr. Blackstone of the Palm Springs Presbyterian Church invited me to hold a class in his church, some forty or fifty miles distant. It was arranged that a class member would drive me each week by car. To my delight we soon had a group of about fifty women, some of them connected with the film world of movie studios, and most of them totally ignorant of the Bible. I was impressed with the reasonableness of one woman's innocent question, "Why did John call Jesus a 'lamb'? Was it because He was so gentle?" This led us to talks on Leviticus and God's preparation for His Son's advent by the symbolism of the Crucifixion. We discussed the cleansing from sin so carefully described in the Old Testament. I had a deep love for this class and·its challenge each week.

It was hard for me to turn this interesting class over to another when God led me to a different region, but I knew that what God had begun in them He would fulfill. And there came to me then the prayer of Robert Murray McCheyne: "God, hold me on with a steady pace."

And shall I fear
That there is anything that men hold dear
That Thou couldst deprive me of
And nothing give in place?

That is not so,
For I can see Thy face
And hear Thee now:

"My child, I died for thee
And if the gift of love and life
You took from Me,

Shall I one precious thing withhold,
One beautiful and bright,
One pure and precious thing withhold?
My child, it cannot be."

Amy Wilson Carmichael

It is important here to add a side note to clarify something. While in England, Europe, and China I had not run into others with the same name, Audrey Johnson. However, immediately after arriving in San Bernardino, I ran into difficulties. At least five people in San Bernardino were called Audrey Johnson. When my bank even mixed up my checks with those of another Audrey Johnson, I recognized something needed to be done. I imagined that possibly there were many Audrey Johnsons in America and if I were to go into public work this would lead to confusion. Therefore after about 1953 I decided to use my middle name, "Wetherell," as my given name, one which my friends use to this day. I reasoned it would be unlikely to find another "Wetherell Johnson" in America. I only mention this because people have asked why I do not use my first name. However, my European and Chinese friends still call me Audrey.

TWENTY-TWO
EARLY EXPANSION

And he said unto them, Let us go into the next towns, that I may teach there also: for therefore came I forth [Mark 1:38].

By 1956 I had been away from England for ten years! Our Bible study class had been meeting for what we now called a "class year." During this time, we had met each week for thirty-two weeks with a final testimony meeting to close our class. No classes were held during summer months. These would resume in September and continue until May when they would close for the summer. To my surprise, in 1956 the San Bernardino class presented me with a generous gift to provide for a trip to England to visit my family, and to return to my favorite haunts in France and Switzerland. It was a very exciting send-off, as the entire class assembled on the San Bernardino station platform to wave farewell. As the train moved out I went to my seat and was met by a lady who said, "You must be a special person. Who are you, a movie star?" I was highly amused, smiling at this flattery, since I certainly felt I was a far cry from any movie star.

To my great delight I was met in England by my beloved sister Kitty and her husband. I was soon with nieces and nephews again, all of whom except one were married. While in England I could not miss the opportunity of spiritual uplift I knew would await me at the famous Keswick Conference, which brought back precious memories of my commitment to the Lord for China. It was wonderful to wander by the lakes and to climb the beautiful mountains in this lake district. The Keswick tent was just as it had formerly been, with capacity for some 6,000 people. I was hungry to be fed spiritually and will never forget Dr. Paul Rees' messages on seeking the fullness of the Holy Spirit. He quoted a final phrase which I wrote in my Bible, "As you expect, so shall you receive."

Traveling in Europe was comparatively cheap in those days. Because of my love for Beethoven's music I visited Bonn, the provincial capital and gateway to the Rhine Valley where history stretches back for two thousand eventful years, even to the Roman era. I rambled through the city and remained spellbound at seeing Beethoven's home at Bonngasse 20, and looked with awe at the piano on which he composed such glorious music.

I then traveled by steamer down the Rhine from Koblenz, where rivers and mountains converge. This is the most romantic section of the Rhine. On either side are ancient castles with fascinating histories. I recalled the legend of the beautiful siren Lorelei as we sailed by. This legend has it that she lured boatmen to their death by singing at this very dangerous place in the river.

My journey continued through France and into the Black Forest in Germany to beautiful Lake Titisee at Hinterzarten. Never do I feel so close to my Creator and Father as in the mountains. I would find out the hotel or rental which had the best view and go to the travel office to inquire the price. I drank in the beauty of the Black Forest, the blue lakes, the mountains and trees like a sponge.

Then I entered my beloved Switzerland! It seems unbelievable today but a class hotel overlooking Lake Lucerne and Mt. Pilatus was six dollars per day, including two meals and a free funicular ride down into the glorious city of Lucerne.

I also revisited my beloved Matterhorn, which had a special

spiritual significance for me. I sat on a rock and gazed at its height which seemed almost to touch the dome of the sky. Again I went up to the Gorengrat by funicular, the highest outlook, from which to view the long range of peaks. I was ecstatic! I walked all the way down the slopes among blue gentians and anemones, past rippling creeks and pine trees, gazing all the way at that mountain leaping into the sky as though aspiring to meet with its Creator.

I did not know of Dr. Francis Schaeffer's work in L'Abri at that time, but while in Switzerland I visited Beatenberg Bible School again, although Dr. Gertrude Wasserzug was no longer there.

Another delightful walk from Lauterbrunmen, the valley of waterfalls, along the path to Murren was indescribably beautiful as I looked over to the magnificent peaks of Eiger, Monch, and Jungfrau. I was enraptured! Always that walk to Murren will be connected in my mind with the words, "I am the Lord thy God which teacheth thee to profit, which leadeth thee by the way that thou shouldest go" (Isa. 48:17).

What a welcome awaited me in San Bernardino when I returned, especially from Miss Hertzler. I soon discovered some changes had been made in the church where our class met. The pastor had joined a different denomination, and a new pastor, the Reverend Bob Pietsch, invited us into his church and gave us a very warm welcome. The Reverend Pietsch later was for many years a member of the board of directors of Bible Study Fellowship.

I again came into contact with Mr. Robert Young, while at a university conference. As he had watched the growth and power of God's Word in the members of the class, he said very thoughtfully, "Miss Johnson, this work is going to grow more than you can imagine. I believe you should (like Paul) consider a more strategic place, such as the San Francisco Bay Area—midway between north and south—which is far more accessible than San Bernardino."

I was also friendly with Mrs. Harold (Kay) Gudnason, whom I had met at the Mount Herman Conference Center and by whose invitation I had held meetings in her home. Mrs. Gudnason visited us in San Bernardino at this time. She mentioned that Dr. Billy Graham would be coming to San Francisco in 1958. She said, "I believe the Bible Study Fellowship would be wonderful for follow-up work." She added, "My church pastor, Dr. Ernest Hastings, is also interested in what you are doing." She suggested I come to Oakland to see Dr. Hastings.

By this time I had been enabled to buy a second-hand car and was learning to drive it! (I remember that as a little girl of six years of age when in Paris I would take long walks with my sister; I thought how lovely it would be to have a little seat that would move *with* me, so I could sit on it instead of walking!) Miss Hertzler had tried to teach me to drive, but after I once landed us in a ditch, she backed out from any more lessons! The husband of one of our leaders kindly took over these lessons, and driving has become a delight to me ever since. One feels as though this is one's own little home on wheels, alone with God, comfortable and able to go anywhere.

I was delighted to visit the Bay Area again with its beautiful forests and blue waters. A friend drove with me to Oakland where Mr. and Mrs. Gudnason lived. They warmly invited me into their lovely home. They took me to the Cow Palace in San Francisco where Billy Graham was conducting his Crusade. As I sat with them I marveled at the eager crowds and the excellent messages given in the power of the Holy Spirit, and I could hardly believe the numbers who came forward to make decisions. After one of these meetings I was personally introduced to Dr. Graham, who told me of his keen interest in Bible teachers. Little did he or I realize that years later one of his daughters would become a teaching leader of a Bible Study Fellowship class.

Mrs. Gudnason introduced me to Dr. Ernest Hastings, who was then pastor of the Melrose Baptist Church in Oakland, a flourishing congregation. Seeing that he did not know me personally at all, I was grateful for the risk he took in inviting an unknown woman to teach in his church. He said he was happy for me to try out a class, and that its continuance would depend upon the elders of the church and the congregation. Meanwhile a lady in his congregation, Mrs. Watson, who was later going away for a month, graciously offered me the use of her home during her absence.

Moving from San Bernardino was a big step for me to take. Miss Hertzler had always felt that the Bible Study Fellowship should take root in other cities beyond San Bernardino. Yet leaving all those very dear friends would be extremely hard. So far I only knew as personal friends Mr. and Mrs. Gudnason in Oakland, and through their great kindness had been made to feel at home. Yet God had given me confirmation to go to Oakland. Who was I to hold back from His leading?

The San Bernardino leaders were disconsolate. "What shall we do for a teacher?" I reminded them of Matthew 14, of how our Lord Jesus gave food to His disciples who then fed the multitudes. At this time Miss Hertzler had taken an early retirement from her educational position because of ill health. Her time was partly filled by special counseling with gifted students. She had leisure time to help with teaching. I then divided the class into four; Mrs. Voss, Mrs. Joy Sharp, Mrs. Vergene Lewis, and Miss Hertzler—all of them trained discussion leaders—each took one-fourth of the class and afterward gave a talk on the passage to their group. This would not be as difficult as teaching a large class. The Reverend Robert Pietsch kindly offered to teach homiletics to the four leaders.

I do not remember how long I stayed in the home of Mr. and Mrs. Gudnason, with its glorious view over the San Francisco Bay. Mrs. Gudnason took me to the Melrose Baptist Church, where I continued as a member for several years. Later I was asked to teach Colossians in the church Sunday school.

Mrs. Gudnason would arrange parties where I could personally meet people who might be interested in Bible study. There were about twenty-five persons present in the first class. I was immediately led to the excellent pianist, Mrs. John (Pearl) Hamilton, who was recovering from a skiing accident, her leg still in a cast. She became a close friend, a teaching leader and staff member. Today she is still deputy director to the new general director of Bible Study Fellowship.

The class quickly grew to about seventy-five members. I first taught the book of Matthew. At the end of the class study, I would ask if any member could list all the chapters of Matthew and name the content of each chapter. Several accomplished this perfectly!

During these early weeks in Oakland the San Bernardino friends would call almost every evening with, "If they don't want you up there, please come back to us." They would also send gifts, which I put toward an apartment I knew I would soon need. Then the time came when I left the Gudnason's lovely home, never forgetting their faithful kindness.

House-sitting in Mrs. Watson's home in another part of Oakland was mind-stretching as I learned to find my way around this attractive city. It was here I began to have a leaders' meeting in the home. My search for an apartment continued in 1958 and into 1959. As I was praying over this, remembering that all my life had been lived in other people's homes, I said to my Father, "Lord, since all these apartments are too expensive or too small to entertain guests, is it possible I could find a home—with, say, a double mortgage?" Almost immediately I discovered a little cottage with two bedrooms, situated at the end of a dead-end street and conveniently accessible to the church.

Needless to say, two mortgages necessitated a visit to the bank. Mr. Harold Gudnason, who was well recognized by the bank, offered to come with me. The bank manager asked, "Miss Johnson, will you kindly tell me your salary?" Knowing he would not understand "living by faith," I said, "I am supported by voluntary contributions toward my work." He asked me to give a rough estimate of the funds per month that, after class expenses, were left to me. After my reply, he said, "I don't see how you can live on that amount, let alone carry two mortgages." I replied that I expected the work would grow. I was quite aware his confidence was in Mr. Gudnason and not in me. However, to God's glory let it be said that never once did I need to call on Mr. Gudnason for financial help, and never once did I default as payments became due. "Whosoever believeth on him shall not be ashamed" (Rom. 10:11).

I could not wait to call Miss Hertzler to tell her I had committed myself to the purchase of a house. Her reply in amazement was, "With what?"

I simply loved my little Laird Avenue house! Someone gave me a dining table and chairs, which had been stored in a garage. At first I slept on a mattress on the floor of my room. Gradually, as I had the money, other things were added, draperies were hung, and reading lamps appeared. Eventually I found a bed on which to put the mattress! It was a homey place and unpretentious. A spreading red hawthorn tree filled my window where birds sang. At last I had what perhaps every woman wishes—a "nest" of my own!

Meanwhile my friend, Miss Hertzler, had no intention of moving from San Bernardino where she had many friends. But to quote her own story, early one morning in January 1959, during her "quiet time," she heard the still, small voice saying, "Miss Johnson's work is more important than your counseling," and she answered, "Yes, it is." She knew from its early growth and present expansion the work would some day become an incorporated organization, and that I would need the administrative assistance in which she had long experience. She flew to Oakland in February 1959, at which time I asked a group of men to meet with me at my Laird Avenue home to form a board of directors. The charter members of our board were Dr. Ernest Hastings, Dr. Horton Voss, the Reverend Robert Pietsch, Mr. Harold Gudnason, Miss Hertzler, and myself. We began plans to establish the official status of the organization and to confirm the name of Bible Study Fellowship. This was the name we had chosen earlier for the classes in San Bernardino and Palm Springs, when we met in Dr. Horton Voss's home.

It was an interesting fact that as we presented the balance of our financial statement at the second board meeting, we had only $101. The method regarding funds, established early, was simply to have an offering plate on a table by the exit door where new lessons were picked up by class members as they left the church. No one would know who contributed, and who did not, but from these earliest days God has supplied our needs. Many a time the chairman of our board has said, "This is the only board I know where the question of how to raise money has never needed to be discussed." Miss Hertzler was always careful to see that the funds were officially audited. Our first auditor was Mr. Alan Brizee, treasurer of the City of Oakland. These early board meetings were a special delight to both Miss Hertzler and me, and we thanked these busy men for giving of their valuable time. They would remark, "Don't thank us, we thank you for the wonderful fellowship we have together."

In June after classes were over in the summer of 1959, I returned to San Bernardino for a visit. Alverda Hertzler had decided to rent her home and move to Oakland. This was a big step for her to take. She had friends of many years in San Bernardino. She loved the home she had built, and had expected always to live there. Now she was moving to Oakland "in faith," coming to an absolutely new work. I could understand the real faith of such a move and knew our God is faithful. Against seeming impossibilities, her house was immediately rented to a fine doctor and his wife, even during the hours we were packing to leave. Again we saw the Lord's perfect timing. When we arrived in Oakland, Alverda stayed with me until she found a suitable apartment not far from my home.

I shall never cease to wonder at our Lord's lovingkindness, His timing, and the key persons and churches He brought to us at such a critical period. No one envisioned the amazing enlargement of an organization of women that was to follow.

Very soon after the class began in the Melrose Church it was attended by Mrs. Marjorie Sommer, who wished to see a similar class started in her Presbyterian Church in Lafayette, a nearby suburb. The Reverend Thomas cordially invited me there. In addition to church members many non-church persons attended. The procedure was the same; leaders from Lafayette would now join the Melrose leaders for leadership class each Monday morning. There were many "first" experiences in these early days, as new classes were introduced in other areas. Once I remember becoming a little confused upon seeing a lady start smoking in the middle of my lecture. She was sitting next to Mrs. Sommer, who also wondered just what to do. Quite unexpectedly this woman turned to Mrs. Sommer and said, "I have never been in a place like this; perhaps I should not smoke now." As time went on she was to become one of our most faithful leaders!

After the invitation to Lafayette, Dr. Robert Munger, pastor of the First Presbyterian Church of Berkeley, asked his assistant, the Reverend Don Moomaw, who prayed at President Reagan's inauguration, to call me at regular intervals about starting a class in Berkeley. At first, I felt my schedule was too heavy to take on any new classes. Besides, our policy was not to begin a new class during a series. But finally realizing the potential in the Berkeley area, I yielded to Dr. Munger's persuasion. In January 1960 we began in Berkeley, our third Bay Area class, beginning with Genesis 12. A fourth class soon began in Castro Valley.

One of the first administrative problems we faced was the production of lessons for the Genesis series. Alverda recalls well the struggle with my old mimeograph machine installed in the basement of my little home. She had no experience in running this machine, but somehow produced the first copies of the by-laws we had formulated for Bible Study Fellowship. Mrs. Pearl Hamilton gave continual typing assistance in these early days. Sometime after our class was established in the Lafayette Presbyterian Church, Alverda discovered they had an offset printing press with excellent type. The pastor very graciously consented to have his secretary produce our lessons on their press!

As I began teaching in the First Presbyterian Church in

Berkeley, I realized the impossibility of continuing to teach four classes, to conduct a leader's class, and to expand the writing of lesson notes. Therefore, Miss Hertzler taught the Melrose class for a brief time. Soon she was needed to oversee the affairs of our general administration, and we then called on Mrs. Pearl Hamilton to assume this class as teaching leader.

I now discovered that the original class leaders in San Bernardino were feeling isolated. The decision to have them come to Oakland resulted in what was to become a policy affecting the future training of leaders. I invited them to come to my home, two at a time. I took them to the Bay Area classes and trained them in teaching homiletics, exactly as I had been taught by my professor, Mr. Roland Hogben, years before. I have not seen anything of this specialized method of teaching in any of the many books on homiletics I have studied. It resulted in the training of teaching leaders to leave a vivid impression of the subject matter, as well as a lasting memory of its outline. It has proven to be one of the most valuable features in the development of the aims of Bible Study Fellowship toward biblical literacy and of my desire that individuals should be incited to follow Paul's example "to declare unto you all the counsel of God" (Acts 20:27). Mr. Hogben gave us this training for Chinese pagans in our missionary years. However, I believe he would be pleased to know how greatly his methods have been used by God through the Holy Spirit to cause class members to delight in their study of Old and New Testament passages. When Mr. Hogben died, his daughter, Dr. Monica Hogben, who is now a missionary in Singapore, gave me his Bible, which I greatly treasure.

The San Bernardino women, Mrs. Vergene Lewis, Mrs. Edna Voss, Mrs. Jean McIntyre, and Mrs. Joy Sharp, were greatly encouraged by seeing other classes develop, especially Mrs. Pearl Hamilton's class. Gradually the Bible Study Fellowship original pattern became formulated into "procedures and policies," which were proving so successful in helping people who were hungry to study the Bible and in appealing to so many new persons attending.

When I spoke at conferences at Mount Hermon Conference Center, I deeply enjoyed the early morning prayer times with other speakers such as Dr. Richard DeHaan, Dr. Donald Barnhouse, and Dr. Henry Brandt. Once Dr. Eugene Nida, the brilliant secretary of translations for the American Bible Society, was present. He was gracious enough to come to hear my message, and because of his love of Bible Study he became deeply interested. As he read the early study materials I had written, he asked to talk to me and gave me excellent advice concerning copyrighting these notes and having them read by some well-known seminary professor. He predicted the work would spread all over America, and I believe his advice to be invaluable.

TWENTY-THREE
GOD'S PURPOSE
AND GOD'S POWER

*So shall my word be that goeth forth out of my mouth: it shall
not return to me void, but it shall accomplish that which I
please, and it shall prosper in the thing whereto I sent it*
[Isaiah 55:11].

It was only after we had moved into the San Francisco Bay
Area that I began to recognize that God was using unexpected
means to expand the teaching of His Word quickly and
beyond all our expectations.

After a period of twenty years of amazing fruitfulness and
enlargement, I begin to see His purpose in this.

Although as compared with other countries, church attendance is comparatively large and there are many truly evangelical churches, the impact on the secular world in regard to
general morality is amazingly little. Indeed believers have
succumbed to the lifestyle and morals of the world even in
such areas where God has clearly stated His unchangeable
will. Take, for example, the matter of divorce among Christians
or the practices of homosexuality, fornication, drunkenness, and wife beating. Why is it that those who call themselves "born again," are trapped into acceptance of these
things? (See Matt. 5:13, "Ye are the salt of the earth: but if the

221

salt have lost its savour, wherewith shall it [the earth] be salted? It [the salt] is thenceforth good for nothing, but to be cast out, and to be trodden under foot of men.")

Why is this? We have wonderful evangelists, we have evangelical pastors with large churches, individuals are saved. As Paul said, "For after that in the wisdom of God the world by wisdom knew not God, it pleased God by the foolishness of preaching to save them that believe" (I Cor. 1:21).

We believe, we are born again, we sing songs to the Lord in the churches, we bring others in to be saved and enjoy fellowship, we give money to the Lord. Yet one all important ingredient seems to be missing: the majority of believers do not *personally read*, understand, and apply the entire Bible for themselves. They are content to be spoon-fed without taking time to discover for themselves the many facets of God's character, and to obey His specific commandments in the Bible.

Our Christian generation has no excuse. We are all literate, but many are *biblically* illiterate, especially in regard to important teaching in the Old Testament.

Personal Bible Study Is Essential. After one is saved, surely the next priority is to know the Person of God and His revealed will through a full knowledge of the entire Bible. When one considers that in the beginning God created men and women *in His own image* and from the beginning communicated with them in a language they could understand, to despise in practice that communication through His "in-breathed Word" (see II Tim. 3:16, NIV), is to fail to perceive His will and to obey it.

All of God's dealings with humanity and specifically the nation of Israel reveals His Person and His will. Symbolism, Old Testament history, teachings of the Prophets, prayer and praise in the Psalms as well as all of the New Testament are vital to every believer's present fulfillment and to an abundant entrance into Heaven (see I Pet. 1:8-11).

What a privilege it is to have an errorless Bible translated into our language in our hands. We live by "every word that proceedeth out of the mouth of the Lord," God said in Deuteronomy 8:3, which our Lord Jesus also quoted. It is not good enough to receive this Word "second hand." One must know and understand God's revelation for oneself, alone. This is the main emphasis of Bible Study Fellowship.

Certainly the earnest pastor cannot do everything. He has his sermons, his visitations, his meetings with elders, and counseling often becomes a heavy item in his overloaded schedule.

Therefore just as God has called out such prophets as Billy Graham to become *an arm of the church,* I believe God is urging organizations such as the Navigators, Walk Through the Bible, and Bible Study Fellowship to cause men and women of all faiths, believers and unbelievers, to study and discern for themselves the whole counsel of God by reading God's entire revelation given progressively in the whole Bible.

However, one can never come to know God Himself in a personal, private relationship by "spoon-feeding" alone. (See *Knowing God* by J. I. Packer.) Warm fellowship in discussion classes encourages the person who is totally ignorant of the Bible. Since Satan is against this all-important study, the discipline of required answers to helpful questions on each passage or book gives the person concerned (believer or nonbeliever) confidence to discover for himself through the Holy Spirit the many facets of the Person of "the God Who is there." Getting to know God through His Word invariably leads to a complete change of life, a conscious responsibility to have an active role in his church and the society in which he lives.

Relationship to Churches. In this sense Bible Study Fellowship aims to become a definite "arm of the church." Churches welcome us. After the beginning of our work in a home, we always hold classes by invitation from the pastor in a church. Unchurched members often join the church where they attend a class; class members say that they appreciate the pastor's message each Sunday increasingly because of a personal understanding of the Bible. Always we try to train church members not simply to warm the church pew, but that each member should ask what he or she can do in his or her own church.

From the earliest days Bible Study Fellowship has been completely interdenominational. Classes are comprised of members from almost all Christian denominations. Discussion leaders are instructed never to encourage members to switch churches. A Catholic priest attended my class for six weeks, and we developed a real friendship. Sometime during the 1960s after Pope John advocated Bible reading, we noticed a great increase in Catholic membership. Priests in one of the Bay Area churches were so impressed with Bible Study Fellowship that any one who taught catechism on Saturday had to be a current member of a Bible Study Fellowship class. Members from Jewish, Christian Science, Jehovah's Witnesses, Mormons, and other congregations have become interested in Bible study. Seeing that all denominations are welcome, Bible Study Fellowship has a truly ecumenical fellowship.

So we do not consider ourselves to be a "para-church" organization as much as an "arm of the church." Many a pastor has written thanking us for the blessing his church has received—even to the extent of saying, "This is the most helpful para-church group I know."

I believe that the work of encouragement, fellowship, and discipline, in regard to individuals knowing for themselves this entire revelation, is a necessity in our biblically illiterate day.

Gradually I realized that although we never advertise and are therefore not well known, nevertheless this work is important as it touches the Body of Christ. (Actually it was Dr. Francis Schaeffer's message at the dedication of the new Bible Study Fellowship property in San Antonio which awakened me to the urgency and importance of this work at the present time.)

We gradually realized that God's constraining impulse and His particular pattern given to a *group of people* after persistent prayer was *because His purpose is* to cause His children to be completely versed in His communicated Word through the understanding given by the Holy Spirit.

The proof of this is seen in His rapid expansion of the work through circumstances we could not have engineered.

The encouragement came in the fruit of completely changed lives and dedication of hundreds of teaching leaders, discussion leaders, and children's leaders who dedicate themselves without salary, thus making a team where the glory never goes to one person but to the Lord. Within twenty years over 100,000 class members have taken the five-year course. Our teaching leaders have shared that when unbelievers and agnostics choose to stay to the end of the five-year series, invariably they are converted through the power of God's Word.

God's Means of Expansion. I have learned by experience that when God leads His servant out, He gives at least one confirming reason for the move, and a "peace of heart" which is spiritual and from Him (*not* psychological). This was given to me and to Miss Hertzler. However, when we moved to Oakland it was in faith and obedience to reasonable signs. Yet at first we walked in darkness concerning our future. One of my very favorite texts is that of Isaiah 50:10, "Who is among you that feareth the Lord, that obeyeth the voice of his servant, that walketh in darkness, and hath no light? *Let him trust in the name of the Lord and stay upon his God*" [italics added].

There was a sense that we walked in faith not knowing what God would do in our new area of life—the Bay Area, where we and the Bible Study Fellowship were almost totally unknown.

Sudden Unexpected Expansion. Very soon after a Bible Study Fellowship class was started in Dr. Hastings's Baptist church, I received a warm invitation to start a class in the First Presbyterian Church in Berkeley where Dr. Robert Munger was pastor. Another class was located in Castro Valley, led by Mrs. Tillman (a former member of the early class in San Bernardino). These three classes, especially that in Berkeley, quickly grew to about 300 members each.

However, I could never have dreamed that God would use that Berkeley class and a class in Lafayette as the first means of "circumstantial expansion." For example, it "so happened" that some ladies who attended my Berkeley Bible Study Fellowship class were in the San Francisco Bay Area because their husbands were studying for their doctorates at the University of California, Berkeley. When the degrees were granted, these ladies who prepared to return East, came to me in real distress. "This personal study of the Scriptures has meant so much to me and others. How much I will miss not having the study."

One lady who attended the Lafayette Presbyterian Church came from Bloomington, Indiana. I recognized in her a natural gift of communication (she was a discussion leader). I suggested, "Why don't you start a class?" She replied, "I just couldn't! I have never spoken in public." I replied, "We will send you lessons, you try with your own friends at first and call me if you have difficulties. You have been an effective discussion leader, God will make you a teaching leader through His Holy Spirit." A few weeks later, after she had gathered together a small group, I received a telephone call, "Miss Johnson, what do you do when after twenty minutes you feel you have finished?" I replied, "Stop! Never try to pad a message." At the time of this writing, this lady is still teaching. She has great facility in communication and is perhaps our wittiest teaching leader, the provider of skits during teaching leaders' seminars! I was delighted to find her letter dated November 19, 1961, in my files. Already she wrote of conversions, delightful discussion meetings, and a growing class of women. Her husband who has a key position in a university now teaches in a Bible Study Fellowship class also.

As I recognized the need for research material for a beginning teaching leader, Miss Hertzler suggested that I send any new teaching leaders tapes of my lectures. Although they always listened to the tape, God would enable them to develop their own style. Very often these new teaching leaders became outstanding speakers.

Another class member whose husband was returning to Goshen, Indiana, was Mrs. Oma Smucker. She too immediately started a class. She is now area advisor for a large region, encouraging new teaching leaders.

Miss Annie Cheairs, who was working for Young Life Campaign in Berkeley, also came to the class. She had a sister, Mrs. Wenger, who taught a Bible class but without the pattern of Bible Study Fellowship (which always results in members *actually studying the Scriptures and articulating their discoveries*). Mrs. Wenger came to Oakland from Little Rock, Arkansas, for training, and wished to involve her class in the concentrated study of Bible Study Fellowship. Both Dr. and Mrs. Wenger are now area advisors after having been involved in the work for twenty years.

A second means of unexpected expansion came about by the moving of a wife and family to another state because of the husband's business connections. The wife asked to start a Bible Study Fellowship class there, and we trained her in teaching methods.

Another kind of expansion appeared in one class I taught. Some class members pledged themselves to bring representatives of every house on their street to the class. They did!

A fourth example of expansion to other states also takes place when a class member writes to a relative of blessing received. This often sparks interest in another region. Someone writes for information about starting a class.

The purpose of explaining this circumstantial expansion is to emphasize that the Holy Spirit of God spreads interest and that it's not necessarily advertising that does it. This is safer too because no glory goes to a particular person.

The teaching leaders give at least twenty hours or more each week to study and meetings and find unspeakable fulfillment in teaching a class of up to 450 members, leading individuals to the Lord and training discussion leaders who could one day become teaching leaders for another class in the area.

Space does not allow me to give all the precious names and stories of the teaching leaders, administrators, discussion leaders and children's leaders of nearly 300 classes and well over 100,000 individuals who have taken the five-year course. But every one of them came into being as a "miracle" of God's circumstantial leading and personal call to a demanding and fulfilling ministry stamped with eternal value.

Before writing more fully about the outworking of God's pattern, I need to record God's supply of needs for printing, new administration buildings, and the supply of finances without any fees required for membership or any appeals made. Actually, one never knows who gives to the little plate at the exit table, or how much, or which persons do not give at all. But the Lord knows all the expenses we must meet, and He sees we have enough to meet them and to allow for further expansion.

Important Administrative Work Undergirded Expansion. God's great gift to me was His gift of Miss Alverda Hertzler. After all, she had not been dean and vice principal of a high school of 3,000 and secretary of the California Dean's Association for three years for nothing. With her long years of administrative "know how," she took complete charge of that end of the work. She attended all classes, organized the business records, and trained the class secretaries (and later class administrators). She supervised the children's programs and bought printing presses that were continually needed to print more material. She supervised the later purchase of new property and was responsible for the excellent administration of future secretaries, bookkeepers, and printers; she even planned (with an architect) new printing and shipping additions to buildings which became necessary. Not only was Miss Hertzler a gift to the work, but God has also blessed us with a precious, enriching friendship in the Lord.

By 1962 I had an abnormally full schedule. I was teaching a training class every Monday for discussion leaders and children's leaders from four classes. On Tuesday, Wednesday, and Thursday I taught classes of 200-300 members of pagans, nominal church members, followers of cults, as well as committed Christians! On Friday and over the weekend I wrote lesson notes and questions amounting to approximately 5,000 words and ten to twelve printed pages. These had to be processed within two weeks to give out to classes both near and distant.

Needless to say the processing of these lessons became an increasing problem as class membership increased. At first Mrs. Pearl Hamilton typed the material and Dr. Hastings's secretary kindly offered to mimeograph the Matthew materials. Meanwhile, Miss Hertzler wrestled with my old mimeograph in the basement of my little Laird Avenue home to produce the first copies of the newly incorporated Bible Study Fellowship By-Laws. Later Miss Hertzler acquired a table-model press for duplicating the lesson notes and questions.

In addition to much enthusiasm by class members, a remarkable spirit of oneness became increasingly evident. One class member, Mrs. Barnhart, offered to have her son run the table-model press we had acquired to duplicate lesson notes in the basement of their home. Soon we discovered that the location of their home so near the Bay created a dampness that affected the lesson paper, causing it to curl. Then another lady, Mrs. Spidell, who lived in a dryer area, offered to locate this press in their basement. (Mrs. Spidell is now an area advisor.) Here the press was operated for eighteen months by volunteers. Since my writing of lesson materials was then only two weeks ahead of the press schedule, my work was urgent.

There was always a group of women who sacrificed time and dirty fingers to keep the press running. Every Monday morning as discussion leaders met, the plea came, "Please pray for the press." It seemed to break down constantly. Mrs. Spidell's basement walls were bedecked with texts of God's promises, such as "Lord, our hope is in Thee." When the press stopped running, workers stopped to pray and then managed to start it again. Printing ink is not easy to eradicate, and those dear women bore many a stain as they gave hours of their time. The lessons got out!

Eventually Miss Hertzler employed the two young men who serviced the press. They took over the increasing production in "moonlight" hours, working Friday night and Saturday. Gradually, as class gifts were received and several years later when we bought our first headquarters, additional equipment was purchased; a new press, a photo copier, collator, and large paper cutter provided for the demands of increasing production for the next seven years.

After volunteers had used the table-model press in Mrs. Spidell's home for some time, Miss Hertzler and I recognized that we desperately needed a headquarters. (Until now the Bible Study Fellowship board meetings had been in my Laird Avenue house.) As applications came to us from persons who wished to start a Bible Study Fellowship class in their area, I saw their need for a week's training in our methods. Also I needed to appraise their ability to teach a class and train leaders. Therefore we urgently needed a headquarters that could be used as an office, with facilities for printing and shipping of materials in the basement and space to sleep orientees from other areas.

We were a bit like the Israelites before the Red Sea. No way seemed open, but we had to proceed! Until that year our income had been only sufficient to cover our regular expenses. But then for the first time we had received more than was required for our general operation. We had learned that one way God guides is by such means. Therefore this was to us a token from Him confirming our step of faith toward the administrative extension of the work. We were looking for an adaptable house in a commercially zoned location. After three months of searching and answering classified advertisements weekly, just three days before the regular meeting of our board, only two houses seemed possible.

The First Office Headquarters. The previous Sunday we had met with a close friend for a long session of urgent prayer. We prayed that God would meet our need. Then just two days before the board meeting after three months of searching, Alverda saw a "For Sale" advertisement for a house on Foothill Boulevard, in a convenient location. When she called, the owner replied, "That ad was not to be in until next Saturday, but I will show you the house." It was the right one!

The purchase of this house was a big leap of faith, but it was in the Lord's timing. The address, 5133 Foothill Boulevard, became our first official headquarters in the fall of 1962. I remember the reaction of our board chairman: "Wetherell, this is a real venture of faith—there is no turning back now." This office-house provided not only office space, but two bedrooms to accommodate the early candidates for teaching leader training. A large basement provided adequate space for press equipment, assembly of lessons, and shipping to classes. Soon our first full-time secretary was brought to us, Mrs. Ruth Stagner, a member of a class in Castro Valley. After a brief time her home situation required that she leave us, and Mrs. Jean Werum followed as office secretary for many years. Jean is now serving as an area advisor in a region in Northern California.

Since we are on the subject of growth, it seems good to give a short review of the printing process through the years initiated by Miss Hertzler, which reveals the amazing growth of class membership in a short period.

After we had used the table-model press for some time, when we moved to the small Foothill headquarters, volunteers ran our first offset press which printed 6,000 pages per hour.

In 1969 when we moved to Skymount, a larger head-quarters, Miss Hertzler planned the first printing addition. There we acquired a press that printed 50,000 pages per hour, and we hired our first printer. A second printing addition was built in 1973 where we added a large collator which assembled 3,000 sets of lessons per hour, mostly run by volunteers. By 1977, we had built a new building of 14,000 square feet on some adjacent land. Then Miss Hertzler purchased a huge press fed by 600-pound rolls of paper which ran off 65,000 double sheets of four pages each. The need for lessons still increased. Today in San Antonio the Production Building, with a work flow and floor plan roughly sketched by Miss Hertzler, production staff, and Mr. Paul Hesson, the architect for the San Antonio buildings, is 27,000 square feet.

At each stage of purchase and new construction, Miss Hertzler would say to the board, "I think this will last us for the foreseeable future." Finally the board replied, "I think we have heard you say this before, Miss Hertzler."

What a testimony this is to the power of God's Word and His Spirit in expanding the work and His gift of an administrator to keep pace with practical needs.

How grateful I am that God called Alverda Hertzler into the work. Although I had charge of the general direction and pattern of the work, the training of the teaching leaders, and the relationship with them (and later with regional area advisors), I could never have handled the other basic requirements of the work.

Ever since she came into the work in 1959 she has completely handled the business administration, without which Bible Study Fellowship would not be where it is today.

She arranged the incorporation of the organization, registration of the name, and copyrights. She supervised all the financial records and the printing and shipping of what grew to be over 80,000 lessons per week.

Sometimes our men orientees occupy high positions in the business world. I was always interested when they expressed

amazement at the expertise of Miss Hertzler's business department and the smooth running of the teaching side of the work.
They always seem surprised that such a large organization
could be run by two single women! Again this is because
"God chooses the things that are not . . . that no flesh may
glory in His presence."

Lord of the great and mighty ocean,
Lord of the pine clad hill,
Lord of those purple mountains,
My utmost being fill
With praise to Thee
Who givest me
Thy beautiful world to enjoy.

Thou who controllest the course of the stars
And the path of the moon on the sea—
Thou who commandest the wind to be still
Lord, rule in the heart of me.
Breathe through my mind
Until Thou dost find
That I will one will with Thee.

A. Wetherell Johnson

TWENTY-FOUR

JOYS OF DEVELOPMENT IN THE BAY AREA

For thy word's sake, and according to thine own heart, hast thou done all these great things, to make thy servant know them [II Samuel 7:21].

The time came when Miss Hertzler and I both realized there would be advantages to our living under the same roof. Although we had no specific "job description" of our responsibilities, we each understood our separate abilities and fields. I had started the classes, had previous experience in China and America in training teaching leaders, organizing classes, and delineating the exegetical five-year series of Bible lessons. Alverda had on the other hand excellent business acumen and was accustomed to American methods and modes of operation; her field was administration. Neither of us had experienced any difficulty in overlapping each other's responsibilities. Without Alverda's expertise and coordination of business and financial operations, the Bible Study Fellowship could not have expanded as it has, reflected in thousands upon thousands who witness to God's power in changing the lives of individuals and entire families. Notwithstanding, I am conscious that the pattern God gave me for the shaping of this work stemmed from early training in London and the years of learning how to look to God for direction by prayer and through His Word as I had experienced these things in China.

In 1962 Alverda and I began our search for a house, particularly in the suburb of Oakland called Montclair. This area was conveniently near our new headquarters, and we hoped to find a home high in the Oakland hills. Alverda looked forward with expectation to building again. First we found a reasonably priced lot, but regrettably it had no view. I returned to my own little Laird Avenue home and prayed. God knew what a beautiful view meant to me, but I realized there were many of His people who also loved nature but who lived without a view. Why should I insist upon His indulgence? At that, I gave my will to His, determined to "be content" (Heb. 13:5).

The next day we returned once more to see the lot minus a view, upon which we had by now almost made a final decision. I remarked to Alverda, "Let's go back by way of the scenic Snake Road." As we did this, to our surprise I saw a small vacant lot with an indescribable view of San Francisco Bay and a deep ravine thickly wooded with a forest of tall trees. There we saw a tiny sign, "For Sale by Owner." We made great haste to telephone the owner and lost no time making our deposit payment! Psalm 37 had very special meaning to us, "Delight thyself also in the Lord; and He shall give thee the desires of thine heart."

Needless to say, the selling price of my little Laird Avenue house had doubled by this time, so that I was able to share adequately in the down payment of our new investment. Alverda had already sold her home in San Bernardino satisfactorily. Therefore, with much excitement we began to plan the new home in which we were to live for nearly twenty years. Alverda, having already gone through the experience of building a home, was aware of the joys and the pitfalls of such an undertaking. I had my own definite ideas about the area that was to be mine. I would need solitude for writing and for teaching preparations.

The design of our home had to adapt to a steep downhill slope and had to be built on two levels where Alverda would occupy the upper floor and I the lower. Then came offers of help from friends around us: the husband of a leader was the head of a lumber-supply company; a talented woman who knew the art of home designing drew plans; and a well-known consulting engineer in San Francisco devoted his skill. It was he who designed the foundation, an especially complex undertaking on such a steep slope. We later learned his design of our foundations with provision for earthquakes became a model for student engineer examinations. Sixty-six redwood steps—often referred to as "from Genesis to Revelation"—led down the slope to a patio garden planted with shrubs and flowers of many colors.

There were facets to building that were amusing as well as testing, and we were constantly reminded of God's faithful undertaking for us. Owing to the two levels of our home, we decided on the necessity of a dumbwaiter which would be electrically operated and serve often to spare us the use of the stairs. But where would we find a contractor with experience in this unusual type of installation? We called a downtown hotel asking, "Do you have a dumbwaiter?" The somewhat hearty reply came back, "Yes! Lots of them. We'd like to get rid of some." God eventually led us to find a "Genie," an electronic garage door opener, which could be hooked up to operate the dumbwaiter.

Again on one occasion when I was shopping in Berkeley in search of a small radio a voice called to me, "Oh, Miss Johnson, you are just the one we want! We are buying a kitchen stove for you, what color would you like?" God's provisions continued in such surprising ways.

I often sat on the rim of our new property, gazing across the wide expanse of blue bay on one side to the deep green forest on the sloping hills, and there I would say, "Lord, I cannot believe after all these years of Your goodness You would give me such heart's desire!"

By January of 1963 our house was finished. Fifty persons who had had some part in its building and helping us move crowded into my downstairs area, which included a wide, open veranda. The chairman of our board, Dr. Ernest Hastings, led in the dedication of our new home. He declared, "I see this house as an extension of the office on Foothill Boulevard—it is part of a ministry—a quiet and lovely place where you will come closer to the heart of God and be able to interpret and teach the Word, not to a few but to thousands." In his prayer of dedication, Dr. Hastings expressed so beautifully what had been in our own hearts, "This home is a gift from Thy Hand, O Lord. We thank Thee for those who have been used to help make it possible. We look behind this and beyond it and see Thee and Thy love gift. We dedicate it to the one end that glory might come to Thy cause. The home which has been given by Thee is returned to Thee, O God, for Thy ministry and Thy directing."

From that day on it was constantly used for Bible Study Fellowship gatherings: board meetings, orientation group sharing (where eighteen potential teaching leaders would meet for training sessions), staff meetings, and Christmas parties! The guest bedroom downstairs allowed us to entertain special guests from time to time. The crowning feature of my home was a mahogany desk built by a friend who was the head of a cabinet company, a desk stretching across the width of one wall, with bookcases built above within easy reach. It was here I was able to write 5,000 words of lesson notes each week without interruption and had the joy of accomplishing my major writing through the years.

Always the Bay was visible from our vantage point and we could often see glorious sunsets, as well as ocean liners at anchor, and the Golden Gate Bridge under which ships sailed to China! Near to us were regional parks of stately redwood trees and lovely ocean beaches. We never tired of escaping to Carmel-by-the-Sea, where a generous class member had a second home which she would loan us for an occasional vacation. Spring would bring its profusion and variety of flowers: rose and jasmine fragrance filled the air; brilliant camelias and rhododendrons caught the eye on almost every street. We picnicked in lovely woods very near our home and in the winter gathered cedar boughs and cones for Christmas.

We made frequent trips to fascinating San Francisco, city of cable cars, famous hotels, and restaurants. For our enjoyment also were the classical music stations on radio throughout day and evening. Members of our classes became our friends, and leaders whom I knew more intimately would take delight in showing us special sights and highlights. One of these was the performance by concert pianist Dame Myra Hess in the beautiful War Memorial Opera House in the city center. I have referred earlier to my sister's study with her, and now was my opportunity to meet her again, but I was too shy. However, I wrote to her my impression of this most brilliant recital and received her lovely handwritten reply, which I keep among my treasures.

Bible Study Fellowship Goes to China. During the time Dr. Munger was pastor of First Presbyterian Church, Berkeley, my class there grew to about 300 members. (It was much nearer our new home.)

At that time Mrs. Caroline Ho and Dr. Wu, who had been on the faculty of the China Bible Seminary, visited the Berkeley class. They requested permission to translate my materials into Chinese and to start Bible Study Fellowship classes in Hong Kong where a new China Bible Seminary had been started. Needless to say, Mrs. Ho would adapt the lessons to Chinese lifestyle.

The board was very interested and decided that we should help with the payment for the first printing. This Chinese Bible Study Fellowship class is still operating in Hong Kong. Recently (1981) I received a letter from Mr. Will Bruce mentioning these outlines which he wants to take over to Taiwan.

New Board Members and an Important Decision. Shortly after this Dr. Munger was called to a church in Seattle. Dr. Harold Englund, who was highly esteemed by the InterVarsity Fellowship, succeeded him.

With the approval of our board of directors, I asked both Dr. Englund and Dr. Dwight Small (now a professor at Westmont College) to join our board.

We were at that time receiving many applications from prospective teaching leaders throughout at least five states and I foresaw the need arising of our having some regional oversight. Remembering what I had seen of organization in China, I recommended to the board that we engage one or two persons to oversee new classes, following the allocation of new teaching leaders who had completed their week of orientation at Oakland Headquarters. These persons were to be called "area advisors."

I recall the excellent advice given by Dr. Englund who had made a study of para-church groups. Seeing that it was a long way to come from Arkansas or Indiana to Oakland for training, one capable teaching leader had suggested that teaching leader candidates might be given their training in their local region. Dr. Englund said emphatically, "No! To divide regions and to 'go national' by setting up regional offices would change the character of Bible Study Fellowship. Every teaching leader should keep close personal contact with the general director by phone and by letter. The future area advisor's work will be to advise headquarters of any real problem in policy or procedure that arises on the field, and be a counselor and supervisor of classes in each region. I foresee that Bible Study Fellowship will grow all over America like crabgrass, taking root in one area and spreading from there. The work will reach as far as it can grow from one central stem." I was amused when my Texas-oriented secretary informed me that the Texas type of crabgrass is often called "Johnson grass"!

I believe this decision proved to be one secret to the strong relationship all teaching leaders have with headquarters. As general director I came to know and love each one and was able to pray for them individually. We are truly a fellowship! When triennial seminars for teaching leaders were instituted, the heart-warming fellowship and testimonies gave evidence to the links that were strongly forged during the week when "would-be" teaching leaders were in headquarters for training.

Later Dr. Englund and Dr. Dwight Small left the Bay Area and our board of directors. They were succeeded by Mr. L. V. Sanderson, a bank manager from Sacramento, and Dr. William Stoddard, pastor of Walnut Creek Church, where I was then teaching our largest class. Dr. Ray Stedman, pastor of Peninsula Bible Church, also joined our board of directors, and much later Dr. Grant Whipple, director of The Firs Conference in Bellingham, Washington.

Transformation of Individual Lives. Underlying all the formal procedures of a growing organization and business matters that seemed to encroach upon our attention were the thrilling, eternal fruits of Bible study and testimonies that came from God's work in so many lives.

One of these testimonies was of a lady studying her lesson questions while under the dryer in a beauty salon. This aroused the curiosity of the woman next to her who asked what she was doing. When told she was preparing her questions for Bible Study Fellowship, she replied, "Oh, my psychiatrist says I ought to mix with some church for fellowship. Could I come?" She came and there found the Lord. She said that previously when tense she had found relaxation in her vodka drink; but now her Jewish husband was intrigued. He remarked, "I notice you do not use the bottle any more. I like the change." She told him what the Lord now meant to her and gave him one of our "Assurance Letters" to read. He read this and from the Bible texts used, found the Lord for himself. I was attending a leader's luncheon just two weeks later where this woman was sitting with a group on the floor, beaming with joy as she told her wonderful story. She added, "This morning my husband said he used to blaspheme with the rest of his office staff, but now if one uttered the name of Jesus in

241

blasphemy he felt as though he had been kicked in the stomach." Such is the power of God's Word when studied!

A delightful story is told of a group of discussion leaders while lunching in a restaurant. Their happiness and radiance were observed by a woman seated alone at a nearby table. She came to them, commenting, "You seem to have so much fun in your 'club.' Could I join it?"

It is my custom at the end of a message (if it is in the context of the passage) to say, "Will you not pray silently now, and then when you get home, at your bedside ask the Lord to give you His text for you, so that you may have the joyous assurance of knowing you are His." One lady was brought by her unconverted friend to my class. I noticed during the lecture that she was in tears; however, I was caught by other inquirers at the end of the lecture, and was not able to contact her casually. The friend who had brought her asked her discussion leader if she had any more information about this "Christian jazz"! Both ladies were given an "Assurance Letter," which gives Bible texts concerning conversion. The two women returned to their respective homes. The new lady knelt down with her opened Bible and gave herself to the Lord. She was so transported with joy that she felt she had to tell her friend about it. Meanwhile, unknown to her, her friend had experienced the same joy of salvation, and immediately felt she had to share it with her friend! The two ladies met totally unexpectedly with the same joyous news in the middle of Orinda Village.

The newest lady gave her husband her copy of the Assurance Letter. Not only was this the means of his coming to the Lord and attending a men's evening class, but he later attended Dr. Ray Stedman's "Scribe School." He is now a pastor in the mountains of Northern California, where the couple is greatly used of God.

Countless thrilling stories can be told of the thousands of lives changed through meeting the Lord in Bible study. One day a lady invited to a class I was teaching on the subject of

Jonah, said, "If she is a fundamentalist and says that the whale really vomited up Jonah, I'm not going." Nonetheless, she came. Knowing there were many, who like myself formerly, would listen only skeptically, I began in low key, speaking of the importance of the "message." Slowly I gave reasons for belief that Jonah's story was an historical event. For example, "Jonah was already a prestige prophet in Israel; Israelites would not be likely to use his name in such a personally disparaging situation." Gradually I came to the words of the Lord Jesus. I concluded the introduction by giving several valid reasons why I personally considered the book to be historic. This lady was converted that day and in time became the teaching leader of a class, and later an area advisor.

Children Are Taught. As classes were growing in number and membership was increasing, many young mothers with children were enrolling for study each week. One day while in our Walnut Creek class Alverda passed a room in the church filled with day-care children, all busy with projects at their tables. Upon seeing this, she conceived a plan that rather than using baby-sitters, we should use the two hours with our three-to five-years olds in teaching.

Shortly thereafter in God's providence, while attending a conference in Mount Hermon, we met Doreen Shaw, a conference speaker. She was one of two specially gifted people God was soon to use in the creation of a children's program. Doreen had had charge of 800 children in a displaced person's camp in Germany following World War II. Her friend, Martie Johnson, had taught psychology at Ft. Wayne Bible College. Together they had supervised an orphanage in Japan and were co-authors of a book on children. Alverda talked with Doreen about possibly helping us introduce a children's study program. Doreen's calendar of engagements was full for two years except (unaccountably) for one free month—the month of August! She consented to compile a manual for use in the construction of the new program and

243

completed a one-year series of Bible lessons for children. That September 1963 Doreen's friend, Martie Johnson, joined our staff, spending a year with us to initiate this new work and writing an additional two-year series of lessons with Doreen's help. She introduced Home Training Lessons, which were a guide for parents in the training of children according to biblical principles. Mothers were eager to receive these each week as they enrolled their little ones in class.

As this Children's Christian Training Program prospered, God brought to us Mrs. Marcella Altmann, a class leader who was also a trained teacher of pre-school children. She directed and developed this program most effectively for eleven years, together with Mrs. Audrey King.

Hundreds of dedicated children's leaders and children's chairmen have carried on this program in their classes through the years. They and other children's staff members have faithfully kept the basic purposes to teach Bible stories and to have children learn simple Bible verses and good children's hymns. Thousands of children have learned that God loves them and cares for them as they have heard His Word and experienced the love of their devoted leaders. A special program was planned for the two-year-olds by a later staff member, Lynn Murphy Casale.

Precious experiences with thousands of little children resulted through the years and in 1981 almost 13,000 two-, three-, four-, and five-year-olds attended their classes each week. One little girl, hearing her father in exasperation say, "Jesus Christ," innocently added, "Yes, the same yesterday, today, and forever—Hebrews 13:8," remembering this portion of the lesson she had been taught and had memorized. I have often wondered what her father thought and have since learned that he came to know the Lord Jesus personally. Another lovely story concerns children who upon hearing that our Lord might come any time in the clouds all rushed to the window to see if He was there. Another small boy who seemed to suffer from an inferiority complex was told Jesus loved him. A picture of Jesus hung on the church wall in the room where his class met. Every day he came he would go to that picture and say, "You love me and I love You." He would point out this picture to other children, "That's Jesus and He loves me."

Mrs. J. O. (Roxie) Fraser. With each new development in our organization and increase of responsibility for the growing number of retreats, seminars, and training sessions, I was more and more aware of my need for assistance. For several years we had been praying for someone whose training and spiritual life would have given her the necessary background for this type of ministry.

During my time in England in 1956, I had renewed my fellowship with Mrs. J. O. (Roxie) Fraser, whom I had known during my years in China.

Following her husband's death during his missionary work with the Miao and Lisu tribes, Mrs. Fraser had returned to England. At first she had been in charge of the Women's Training Department of the China Inland Mission. Later she became principal of the Mount Hermon Bible and Missionary Training College in London.

Mrs. Fraser was very interested in our work, so much so that she decided to resign from her position at Mount Hermon Bible College to come to us if this was God's will. Following a very warm recommendation from the late Dr. Martyn Lloyd-Jones, the board voted to invite her to join the staff. Mrs. Fraser had previously promised to return to England after six months to visit with her married children who were then returning from the mission field. However, we hoped she would return to Oakland after that.

To my great joy, Roxie came to live with us for six months. She was an invaluable help. She taught classes in the Bay Area, where she was greatly used of God to win many unconverted to the Lord. She told us later that her time with us was the happiest time in her life since her husband's death.

She and we had hoped she would return after visiting with her family in England. However, they needed her help so much that she was unable to return. But her heart remained very deeply in Bible Study Fellowship ministries until the time of her death.

Mrs. Fraser's husband was one of the outstanding missionaries in the history of the China Inland Mission. A brilliant musician and an engineer, Mr. Fraser was also a pioneer missionary to China's far western province, working with his colleagues to give them the whole New Testament in their own language.

TWENTY-FIVE

THE AMAZING
OUTWORKING
OF GOD'S PATTERN

Commit thy works unto the Lord, and thy thoughts shall be established [Proverbs 16:3].

Establishment of Men's Classes. Although the growing number of classes was made up primarily of women since the time the Lord called it into being, the husbands of some of these women began to ask if they too might have similar study in evening classes. I recognized that the scriptural principles of balanced family life were disrupted if the wife was ahead of the husband in Scripture knowledge.

During the early days in our Oakland expansion, Dr. Richard Smith started a couples class in the basement of his home. He is a very earnest Christian and a successful physician. He made a practice of hearing his patients' medical history and then asking, "Seeing that your belief in God is also an important part of your life health, would you share with me something of your religious history?" His patients loved him.

Apart from the blessing of his classes he will always be remembered in Bible Study Fellowship history for a most unusual event. In winter he would have a cheerful fire burning in the fireplace and would customarily stand in front of it while meeting with his class. One night, after a busy office day and having gone the previous night without sleep (because he had been called out to deliver a baby), he was very tired. Without warning, he fell asleep during his lecture and as his class looked on, dropped backwards into the fire! There was no harm done, but there *was* much mirth! Today he is engaged in the training of medical students in Saudi Arabia.

I realized gradually that if men were to have evening classes it would be better to have men only, instead of couples, as the teaching leader would be able to deal with specifics which might be more difficult when wives were present. At first we encountered some minor problems. I found (as might be expected) that men were inclined to dispense with some of the established procedures which we considered to be a key to the ministry, but which they considered as "suitable just for women." In the men's classes there were such things as discussion leaders who would allow members to express opinions on a passage even if they had not attempted to study (nor written down their summarized answer to questions)! This troubled me. I knew that such an attitude would ultimately erode the women's classes, where they were increasingly enjoying what they now called "the discipline" of Bible Study Fellowship procedures.

I brought this problem to our board and felt supported by the reply of Dr. Ray Stedman who as a board member and pastor said, "Miss Johnson, you train women leaders; you will have to train the men also. If they wish to hold a Bible Study Fellowship class, they must follow the procedures." This caused me to have second thoughts. Although I have never had difficulty about speaking to mixed audiences when invited, I have always acknowledged God's pattern of leadership in theology as given to men. At the same time, I have felt comfortable with writing lesson notes for study because always I have at least fourteen commentaries to corroborate the exegesis I felt God gave me, as well as the advice of Dr. Everett Harrison of Fuller Seminary who reads all my lesson notes.

However, Dr. Stedman pressed his point, "Wetherell, this is in order for you to train these men in basic techniques since it is *they*—not you—who are asking for inclusion in these classes."

Soon thereafter I invited twenty-five potential men class leaders in and near the Bay Area, who came to my home at 6:30 every Saturday morning. I prepared a light breakfast, and by 7:00 we were all on our knees in prayer. On one occasion a member arrived late, having come a considerable distance. I said, "Gentlemen, if you wish this class to begin later I will agree, but kneeling in prayer is all important, and if we settle together on a time, we must respect the majesty of God with our punctuality." Never again was this a problem!

I learned a great deal in the five years of meeting with these key men who became the leadership of what developed into the division of a "men's work." Some men considered the questions in each week's study to be overly geared to the feminine temperament. After listening to examples, I learned increasingly to create questions which would fit both men and women. During those five years together we developed a meaningful relationship. Gradually the men's evening class followed the same basic pattern as in the women's classes, but with allowance for men's business schedules. Always the men discussion leaders meet early Saturday morning. Even though it might be hard for men to sacrifice the one morning on which they might be able to sleep in, one needs to recognize that if one is to accomplish something for God, one cannot by-pass His Cross and denial of self if one desires His fruit.

By 1970 men's classes represented a good portion of the total attendance of our 60,000 women and men. Perhaps the first outstanding class of men only was in Seattle under the leadership of Mr. C. Schuker. When I visited them there were about 300 in attendance, the largest group of men to this date. (There was also one discussion class for college students.) They had no class pianist but heartily sang a cappella songs of praise and joy that brought tears to my eyes. The teaching leader's lecture was excellent.

Dr. Robert Stevens came onto our staff for a short time to lead the men's work, but during that period we did not have enough men in our classes to warrant a full-time staff member. We very much appreciated his services. He later developed his own organization called "Church Bible Classes."

After this period, men's classes gradually grew to large numbers. For example, in Minneapolis under Mr. Robert Glockner's leadership, there were three classes with a total of 900 men. As years progress, most of our men's classes have continued to grow to 250–400 men. It is interesting that teaching leaders tend to be medical doctors, lawyers, and presidents of business organizations. Perhaps this is because such professions allow for more flexible adjustment of hours.

At first, most men came to a class because of the change of attitude they had seen in their wives who attended day classes. I always remember very early in the work a woman's testimony about the study of Genesis. She was a very strong individualist and said, "I have never before understood the biblical pattern of a wife's role. It has changed my home." Her husband became a member of the Walnut Creek Men's Evening Class. He now is president of a ministry to prisoners. Serving with him as one of his key managers is a young man who was converted while attending our first young adults class in Oakland.

A lawyer, at an evening party gathering just before I left Oakland, said very strongly, "Miss Johnson, you need to realize that the changed lives of the wives is that which brings most men into my class." However, I prayed that this would not always be the principal cause. Now, men ask their men friends and business associates into a class. A businessman, accustomed to the majority of women in churches, is enthralled when he comes for a first time to a class of 300 men, excited over their Bible study—men from all walks of life. He feels there must be something to Bible study, for he knows how hard it is for a man who is occupied in business all week and who has family responsibilities to make time for solid Bible study.

I think of one precious story of an orthodox Jewess which has special significance to me because of my profound interest in Israel. This lady's mother-in-law warned her husband that attending such a class might be dangerous to her faith. However, she received the Lord Jesus as Savior and her life was completely changed. Her husband was so intrigued that he attended a men's evening class. He too became a "completed Jew." Both of them later became teaching leaders, and now the husband has decided to go into the Jewish Bible Society full time. He took seminary training in preparation for his new ministry, and because we are considered as a lay Bible school, he and others in similar situations received course credit.

Another class teacher, a heart specialist, while teaching his class one evening observed a man just two rows in front of him who looked as though he were having a heart attack. Believing daringly in the Lord, he stopped his lecture and said, "Satan, I command you in Jesus' name that you stop hindering this meeting." Immediately the man was completely recovered. Yet that teaching leader had not long been converted himself. He is now an area advisor in the men's division of Bible Study Fellowship.

One man recently converted in the class had found his relationship with his children completely changed. He said, "My children would say, 'I love you' but never, 'I like you.'" Now he could show his love for his children and frolic with them. His delight knew no bounds when his little boy said, "Daddy, I like you and I love you." One day his little girl was on his knee while he told her the story of the death of Absalom. She was very intent, and he waited for some "profound" utterance when finally she simply said, "But, Daddy, why didn't he duck?"

It is at discussion leaders' retreats and at teaching leaders' seminars during testimony meetings that we truly see the demonstration of what God's power has wrought in the lives of men class members. To me it is like adding the quality of bass notes so necessary to music, harmonizing with the treble

251

testimonies of the women. The men exhibit a total oneness in the fellowship, recognizing their fulfillment and leadership in both home and church. Most important is it that these are the men to whom the church pastor looks for leadership. I know several Sunday school programs which have been altered to adopt something of the pattern God has given Bible Study Fellowship.

In 1967 my work as general director and Miss Hertzler's work as administrator were very heavy. Sometimes I had leaders' retreats in faraway states every weekend from February to May, in addition to teaching and writing. On the other hand, there rested on Alverda the responsibility of the production of thousands of lessons to be printed and shipped to all parts of the United States. She handled all financial affairs and was secretary to the board of directors. Added to this, in the summer of 1967 we would spend hours together revising the teaching leader's manual of procedures and policies and helps so that it could be printed that fall.

Miss Hertzler's Illness and God's Provision. Perhaps this heavy assignment accounted for the fact that when Alverda went with me to Mount Hermon where I had a week's speaking assignment, she suffered extreme pain around the region of her heart. I could not leave the conference because of my assignment. A friend therefore kindly drove her home where she telephoned my doctor. As soon as Dr. Helen Christensen saw her, she immediately put her in intensive care in the hospital. She had had a coronary thrombosis. I was indeed thrown upon our faithful Lord; I wanted to be with her but could not leave because of my engagements. The question incessantly in my thoughts was, "Will she be able to resume her work? In any event, is her work too heavy now for one person?" Although Alverda was eight years older than I, her mind was extremely alert and her administration was invaluable. (Eventually she had a remarkable recovery which we knew the Lord gave in answer to the prayers of our people.)

Therefore I talked with the director of Mount Hermon Conference Center, Mr. Bill Gwinn (who later became a member of our board of directors). He suggested the name of Miss Marguerite Carter, who was then in Canada. She had for many years held an important administrative post in Gospel Recordings of Los Angeles. After prayer, telephone calls, and correspondence, she eventually arrived by car from Canada while Miss Hertzler was now at home convalescing from her illness. I shall always remember the day Marguerite arrived at our front door, young looking, gay of heart. We later learned of her spiritual ideals and excellent administrative abilities. Again we realized the truth of Romans 8:28, "All things work together for good to them that love God, to them who are called according to his purpose." Marguerite was a great help from the beginning, and eventually through her we found a larger building for office accommodations and an orientation house as the classes increased.

The Important Pattern of Training Leaders. At this point it is important to explain the philosophy and procedure of the pattern given by God as the secret of God's blessing in the amazing expansion of the work in less than ten years. This lay largely in the fact of each teaching leader's dedication and reliance upon the Holy Spirit's power.

Before I was forced to leave the work in 1980 because of cancer, we had 270 teaching leaders (women and men) who gave at least twenty hours each week in preparation of the lesson and teaching discussion leaders' classes and classes with membership limited to 450. This is always without any remuneration, advertisement, or public recognition. As a team we were all determined that all glory should go to God, and the work therefore should be "low key." Discussion leaders and children's leaders also gave considerable sacrificial time as well.

Needless to say, the original and subsequent training of these teaching leaders is all important.

Training of Prospective Teaching Leaders in Oakland. Teaching leaders and substitute teaching leaders (who would also help carry the administrative duties of the class) were invited to headquarters as candidates for acceptance. In most cases they paid their own transportation to headquarters in Oakland. At first some were accommodated at the Foothill office, others in the home of friends. During this week, the staff and I grew to know each candidate's personality. Since the teaching leader is the key to a successful class, personality was all important and I, as well as others, considered their gift of communication, spiritual outlook, and agreement with the principles of procedures and policies. We considered these four orientation sessions each year of vital importance.

Candidates would arrive in Oakland often half scared! Some of them had never taught publicly in their lives. Therefore our first mission was to make them feel accepted and at home. Marguerite Carter and Mrs. Pearl Hamilton would meet them and often have a scenic evening showing off the sights of San Francisco.

As the work grew we purchased three orientation houses, all located within easy access of headquarters and my home. Each of these houses was occupied by a staff member as her residence throughout the year, which she shared with each group of orientees during their week in training. These homes provided a natural home atmosphere for the increasing number of candidates in these groups and gave opportunity for trainees and staff to enjoy a fellowship and love that carried into each class. Again this proved to be the pattern of Bible Study Fellowship.

On Sunday night these groups, which grew from ten to twenty persons, would crowd into my living room. After a welcome and prayer they would identify themselves in any way they chose. Mostly it would be, "How I came to know the Lord" or "My first contact with Bible Study Fellowship." I think I loved this session second only to my teaching of God's Word. As each one spoke, unconsciously he or she revealed his or her personality, and many very interesting stories emerged. Always a very large percentage of these orientees had been converted at Bible Study Fellowship meetings.

During orientation week all the visiting candidates attended classes, including my own, and studied administration and class finances with Miss Hertzler. These sessions also included the study of homiletics in workshops and an entire day of the teaching leader's manual, where I explained the "whys" of some procedures. It seems our work has progressed—first with an existing problem and prayer as the means of a solution—resulting in a proven procedure, or, if it involved a decision of the board, a policy! God gave the pattern of Bible Study Fellowship, and our glory is that no one but He has the glory! *The teaching leader is the key to each class*, although I am known in each class by the study of my lesson notes. The teaching leader is very dependent upon the class administrator, discussion leaders, and children's leaders; we are a fellowship led by God's inerrant Word.

At leaders' meetings we do teach leaders some of the techniques of speaking which is called "homiletics." Among other techniques, some people like to stress having three divisions of the subject beginning with the same letter for the purpose of memory.

Personally I do not often use this technique, although I appreciate its value. Many of our discussion leaders, however, find this a tantalizing "brain teaser." At a recent teaching leaders' seminar I sat next to a teaching leader who told me this delightful true story which I thought was too good to omit. Actually, it is his wife's story.

When I was a discussion leader in Bible Study Fellowship, I had always wanted to do my homiletics using alliteration. I loved it when others gave their subject sentences of ten words or less using all "P's" or "S's," etc., but my mind just didn't seem to operate in those channels. I prayed specifically, "Lord, if it is Your will, please bring an alliterated subject sentence to mind." Well, week after week, no such sentence came. Then one morning at 2:00 A.M., I awakened, and all at once a sentence came to mind concerning the Flood in Genesis 6–8.

Ecstatically, I began shaking my husband, Bill, who is the teaching leader for the Memphis Men's Evening Class of Bible Study Fellowship, and said, "Wake up! Wake up! I've got a homiletic!"

Bill awakened from a deep slumber and said, "Take two aspirins and maybe it'll go away."

I replied, "I'm serious, Bill."

So he patronizingly said, "Okay, what is it, Diane?"

"Get this! 'Righteous Remnant Rescued from Ruin to Restoration and Replenishment.'"

Bill says, "That's great, Honey, really great. Now go back to sleep."

So I then rolled over with much self-satisfaction, thanking the Lord for my subject sentence which had come after weeks of laborious thought.

No more than sixty seconds later, Bill punched me and said, "Submissive Sweetheart Startles Sleeping Spouse Spouting Scripturally Sound Spiritual Sayings!"

Now I ask you—was that fair? My alliteration, which had taken me weeks, was topped by my husband in less than one minute!

At the close of each orientation session Wednesday night, we all went out "on the razzle." By this time the orientees had become so close in their fellowship that future meetings were like a college reunion!

On the day of departures I had personal interviews with each candidate. Each one would receive confirmation of acceptance, or if not, some gentle suggestion of another position of service in Bible Study Fellowship. We became intimately acquainted and subsequently frequently communicated by telephone and letter. Also area advisors would visit classes, and help teaching leaders by instruction and fellowship.

Often I comfort new teaching leaders by telling them how Satan attacks me before speaking in a class. Yet once one is in the pulpit with a well-prepared outline and is alert to the varied expressions of the audience during the message, the Holy Spirit takes over, and teaching the Bible becomes quite definitely the most exciting, delightful, and fulfilling work one ever does. Then to hear of changed lives gives an unspeakable exhilaration. I am always careful to turn aside any suggestion of praise, remembering that "God will not give His glory to any other." This is also the reason we never advertise or solicit, for fear of touching "the glory of God" (Isa. 42:8). I have learned to simply forget any kind of praise, and always feel helpless without the Lord's gift of power to speak.

Sometimes I lie awake at night marveling that God would do so exceedingly above all I had prayed or even imagined! One poem particularly comes to mind:

> O God of stars and flowers, forgive our blindness;
> No dream of night had dared what Thou hast wrought.
> New every morning is Thy lovingkindness
> Far, far above what we had asked or thought.

Amy Wilson Carmichael

Leader's Manual and Discussion Leaders. When we received more applications for new classes far from us, I felt the time had come for us to compile a leader's manual which they would study and take home with them. This would be a further development of assistance to them.

At first, when Mrs. Schaap began her class, I sent a tape of my lecture to her. This aid, which was later made available only to teaching leaders, became a helpful resource material to them through the years. It assists teaching leaders in their teaching until they are confident to develop the particular way of communicating a message which the Lord gives individually to them. When we compiled the manual, we asked leaders to give their contribution to its composition. I remember Mrs.

Katherine Plate of Berkeley inviting several friends to her country home at Mount Hermon Conference Center, where we discussed and decided upon some basic rules which we thought necessary for our unique method of study. Although the atmosphere of each Bible Study Fellowship class would reflect the teaching leader's personality, part of the "family" fellowship among the classes was derived from the fact that to attend one class—whether in the Bay Area or elsewhere—it would be basically the same since each class would follow the pattern God gave us, and the basic structure, later known as "Policies and Procedures."

In time there were manuals for class administrators and children's leaders, and separate manuals for men's classes.

Training of Discussion Leaders. I taught new teaching leaders that the key to a fruitful ministry lay more in their training of discussion leaders once a week then even in their lecture. Discussion leaders developed a relationship with each member of the small group. This fellowship counts particularly in the life of a new member who is perhaps totally unacquainted with the Bible.

I loved my own discussion leaders' class. They were committed to answering all questions. Discussion during the prolonged period was open. "No holds were barred" as I dealt with their theological questions. They were taught never to say "that's wrong" to a class member, nor to give out any answers. Instead they were to look around and ask if another member might have a different opinion.

In addition, every discussion leader was required to submit an outline of the passage to be taught. This often served to discover potential teaching leaders. Always the teaching leader gave her own outline.

I came to know everyone in my discussion training class as close friends. It is always thrilling to watch their (often unconscious) spiritual development.

We always kneel for prayer, which continues usually for at least thirty minutes. I do not believe kneeling is just a matter of form; there is something of earnestness, of recognition of the majesty of God (consider that the Lord Jesus and Paul knelt) that our Western, comfort-loving Christians seem to lose. Most leaders had never knelt in public prayer meetings such as these. They came to experience a new delight in the power of corporate prayer. We became intimately close. I sensed that any teaching leader's effectiveness depends very largely upon the spiritual quality and dedication of each discussion leader who led fifteen class members. Each discussion class has a prayer chain for those who wished to participate each week.

Regional Retreats. Just as the first "stepping stone" of the Bible Study Fellowship began with five ladies in San Bernardino and later moved to Oakland, so our first retreat for leaders began in a small way in 1964. Dr. and Mrs. Wenger invited me to hold a retreat in Little Rock, Arkansas, in a beautiful resort called "Petit Jean Park." It was wonderful for me and them to get to know each other in fellowship. Dr. Wenger and his wife have been a wonderful help down the years. He started a men's evening class in Little Rock.

Mrs. Smucker, whose class was 800 miles away in Indiana, also brought two carloads of leaders. We met together in sharing and teaching, and I realized the great value of this relationship with classes who were far away from headquarters.

During this first visit to Little Rock, I met there a very interesting lady, who told me her story. She was so moved by the study that driving home from the class she stopped by a tree. Looking up at it, she prayed, "Lord, this tree represents to me the Cross where You carried all my sins. I now commit my life to You and ask You to come into my heart." She has for some time been a teaching leader in that region. At that time she took me to see some of the beauties of the area. For the first time I heard the haunting call of the whippoorwill in Little Rock's lovely woods and saw the brilliant red cardinals.

As the work grew, we recognized the importance of establishing a close relationship with all the leaders of classes, through "Regional Retreats." Actually these leaders' retreats constituted one of the heaviest items in the general director's program. There were usually seven retreats between March and May. This meant leaving the Bay Area for each retreat from Thursday to Sunday.

However, this constituted one of the greatest blessings in the work. Leaders were able to develop a close relationship with other classes in their region. We from headquarters came to appreciate the leaders as our own friends.

The regional schedule was arranged so that leaders from every class would be able to attend at least once in three years. From February to May, Mrs. Pearl Hamilton and other staff members would travel with me to one place or other, for example, Estes Park, Colorado; Asilomar (near Carmel), California; Seattle; Portland; Pipe Stem, Virginia; Fort Wayne, Indiana. From 300 to 600 teaching leaders, discussion leaders, and children's leaders attended each regional retreat. Often the membership of individual classes wanted to help financially in gratitude for all they received from their leader, and we had ways of being sure that no leader missed attending a retreat for lack of money.

These retreats are most productive. Each class is always publicly recognized as the teaching leader introduces them. This gives a sense of unity to every class in that region. Each morning and evening I would speak on ome special theme, with special teaching on subjects outside the five-year study series. For example, one year I taught the book of Leviticus, without which one cannot grasp something of the full meaning of Christ's Cross for remission of sins and God's principles of worship.

At other retreats, I taught the book of Psalms as "God's Manual for Prayer." Other subjects would be on "The Fullness of the Holy Spirit" and "God's Inheritance for the Believer According to Ephesians and Colossians."

Members of the staff gave special training workshops for discussion leaders and children's leaders.

In the afternoon, complete silence is observed from 1:00

P.M. to 4:00 P.M. A few heart-searching questions are given out to each person to help with a private time with the Lord in these lovely quiet places. Afterward, the leaders gather together in small groups of five persons (chosen by themselves) to converse and pray together. This is called "The Fellowship of Fives."

In the evening after the message the whole meeting is thrown open for testimonies (three minutes each). Often the men lead. Many of these testimonies were so moving it was hard for me to keep back the tears. To most leaders their regional retreat is one of the highlights of Bible Study Fellowship, as God reveals Himself in others (especially in those times of silence, when each person can be alone with Him).

Out of many varied events regarding the regional retreat, one or two stand out in my mind.

Once we were at Houston Woods early in the year, and there was such a heavy fall of snow we feared for the safety of leaders on the way. I called headquarters for prayer. Little did I think of Miss Hertzler's practical gift. She immediately called the Ohio Highway Patrol Office in that area and explained the situation! Our leaders were led into the meeting place by snowplows, and increasingly realized their protection when they passed other cars (not of our group) lying abandoned in a ditch. It was a very heavy storm. I do not believe anyone else on our staff would have taken such initiative, and we laughed as we blessed God.

On another occasion, also in snowy weather, I was traveling alone. As we landed at Fort Wayne, Indiana, the snowbanks were high and visibility was low. The pilot hit a snowbank, and the wing where I sat by the window was broken. Miraculously, the pilot immediately lifted the plane and headed for Chicago, the nearest place for repairs. The passengers were scared, and wine was freely given to all who needed "a sense of security." The man sitting next to me said, "Aren't you scared?" I said, "No, God is my Father, and I am in His hands. I am praying for the pilot."

When we arrived in Chicago, all the fire trucks were out in

261

readiness. Another plane was provided for transportation. Again at Fort Wayne everyone connected with us was praying. God answered prayer and we arrived safely in Fort Wayne. (Some passengers preferred not to try a second time!)

Once in Colorado, a new men's discussion leader who was passionately fond of mountains decided to skip out just before my evening message. (Perhaps a woman speaker had its drawbacks!) Later he told one of our staff of his experience. It so happened that as I stood to speak the sun was flooding the stained glass window behind me. I began by prayer, "Father, what is man that Thou art mindful of him, and the son of man, that Thou visitest him?" Evidently the Lord spoke to him during the prayer. He even forgot his passion for mountains, as God revealed Himself to him in a new way.

I was always deeply touched by the sincerity of several husbands who at the testimony time would share the fact that before they were converted they were jealous of their wife's new deep love for the Lord. After as they witnessed the changed attitude and life, they hungered for something to meet their own need. This resulted in conversion. To me the fulfillment came when we saw them greatly blessed in ministering to other men.

Training by Triennial Seminars. Our teaching leaders, whose commitment and sacrificial ministry was inspired by the power of the Holy Spirit, needed spiritual renewing and fellowship with other teaching leaders from all regions and countries.

Therefore I decided to initiate triennial seminars for teaching leaders only. These last four days, and are always held during the month of January. The response is always 100 percent and the blessing is indescribable. The teaching leaders live with others who share the same problems and joys. They are made aware of the power of God's living communication of Himself. They meet all the staff.

We engage prominent speakers who invariably give enriching spiritual teaching. For example, the speaker at our first seminar in 1969 was Mr. Roy Hession, author of *The Calvary Road*. At this first seminar we had only seventy-eight teaching leaders, out of which seventy-five attended.

In 1971, Mr. Joe Carrol of the Evangelical Institute of Greenville (South Carolina), gave a very searching message concerning the Cross for believers. One hundred and four teaching leaders (99 percent) attended.

In 1973, Dr. Paul Rees spoke on "Encounter with the Holy Spirit through Ephesians." In spite of a flu epidemic, 148 teaching leaders attended from all over America, England, and Australia. Dr. Rees emphasized present-day social problems and gave a broad vision which was greatly appreciated, as heard in the evening testimony meeting.

In 1976, the Rev. Michael Baughen, rector of All Souls Anglican Church in London (formerly Dr. John Stott's church), came to America for his first visit. He spoke on the Life of Moses. Mr. Baughen is very easy to know personally, and our teaching leaders were very blessed by his messages. He is also very musical. He has published a hymnbook of music to the Psalms. He played these to us, and taught us beautiful harmonies which seem to perfectly fit the words of the Psalms. Our staff and many others use this hymnbook called "Psalm Praise."

In 1979 (my last year as general director because of cancer), the teaching leaders begged for another seminar with the Reverend Michael Baughen, who came with his wife and spoke on the subject of prayer. Two hundred and sixty-six leaders attended. (It is interesting to see from the increasing number of leaders the growth of the work!)

Perhaps one of the highlights of that seminar was the communion service. Two hundred leaders sat in three concentric circles with Michael Baughen. He gave the "bread" to me and I passed it on to my neighbor, saying, "Peace be to you," until all had partaken of "our Lord's human life in the flesh."

We gathered together at a table for the wine. After we sat down, Michael prayed. He suggested, "Let us show our love to one another and tell each other why we love him or her. It is scriptural to embrace one another, if you feel so led."

I have never witnessed a scene of such expression of love. The joy, peace, and love of it all will never be forgotten. Michael Baughen sent me to the seventh heaven when he told me that this was the most responsive audience he had ever ministered to!

At each seminar the speaker and I both gave morning and evening messages. Other members of the staff gave workshops on homiletics, children's work, and other subjects.

During the seminar a question box was used, and an hour was set apart for answers. In addition to this, another hour was used when every teaching leader filled out a "Theological Quiz," which was conducted by a staff panel.

After lunch there was a rigidly enforced silence when everyone went out with a "self-evaluation" sheet with a suggested passage of Scripture and some private "self-evaluation questions."

It is wonderful to see 266 individuals finding solitary places to pray alone with the Lord for three hours.

After this we all assembled in groups of five to share whatever we wished with each other.

The peak of the day was the testimony meeting after the evening messages.

There were dramatic events at seminars, each of which accentuated the love we had for each other. One tragic circumstance was when a men's teaching leader, a medical doctor traveling with his wife, had a car accident which completely paralyzed her. His profound grief and godly attitude impressed us all, and the poured-out loving concern is impossible to describe.

Another medical doctor, Dr. Wenger, with us from the earliest days, who used to lead our communion services, suffered a detached retina and was almost blind for a considerable period. God restored his vision through laser treatment, but none of us can forget his submissive triumph through those long months of immobility.

Unfortunately, I omitted to keep a diary of Bible Study Fellowship years or notes of testimony meetings. Mrs. Hamilton remembers some unusual points. She remembers all the names, but we refrain from using them.

For example, one teaching leader said, "Finding Bible Study Fellowship is like finding a life work."

Another, a senator's wife said that she had never expected to see so many sunrises as she now saw since she started getting up early to meet with her Lord.

One man said that he "did not like people" until he came to Bible Study Fellowship.

Purpose of In-depth Training. The reader may wonder why the author gives so many paragraphs concerning the training and extra teaching of leaders.

The reason is that we have found that if we want spiritual quality this is *all-important.* One cannot give out more than what one has received, and superficiality in Christian work results in superficial fruit.

It is not enough to lead individuals to receive Christ through the Holy Spirit at new birth. Paul states, "As you have therefore received, . . . *so* walk ye in him" (Col. 2:6). It is not enough to persuade believers to study the *whole* Bible for themselves, discovering thereby God's Person, His character, and His will for His children (see John 14:23, 24, TLB). God's will for the whole Body of Christ is *that it be "fitly joined together* and compacted by that which *every joint supplieth,* according to the effectual working in the measure of *every part,* [making] increase of the body unto the edifying of itself in love" (Eph. 4:16, italics added).

After a class has been established, usually one-third to one-half of its membership is not yet converted. Many men and women come to class with heavy hearts, frustrated over the meaninglessness of life. Usually a "friend" asks them so persistently that to get "free," they say, "I'll come this once." Then as they feel the atmosphere and are brought into contact with the *powerful authority* of God's Word given out in the lecture, they are won over. "I somehow felt I *belong* here," one said. "This Christian joy has meaning. I need these nice people and a place to bring my children." Since all of humanity has been created in the image of God, if one does not repress it, there must be a recognition of God deep within the heart. (See Rom. 1:18–20, TLB.)

After conversion, the fellowship of ten to fourteen others (discussion class), where each opinion as to the passage studied always receives interested attention, creates growth. Each "joint builds up the other."

Added to this, the discussion leader's personal interest in *each member* (often through telephone calls) and the optional sharing of problems for a prayer chain gives a sense of "belonging and acceptance," and an experience in articulating one's belief to one's family and peers.

However, the discussion leader must learn by experience among other leaders before he is able to create that same atmosphere. Nothing is so heart-warming and meaningful as to have fellowship by talking of what the Lord gives to us who meet Him in His Word.

Surely this is how our Lord Jesus trained His own disciples. He took them alone (see Mark 6:30; 8:7–13; John 13–17). He sent them out to others, to give out what they had received. They came back to Him and shared their experiences. Later Paul, John, and Peter operated in the same way with ardent love, discipline, and personal example, as we see in their letters.

I believe God has a message for this age when "Christians" are increasingly caught up in the "love of emptiness" and pleasure-seeking. Even believers show a certain resistance to accepting a trial as allowed by God for good. Much less is there the attitude of rising to God's call to triumph in the midst of trial. Instead, even believers are apt to follow the lifestyle of this generation "to take the easy way out." For example, the unbeliever says, "Marriage is difficult, let's get a divorce." Unfortunately, in our day the believer is apt to fall into this same deceptive trap.

Therefore Christians of today need help. They need study, they need discipline, they need fellowship and love from others like themselves to become true disciples of our Lord Jesus Christ. I was recently told of a young mother with several small children who had told her neighbor, who was a very mature believer, that she planned to attend Bible Study Fellowship. Her neighbor, knowing of the young mother's busy days and undisciplined lifestyle, commented, "You'll never make it. It requires a lot of discipline and time." This young "undisciplined" mother was overheard about six weeks later commenting to another woman who had never attended, "You just must come. I was told I couldn't do it, but I am and I'm getting so much out of it, and I'm even getting organized at home!"

Many persons who were converted and nurtured in this way in Bible Study Fellowship classes for five years are now on mission fields. Some have initiated a fruitful prison ministry. Men have gone on to seminary and are now pastors in many denominations, including the Episcopal Church. Others have initiated needed social ministries. One lady in my Walnut Creek class was convicted when I said, "What are *you* doing for the Lord?" God led her into a most neglected ministry of helping and teaching retarded adults, a ministry which has greatly grown and been blessed by God.

During almost every lecture a challenge is made "not just to warm the church pew." "What are you doing for Christ in changing family and your own region in society?" Many pastors are shocked when a church member who has previously warmed a church pew asks, "Is there anything I could do to help?"

Building up the Body of Christ and reaching the ordinary

man in business who is unconverted take careful training; and this is why I've provided this rather prolonged explanation of the God-given pattern and blessing concerning the extra training of leaders.

TWENTY-SIX

SUDDEN DIAGNOSIS CHANGES PLANS

Thou art the Lord Who slept on the pillow,
  Thou art the Lord Who soothed the furious sea;
What matter beating wind and tossing billow
  If only we are in the boat with Thee?

Hold us in quiet through the agelong minute
  While Thou art silent and the wind is shrill;
Can the boat sink while Thou, dear Lord, art in it?
  Can the heart faint that waiteth on Thy will?

Amy Wilson Carmichael

By 1968 it was obvious that we needed yet another move and a larger headquarters than that of "Foothill." We needed a new printing press and a building to accommodate a larger staff of workers.

Alverda Hertzler and Marguerite Carter began a search on all sides for a suitable building or vacant lot for this larger facility, yet seemed to find nothing.

For our summer vacation in 1968 Miss Hertzler and I had decided to rent in our beloved Switzerland a small cottage, which in French was called "The Nut House." To our advantage, the American dollar was at a premium! One day we took from our mailbox a letter from Marguerite, illustrated with snapshots describing a beautiful property she had found. It was located on a high promontory commanding a magnificent view and held possibilities for future expansion. We were thrilled, knowing her acumen, and returned to Oakland soon afterward. We learned there was a project of the Nahas Company of Oakland to develop an office park on some acres of land high in the hills situated opposite their own offices. We would purchase the first plot in the proposed development, contingent upon its being commercially zoned. The price offered on this undeveloped land was more reasonable than any other property we had considered.

After much prayer, our board of directors determined that we should proceed and trust God for His continued wisdom to plan and build the type of headquarters we needed. Everything seemed to move along smoothly toward our goal. Only one obstacle remained—the approval of Oakland's Planning Commission for commercial zoning of land for an office park in this location. All indications led us to expect that the Nahas Company's application would be passed without hindrance. Our expectations were high.

Then came the disappointment and seeming end of all our hope. Oakland's Planning Commission flatly turned down this petition, bringing us to what seemed a "dead end." Our dashed hopes could fall only upon the firm foundation of the knowledge of God and former experiences of His faithfulness. Alverda said, "I don't know what to do. Marguerite and I have combed every possibility." I replied, "Never mind. This is the Lord's work, and He does not shut a door without opening another."

Although we completely trusted God, there was one nagging regret. On the following day, when we were to open our first teaching leader's seminar in 1968 (attended by seventy-five teaching leaders from across the United States), we would not be able to give the good news of a completed transaction for which they too had been praying.

Then our loving Father worked beyond anything we had

asked or dreamed! On the very day while we were busy packing to leave for the seminar the vice president of the Nahas Company called us with their offer to sell us their own office building—across the street—with its beautiful landscaped gardens and unusually artistic offices. They were more elaborate than we would ever have planned, surpassing our expectations for both suitability and attractiveness!

In days to follow, as class members, leaders, and others visited us, I always felt a little apologetic when showing them these offices which were more elegant than we would have built, but always they responded with excitement and praise for the wonderful thing God had done. I felt led to call this gift of His, "Skymount"; it was situated on Oakland's skyline, and to the discerning and alert there was a spiritual significance in such a name!

This was indeed another step of faith; we needed to trust God not only for the initial purchase but for the addition of a printing and shipping wing. In God's faithfulness, spontaneous gifts came in—many represented real sacrifice. As we began to build and payments were needed at certain stages, we found that God provided sufficient money at each stage until the entire project was completed. Not all the sacrificial gifts had been that of money; labor and talent were donated in practical ways. Miss Hertzler poured energy and hours into negotiations and planning. The architect, builder, and members of the Walnut Creek Men's Evening Class had a deep personal interest in the construction. Class members and volunteers contributed materials and did the painting and landscaping.

Finally the dedication day arrived; eighty persons, the board of directors, the staff, and others who had been especially interested in the building attended. I told the story of God's goodness and our venture of faith, and then announced, "And . . . it is all paid for." I wish all who share in reading this story could have heard the gasp of praise that echoed through that room!

In 1970 I read a book of Christian work in Switzerland which deeply impressed me. This was *L'Abri* by Mrs. Edith

Schaeffer. Her early experiences as a missionary's child in China naturally caught my attention. Following this, I discovered that the story of the founding of L'Abri (very near the time of the first classes of Bible Study Fellowship) was an absorbing history of God's miraculous leading.

I took the unusual step (for me) of writing to Mrs. Schaeffer, telling of my appreciation of her book and Dr. Francis Schaeffer's work.

I received a gracious reply, giving me a very cordial invitation to visit her and to learn more about the L'Abri work.

Since I have deep roots in Switzerland as well as France, Alverda and I were planning to visit the continent again, combining the trip with the need to confer regarding the new classes in England. We decided to accept Mrs. Schaeffer's kind invitation, little realizing at that time the enriching fellowship which would follow.

A smallpox shot was required for travel to Europe. Therefore I visited my doctor, Dr. Helen Christensen, for this purpose. What a shock it was to learn that I did not need a smallpox shot now, but urgently required surgery! As she examined me, Dr. Christensen immediately diagnosed an extensive breast cancer. Within that same week, instead of flying to the beautiful Swiss Alps, I was undergoing radical surgery in Alta Bates Hospital in Oakland.

This was most unexpected since there is no record of cancer in my family, and I was working hard and feeling well. Although I longed to get to Switzerland, yet I knew that my Father Who created me would not have allowed this illness to occur except for His own good purpose. I had a good doctor and a good surgeon. My heavenly Father was good to me in that a friend, a qualified nurse of another hospital, received permission to care for me all night after the surgery. It was a comfort and spiritual delight to have Marylin Flood with me that night.

Another of the great consolations from the Lord at this time of illness was that I received a flood of many hundreds of letters from teaching leaders and class members. Their stories of changed lives and conversions through Bible study and their spontaneous love for teaching leaders, for fellow class members, and in finding help from lesson notes made me realize as nothing else how God's Word was drawing individuals into intimate relationship with Him to joyous witness and restored family circles.

Among the many meaningful letters and notes, I read such things as, "Bible Study Fellowship has been a lifeline; from complete ignorance of the Bible I feel now like a sponge, eager to soak it up."

"Every single aspect of my life has been changed since I joined Bible Study Fellowship and learned that I could spend the rest of my life with Jesus Christ at my side. I didn't know!"

"Bible Study Fellowship has allowed me to open my life completely to the Lord's leading; even though it may mean a complete change in direction. My husband and I have become willing to give ourselves to His leading, without being concerned about loss of physical security, because we are secure in Him."

"First I came to class for a time-killer; little did I know I would find eternal life."

"I praise the Lord for the discipline I have received through Bible Study Fellowship. Now I cannot bear to miss a day of study."

"Women at first thought the studies were too hard and disciplined, but later they share that the discipline is the best part! And . . . I know why . . . you made them get close enough to touch God through His Word. It is really thrilling to be a teaching leader . . . to see God's Word strengthen and change lives. I suppose it will not surprise you for me to say it usually changes me before I get to teach others!"

"This is my third year, and the Scriptures mean so much to me now. Of course my relationship with Jesus has become the most important thing in my life. He is the center of our home, and Bible Study Fellowship has helped me see the lack of spiritual things I have neglected to teach my children. So now I share what I am learning with them, and this year they have started reading their Bibles on their own. My son made up a little motto, 'a chapter a day keeps the devil away.' When I first began Bible Study Fellowship my husband did not know the Lord personally, but he saw the change in me and wished that every day were class day because I was different. The following year he gave his life to Christ. My husband and I are as different as night and day, but now we share the most wonderful love through Christ."

"My husband, who is Jewish, is now enrolled in the men's Bible Study Fellowship and is learning about the Lord. We now have a family altar of fellowship and praise God each morning before our family leaves home. While trying to find the answers to questions in his weekly study, my husband said, 'This is just like going on a treasure hunt.' All my life I have been searching for 'The Word,' and now I feel that I have found a way of studying it for the rest of my life."

"I was new to God's Word and I was shocked to see so many women interested in studying the Bible! The love, joy, and excitement of being there was overwhelming. Since that day the same love, joy and excitement of studying God's Word with others that love Him, is mine. Through your love of God I have the gift of a vital, alive relationship with the living God."

Although in these hundreds of letters that poured in there was a personal concern and affection for me expressed, my greatest joy was that they were indicative of the power of God's Holy Spirit through His Word, more than I could have ever realized!

With God's help, I made every effort to recover as soon as possible. My doctor was surprised the next day to find me exercising my arms on the bar, exercise that would prevent my arm from looking deformed. I knew God had placed me there for His witness, and I had time to meditate on Him and enjoy visitors. It was a relief when the surgeon said they had eliminated all the cancer cells, and he presumed that I would not have any more trouble. I know this was due to the many prayers throughout our classes.

I would not write so much about this operation were it not that today I am continually hearing women who are greatly distressed when they receive the same diagnosis. My aim is to encourage them from my own experience. After barely a month, the surgeon gave me permission to travel to Switzerland, although the wound still was open and needed dressing.

The SAS airline was very good to me, and we enjoyed the trip over the North Pole. In God's providence we found a hotel at Lucerne with a balcony overlooking my beloved Lake Lucerne and Mt. Pilatus and other mountains all around. We loved the boat trips on that long and most beautiful blue lake. Then I felt we needed to rent a car. It was easier for us to travel that way with our luggage. I drove many miles. On the way to L'Abri we drove around Lake Thun, through beautiful Gstaad and some high Swiss passes. Eventually we arrived at Villars, where I found that my French as a second language helped us find the whereabouts of L'Abri.

After locating L'Abri, it so happened that Dr. Francis Schaeffer was away for some speaking engagements, but Alverda and I spent a delightful time with Mrs. Schaeffer. As we compared notes concerning the work for God we each had been given, in America and in Switzerland, Mrs. Schaeffer said, "I think the Lord has brought us together for a special purpose." This proved true far beyond our expectations!

I was moved by all I perceived of self-sacrifice in their work in L'Abri; Dr. and Mrs. Schaeffer lived in a chalet called Les Melezes, where they had constant interruptions from students all over the world who came for study of God's Word and Christian philosophy. Students often had to bundle up on the floor to sleep at night, either at Les Melezes or some nearby chalet where L'Abri workers provided accommodations— which might even result in a long line-up to brush their teeth in the morning! They listened to Dr. Schaeffer's tapes and were encouraged by him in the evenings when they met in the little chapel to ask questions regarding humanism or aspects of the Christian life. His answers were always gracious, understanding, and full of spiritual enrichment. In years following I took students and staff to L'Abri to receive his rich enlightenment.

During this first visit with Mrs. Schaeffer I saw their personal "home" was in one room. There was a double bed on which Dr. Schaeffer typed all his books, and a collection of classical music to drown the noise of the washing machine next door. I had seen much self-sacrifice for others in China but nothing more real and unselfish than what I now perceived. I longed to do anything I could to help in any way; Mrs. Schaeffer told me that the following year they would have engagements in the United States for many months, with just one week's break. This gave me an idea. They had not had a holiday for some time. I wondered, would they like to rent a cottage in peaceful Carmel-by-the-Sea where they would rest for a week? Her face literally shone—"*Would* we?"

After we returned from Switzerland we made arrangements for a place of quiet retreat in Carmel. We met Dr. and Mrs. Schaeffer upon arrival in San Francisco; he was dressed in his very distinctive Swiss holiday attire. We enjoyed enriching conversation with them both as we drove them to Carmel. This was the beginning of one of the most precious friendships we have ever had.

Dr. Schaeffer Encourages Single Young Adult Classes. For several years, inquiries had been made concerning classes for young adults. We recognized that the theological teaching and questions of the lesson notes and lectures were beyond the capacity of most high school students. But what about the college students and unmarried young adults? I hesitated for some time, remembering the fine organizations already existing for this age group, such as Campus Crusade, InterVarsity, and other missions for that generation. Yet the pressure for a "lay Bible school"-type of student approach continued.

When the board asked us to look into it and try some experiments, I felt we should not meet in a church until God had confirmed His leading as to whether He wanted us to work in this area.

Some time before, almost unnoticed to the upper Skymount offices, a building just below us had been vacated and was for sale. A friend, Mrs. Winter, brought it to my attention, saying, "Your offices are full. Surely this building just below you would be ideal for growth."

We realized we needed more offices, especially for the teaching staff, which was increasing, for workshops for teaching leaders, for get-together gatherings for about twenty-five area advisors, and for our periodic classes of twenty orientees each.

Most of all, as I looked at the offices, an area for a lounge, a kitchen, and a large hall, I thought, "Wouldn't this be an ideal place for a young adults class?

Knowing that Dr. Francis Schaeffer understood student needs better than anyone I knew, I asked him if he could arrange to visit us. He graciously came to help us with this important decision and to look over this property, especially the large hall. When I asked him if he thought students would be interested and willing to give their precious time to such serious study, I can see him now standing in the middle of that empty hall, appraising the situation. He said, "Wetherell, if the board is willing, I urge you to go ahead. This would be a perfect set-up for students, and I am convinced they would revel in the Bible study presented." Therefore, with the favorable consent of our board, we undertook the acquisition of this annex to Skymount!

Mrs. Pearl Hamilton and I, after a long time of discussion and prayer, began this new venture with young adults, aided by leaders of their age whom we trained. The Reverend Mike Ladra was an early staff man who contributed much to its development. God answered the prayers of our teaching leaders and class members.

The construction of this new program involved some adjustments in class structure; we tried to enroll an equal number of girls and young men, although discussion groups temporarily separated them. After the lecture time was given, they assembled together to ask questions or to give testimonies as to what God had given them. Class commenced at 7:30 P.M., but no time limit was set for closing of the class. Afterward, refreshments were served, which gave opportunities for men and women to become acquainted and for personal counseling.

There were many conversions. I well remember a young man openly testifying to his receiving Christ at a previous meeting. He "ran off" with my young secretary, and they now have a beautiful Christian home. Not only that, he is engaged in a full-time work for leading prisoners to the Lord and helping them in other ways.

Marriages were so frequent that almost all of our leadership had to be changed each year, as this was an "unmarried class." It was delightful to see new homes founded upon a biblical basis.

In order to stabilize and deepen theological knowledge in both students and staff, some summers Miss Hertzler and I would take a group to study for a month under Dr. Schaeffer at L'Abri. Those who could paid their own way; otherwise, we helped with their travel.

That was a delightful experience. I introduced them to mountain climbing and the ski lifts and was available for counseling. I don't know who enjoyed it most, they or Miss Hertzler and I.

The theological training of Dr. Schaeffer led several to think in terms of full-time Christian work and seminary. Most of all they saw true sacrificial living on the part of the entire L'Abri staff and returned home with new vision.

TWENTY-SEVEN

OUTREACH TO
OTHER COUNTRIES

*Enlarge the place of thy tent, and let them stretch forth the
curtains of thine habitations: spare not, lengthen thy cords, and
strengthen thy stakes* [Isaiah 54:2].

After returning to Oakland, I was still heavily engaged in
overseeing the teaching division of our work and continued to
teach a class of more than 400 women in Walnut Creek. Miss
Marguerite Carter was by this time occupying one of our
orientation homes, and had invited her two dear friends, Mr.
and Mrs. J. Stuart Mill, from Australia for a short stay in
Oakland. Mr. Mill was then director of Gospel Recordings,
Incorporated, in the Australasia area. Mrs. Mill was chairman of a greatly blessed women's organization, the Australia
Christian Women's Conventions. Mr. and Mrs. Mill were
interested in the ministry of Bible Study Fellowship and at
Marguerite's invitation visited our Walnut Creek class the
day of my lecture on the topic of Romans 7.

Knowing that Mr. Mill naturally preferred men speakers in
the pulpit, she was somewhat apprehensive when instead of
my usual fifty minutes I went beyond the time. At the close of
this study, Marguerite turned to Mr. and Mrs. Mill, somewhat
anticipating that he would by this time be ready to leave, but

was delightfully surprised when instead he said, "I could have listened for another two hours!" The importance of this remark and interest was that when Mrs. Mill arranged to invite me as conference speaker to the Australia Christian Women's Conventions, we felt it was also with the strong support of her dear husband. To receive an invitation to speak to this large group of women in Australia was most exciting.

Apart from the personal joy in traveling to new and beautiful parts of God's creation, God led me to believe that this visit might be the forerunner of an important extension of Bible Study Fellowship.

The Qantas plane on which I traveled was almost empty. I therefore had a very restful trip and received royal treatment. It was beautiful too. I saw the Southern Cross, and in the early morning, reveled in the lovely bush and forest country which clings to the coast line of Australia nearly as far as Sydney Harbor.

I was met by a gracious group of Australians, including Mr. and Mrs. Mill, and was taken first to their home where the view from their windows commands the breathtaking sight of Sydney's magnificent harbor and the shell-like architecture of the Opera House. It was as though the wonderful scene came right into the room.

Throughout the conventions I was impressed with the warm, friendly atmosphere to which Christian women had brought unchurched and non-Christian women to attend; the meetings were well-attended and excellently organized. In the presence of such kindness I felt at home in this most beautiful country.

Near Sydney I spoke to large audiences at "Stanwell Tops" on the coast. Another meeting was in Newcastle. Later I spoke in the clean and spacious Australian capital—Canberra. We traveled by car, with the Dandenong mountain ranges in view, to Melbourne, which is almost European. Indeed to me it had something of an English atmosphere!

In each city the audience was very responsive, and when I

mentioned Bible Study Fellowship, I discovered a real hunger for similar weekly meetings.

Following the Melbourne engagement, we went on to Adelaide. Adelaide was blessed by the services of a qualified surveyor when the streets and layout were planned in 1836. As a result it is said to have one of the most beautiful town plans in the world. There is a charm and spacious grace about this city with many beautiful churches. (I rejoice that we have good Bible Study Fellowship classes there now.)

My stay in Australia, Tasmania, and New Zealand, was not all work. Dear friends took me sightseeing. I fell in love with the koala bear (to the extent that Mrs. Mill gave me a replica of one to take home!). I enjoyed holding little kangaroos in my arms!

Tasmania is the "Emerald Isle" of Australia. Although only 190 miles wide and 180 miles long, its rolling hills, lovely alpine lakes, and dramatic seascapes take one's breath away.

After our arrival in New Zealand and after I spoke in Auckland, Mrs. Scott, a convention representative, gave me a tour of the Northern Island. I was fascinated again with its almost English atmosphere and a very low key way of life. Mrs. Scott took me to the beautiful Lake Rotora Natural Park, and Waitomo Caves. I was deeply interested in the Maori tribes as we met personally with some of its members.

In Australia I traveled mostly with Mrs. Grace Collins and Miss Jean Raddon, newly arrived from Nepal where she had been a missionary for several years.

We three were together on a somewhat eventful trip to beautiful Hawkesbury River Bay, a "must visit" for all tourists.

The parking area was small, and not many tourists were there. After parking the car, Mrs. Collins said, "We will not be long. It is safe to leave the car unlocked. Let us put our handbags under the seat." Famous last words! As we were on our way back to Sydney, dear Jean Raddon suddenly said, "Christians or no Christians, who has my bag?" When we looked, to our dismay we discovered that all three handbags were missing. None of us carried much cash, but my handbag held my passport, traveler's checks, and other important papers.

What should we do? We prayed. I prayed that "whoever had stolen our bags might decide to take the cash and leave the bags at the parking place." So we returned, but no purses were there! Suddenly I remembered that my bag also contained my hotel key which could give the thief access to all my belongings in my room. Immediately I telephoned the hotel. They replied, "Miss Johnson, we are so glad you called. We have just received a phone call from a couple who were taking guests out into the bush near Hawkesbury River. As their car traveled slowly along an unfrequented dirt road, one of them noticed a handbag lying under one of the bushes. They decided it might be important so they stopped to investigate. To their amazement they found three handbags emptied of cash, but with other articles left seemingly intact. Your hotel room key was there, so they phoned this address. They gave their address and suggested you could see them now at their home."

Imagine our excitement and also the excitement of our Good Samaritans when we arrived. All the things in the three bags had been mixed up. Mrs. Collins said, "Whose comb is this?" Miss Raddon commented, "This lipstick is not mine!" I said "This address book does not belong to me." Our hosts sat laughing. Then we talked of our prayer and they told us of how nearly they had passed by, ignoring the bags as none of their business. We had the impression that the finders were not professing Christians, but they were interested in our testimony and immediately introduced their son, who somewhat against their aims for him, had chosen to attend Bible school. We all felt God had meant this event as an encouragement to him, as well as a blessing to us, as we persuaded him to speak about himself.

While in Newcastle, north of Sydney, I spoke at one of the convention luncheons. Out of courtesy the hostess had placed an attractive Chinese woman next to me at the table. I talked to her in Mandarin, asking if she had ever been in China. I told her I had taught in a seminary in Shanghai. She beamed and said, "My husband and I are graduates of a seminary." Then she named the China Bible Seminary. When I added, "I was there," she looked at me in amazement and said, "Are you Yang-Chiao-si?" What a reunion! She and her husband were among the students of my class. Nothing under Heaven could have thrilled me more. She vanished quickly and returned with her husband, Mr. Ts'ai, who was at that time the pastor of a Chinese church in Newcastle. At the close of my message we met again and together wept as we talked of years past and of the continuing grace of God. Other times of meeting my Chinese students have happened in my travels in recent years. To me these moments are as precious as meeting members of my own family.

Before leaving Australia, Mrs. Grace Collins and I had a long talk together. Her committees were eager to have Bible Study Fellowship classes in Australia. At the same time Miss Jean Raddon had indicated to her that the Lord was leading her to leave her mission in Nepal and that she would be open to work in Australia. The Australia Christian Women's Conventions needed more key staff, and Mrs. Collins' work as director was becoming very heavy. However, at this point nothing had been resolved. It was then that Mrs. Collins and I felt of one mind together that the Lord was leading us to ask Miss Raddon whether she would be interested in working half-time with the conventions and half-time with Bible Study Fellowship in the formation of Australian classes. I suggested that Mrs. Collins and Miss Raddon come for about six weeks to the U.S. to get a full perspective of the basic pattern and operation of the work of Bible Study Fellowship and to meet our teaching leaders. We would also continue our good fellowship together.

When I talked alone with Miss Raddon, we both had a wonderful surprise. I asked about her life story. She mentioned among other incidents that during World War II she

283

had been stationed at Colombo, Ceylon, as matron of a hospital. I asked, "Were you there when the Japanese internees were housed for a time at the hospital?" Her eyes grew big as we took a long look at each other. With astonishment she said, "Are you the Audrey Johnson with whom I enjoyed real fellowship in Christ?" I said, "Can it be you, and we never recognized each other all these weeks?"

All my life I have found God is so wonderful in bringing together former acquaintances after many years, friends who have become involved in His work.

After Miss Raddon joined our teaching staff on a half-time basis and returned to Australia, she soon sent fine applicants to California for orientation. There were men as well as women. It was good to have different nationalities with us, and we enjoyed their humor and eagerness. They returned to shepherd excellent classes under Miss Raddon's supervision. Gradually, however, Miss Raddon's work with the Australian Christian Conventions increased so much that she had to give her full time to it.

As the classes grew, Miss Marguerite Carter and I went out to Australia for their first leaders' retreats in Sydney and Melbourne. We made more friends and the retreats were set in beautiful areas.

By this time we realized that we needed an office and secretary for storing lesson notes, general supervision, and meeting people who wished to become new leaders. God led us eventually to ask Mrs. Cheryl Hutchinson, who had held a class in Melbourne for some time, to take on this responsibility. We see her at least once a year for area advisors' meetings, and also for a teaching leaders' seminar. I have many other dear friends in Australia, and I look forward to one day going out again.

Not only did God open a door in Australia, He also opened doors for Bible Study Fellowship to be started in other countries. Perhaps because of my British background, I longed to see classes commence in England too. I felt that if I or some full-time English worker could live there, classes would soon develop. God had another way! Mrs. Ann Cook, whose husband had given a year of medical service in a hospital in Seattle, was formerly very bored with "Bible classes" but had been persuaded to attend Bible Study Fellowship "just once." She was so delighted with the format of our study that she offered to assist in the children's classes, which meant she also attended the Monday morning discussion leaders' meetings. Her husband also became interested and attended the men's evening class with some of his fellow physicians.

It was Dr. Cook's desire, as well as that of his wife, that a class should be started in Liverpool when they returned, to the extent he paid for her travel to California to attend a teaching leaders' orientation session. Mrs. Cook is a delightful person, and very quickly a large class began in a Methodist church in Liverpool. I was delighted to catch the enthusiasm—especially when travel had to be by bus or on foot. This first class was soon followed by a men's class (taught by Mr. Alan Morell, who knew many of my friends from my youth) and another day class in an adjoining suburb. Classes continue to be added.

Some time after this, Miss Hertzler and I attended the Mittersill InterVarsity summer sessions in Austria for students from many countries. I was invited to speak. In addition, I was asked to tell something of the work of Bible Study Fellowship. This resulted in a deep interest by Mr. and Mrs. Bentley Taylor, who at that time were still working with Overseas Missionary Fellowship. I had known these friends for many years. They lived in Hereford, a charming ancient city in the Cotswolds of England. Mrs. Bentley Taylor had a prayer group and stimulated them to hold a Bible Study Fellowship class (although she did not feel led to teach it herself). This led to my visiting Hereford as well as Liverpool, with the result that two ladies came to California later to complete their training in orientation study. The class in Hereford was held in a great, historic Anglican church. When I visited the class I sometimes wondered how it could be heated comfortably in winter!

A young English woman, Miss Ann Horsford, had joined our staff in 1972. She had been a staff representative for the Navigators, and her experience was a great support in the teaching division of our work. Her annual vacation visits to be with her mother in England gave opportunities to assist teaching leaders of English classes.

In mid-June 1977 a retreat for all English leaders was arranged at a lovely old manor house situated in beautiful, landscaped grounds in the north of England. This gave to them the sense of oneness and fellowship, not only among themselves, but similar to that which existed in our American classes. Alverda and I joined Ann Horsford in Liverpool where we met with the leaders. Later we drove up to the retreat.

Afterward, Alverda and I enjoyed a lovely visit to the Lake District. We longed to drive on up to Edinburgh and Loch Lomond, which we had visited on a previous trip, but we could not. At that earlier time we saw many scenic delights of Scotland, including Holyrood Castle and the Tattoo at Edinburgh Castle, a magnificent spectacle of massed bands, bagpipes, and military maneuvers displayed against the background of the lighted castle. The pageantry, color, and music were truly indescribable. This was a year when a realistic "storming of the castle" was staged, with cannons firing and smoke of battle rising! The ceremony ended with the impromptu singing of Psalm 23.

Classes throughout the U.S. had grown to such an extent that in 1979 they were established in over forty states, including Hawaii, where there is now both a day and an evening class.

A most interesting outgrowth of a class in Washington State resulted in the spread of classes to Canada. Mrs. Irene Baker, whom Alverda and I had met years ago at The Firs Conference, had taught a day class in Blaine near the Canadian border. Canadian women pooled their cars to drive across the border and pass through customs each week in their eagerness to attend Mrs. Baker's class, and some to attend a leaders' meeting as well. The story is told by the children's chairman of a small Canadian boy who during class procedures did not salute the flag. At first his leader ignored him, but finally in curiosity asked him, "Why do you not salute the flag as the other little boys do?" Almost in tears he stubbornly replied, "It isn't my flag!"

Finally, ladies from Vancouver came to Oakland for orientation. There are now two classes in Vancouver, and more inquiries are coming in. It is always a delight for Alverda and me to visit Canada, especially Vancouver and beautiful Victoria. After passing through Vancouver, we would then drive on to the glorious Canadian Rockies. One of my favorite views is that of Lake Peyto from which one gazes over to "the land of far distances."

Although we gained some classes in Canada, we lost a Canadian staff member, Miss Marguerite Carter, who had been with us for eight years, giving valuable assistance on the administrative side of our work. In 1975 she retired. For circumstantial reasons she needed to return to her homeland in Canada and to be with her family for a prolonged period. We missed her, for she was a personal friend as well as a key member of our staff. Our personal friendship has continued through the years. (She came to San Antonio recently and gave two months of her time to typing part of this manuscript.)

TWENTY-EIGHT

GOD PROVIDES HIS FUTURE
LEADER AND A NEW LAND

Green pastures are before me,
  Which yet I have not seen.
Bright skies will soon be o'er me
  Where the dark clouds have been.
My hope I cannot measure
  My path to life is free:
My Savior has my treasure
  And he will walk with me.

Anna L. Waring, 1820-1910

For some time I had been looking forward to finding a
replacement (in case of emergency), who would be trained in
the work. Yet nothing had worked out. God knew that when
the emergency came He already (unknown to me) had His
own choice.

To explain something of the circumstances of how God
worked out His purposes, it is necessary to go back in years to
the beginning of the work in San Antonio in 1969.

Mr. and Mrs. Larry Heppes had been in Bible Study
Fellowship classes in Oakland. Mary Heppes was in my
Walnut Creek Leaders' Class. When they moved back to

their original home in San Antonio, Mary particularly was determined to spark a Bible Study Fellowship class in this area. Eventually, from the spring of 1969, Mrs. Monica McGann taught a women's class for two years, but had to leave when her husband began conducting evangelistic meetings in other parts of the U.S.

I remember going to the home of Mr. and Mrs. Heppes in San Antonio in 1971 where a group was gathered for prayer to find a replacement for the class. Meanwhile Mr. Larry Heppes had started a men's Bible Study Fellowship class.

When we were searching for a replacement for Mrs. McGann, no suitable leader was found, so the women's day class was discontinued. But a group of women prayed. More than a year later Mrs. Robert Jensen moved to San Antonio, and God laid it upon her heart, as a result of seeing the lesson notes and the pattern of the work, that He was asking her to restart the class in 1973. I well remember her coming for orientation classes and was impressed by her life in God. Like myself in 1952, little did Mrs. Jensen realize that her leading from God to take a class would one day result in the position she now holds.

Later, when I came to appreciate her gifts increasingly, we asked Mrs. Rosemary Jensen to be an area advisor for Texas. Under Mrs. Jensen's capable advisorship, new classes for men and women started not only in San Antonio but in several other Texas cities.

Had it not been for another unexpected attack of cancer, I have good reason to believe I would still be general director of Bible Study Fellowship. Presumably we would have been searching for more buildings for the growing work at Oakland Headquarters.

At the end of 1977, I was suffering considerably from what I thought was shingles. We had an area advisors' meeting in Oakland, which Mrs. Rosemary Jensen attended. Her husband, Dr. Robert Jensen, had very kindly sent me some medication for shingles. It touched me that he should think about it.

I visited my doctor, who on examination expressed surprise, since for seven years there had been no complications from the radical operation or symptoms of cancer. But now the symptoms were there. An X ray revealed a collapsed vertebra in the spine, and cancer spread to four vertebrae in the upper spine.

When Dr. Jensen heard of the definite diagnosis, he and Mrs. Rosemary Jensen invited me to stay in their lovely home in San Antonio and take extra tests at the state hospital where Dr. Jensen had some excellent specialists. This was in January 1978. Meanwhile God had revealed another aspect of His leading. While I lived with Dr. and Mrs. Jensen, I became conscious that God had blessed Rosemary with spiritual depth, a gift of speaking, and a gift of administration. Besides being a former missionary in Africa, she had been a Bible Study Fellowship teaching leader and then area advisor for six years. As I listened to her telephone counseling with some of her class members, I wondered if this was not the replacement God would choose, since no one knew how my cancer would develop. Yet she lived in San Antonio, and Bible Study Fellowship headquarters were in Oakland, California.

It was decided that I should take cobalt treatment at the University of California Medical School Hospital in San Francisco, which was at least an hour's drive from my home. Friends kindly drove me over, and usually between the waiting period and the treatment we spent up to five hours a day. Mrs. Pearl Hamilton, Miss Hertzler, and other staff members faithfully carried on the work at the office.

I was pledged to speak at four weekend retreats that spring, yet at that time I could take only liquids and was physically very weak. This is where one proves God's faithfulness. I remember taking cobalt five times a week, then leaving for a large leaders' retreat at Asilomar, California, with Pearl Hamilton and other staff members. God wonderfully undertook, and nothing was left undone because of cancer.

Then there was another five days of cobalt treatment. After this we again went on the road to the Houston Woods, Ohio

Leaders' Retreat; the Green Lake, Indiana, Leaders' Retreat; and lastly, the beautiful Pipe Stem Leaders' Retreat in Virginia. Mrs. Pearl Hamilton was with me all the time, and I was wonderfully upheld. I believe everyone knew that I was there because of adequate strengthening from God in answer to many prayers. Pipe Stem had a beautiful vista and a ski lift that went down to a glorious stream where we rested one day before the leaders arrived. My wonder at God's undertaking beyond all one could ask or think gave a confidence which otherwise would have been impossible.

Of course our class members were shocked to learn about the new outbreak of cancer. So many letters had arrived that I needed to thank them for their earnest prayer and to give reassurance of God's faithfulness. I sent the teaching leaders the following letter to share with their classes:

> This was an unexpected shock, as I have a full schedule ahead. Our loving Staff has prayed for me around the clock, and I sought God for His leading. When any physical problems occur, I believe there are four possible lines of God's purpose in them:
>
> 1. Christian workers are warned to expect attacks from Satan—physical, circumstantial, and spiritual. God allows this to train us to resist Satan by prayer and claiming God's promises.
> 2. God sometimes wishes to train our *faith* when in answer to prayer He miraculously heals us without any medical remedy.
> 3. God sometimes leads us to make use of modern scientific medical remedies, yet the true healing power comes from Him, our Creator.
> 4. God sometimes says "No," as He said to Paul when Paul prayed three times concerning a "thorn in the flesh, a messenger from Satan to buffet me" (II Cor. 12:7-9, NIV). However, God gave Paul a wonderful promise: "My grace is sufficient for you, because My *power* is made perfect in weakness."

After prayer, I felt led of God to take the treatments prescribed by doctors—cobalt treatments beginning February 13, 1979, in San Francisco.

Because so many of you, our beloved Bible Study Fellowship family, suffer in different ways (financially, physically, with personality and family difficulties, perhaps suffering spiritual depression or persecution), I rejoice in God that in my present suffering I am sharing this with you.

I believe Christ is coming soon, and He still has much work to do in "conforming me to His image." He promises in Romans 8:28, 29 that *all* things (the *bad* as well as the good) work *together* for good to those who are called according to His purpose. We must never *waste* the purpose of suffering by unbelief in His covenant lovingkindness. Therefore I am eagerly looking forward to what He has for me and through me for you in this situation.

However, please pray for me. Pray for a miracle of healing (if this is His will). Pray for strength during these days of treatments, as I believe *He* wants me to complete this year's schedule and has a further ministry for me in Bible Study Fellowship.

Please remember Miss Hertzler, too, in this crisis.

Yours lovingly and joyfully in Christ,
A. Wetherell Johnson

While I was taking meetings and concluding the cobalt treatment, I kept thinking and praying about my replacement and Mrs. Rosemary Jensen.

Already, Dr. and Mrs. Jensen had been invited to attend the March 1978 board meeting. Dr. Jensen gave a medical report on my medical situation, and Mrs. Rosemary Jensen, as area advisor for Texas, gave a report on classes there. At the next board meeting in May of that year it was voted to invite Mrs. Jensen to become a member of the board.

Later in August while Miss Hertzler and I were on vacation in Santa Barbara, I received a letter offering the Bible Study Fellowship a gift of ninety-five acres of land for building administration buildings for Bible Study Fellowship in San Antonio. To me this seemed to be another confirmation from God regarding Mrs. Jensen's leadership. I presented it to the board at the next September meeting.

Later a committee from the board, including Miss Hertzler and myself, were taken by helicopter to envision the entire ninety-five acres of property on a lovely hilltop adjoining San Antonio. It was beautiful, with many trees and grassland. Yet we all recognized the problems of building a road of access and the problems of building the large administration buildings which would be required.

The board was gracious but also very concerned that we make no mistake about a move to Texas. None of us wanted to leave Oakland, California, where we had our beautiful headquarters for so many years as well as the lovely orientation houses, where we had experienced such blessing in the work.

They needed to give much prayerful consideration before contemplating such a tremendous move which would affect all of our staff. On the other hand, the Bible Study Fellowship was growing to such an extent that almost immediately we would need once more to look for some land on which to build in Oakland, and there apparently was nothing suitable available.

I continued with my duties half-time, in leadership office work as well as teaching the young adults' class in the evening with God's enabling.

On September 10, 1979, the board of directors decided that God was leading the Bible Study Fellowship to move to San Antonio under the leadership of Mrs. Rosemary Jensen. Mrs. Jensen would take office in January 1980, when I would become founder and general director emeritus and Miss Hertzler, administrator emeritus.

Mrs. Rosemary Jensen came to stay often at our home in order to get some idea of the headquarters' work, and to become acquainted with the staff. This involved being present through the new orientations and area advisors' meetings. Also our personal friendship grew. She hoped we too might move to San Antonio, and we felt this would perhaps add to the sense of unity of the work.

How wonderful to recognize God's hand in my recurrence of cancer. Not only did it make me more dependent on Him, but in this way His will concerning the future was gradually revealed, and today we see how marvelously this transition of leadership in the work has prospered.

On December 1, 1979, which happened to be my birthday, the staff and area advisors urged that we hold a regional meeting in the arena side of the Oakland Auditorium. (Mrs. Pearl Hamilton tells me now that I fought it all the way as being too personal!) However the staff was adamant.

There were 5,000 to 6,000 of our Northern California membership from as far north as Eureka and Sacramento and south from Fresno. This was the first time many class members who weekly studied my notes and questions had seen me. It was a real time of rejoicing. Area advisors from all regions were also there since we were to hold an area advisors' meeting the next morning. A large banner above the stage read, "To God Be the Glory." The organizers of the rally had difficulties because there had been a wrestling match the night before, the workmen were still trying to get things straight at 7:00 A.M. while the audience was beginning to arrive at 8:00 A.M.!

Mr. Harold Gudnason (on our board of directors) acted as master of ceremonies, and I introduced Mrs. Rosemary Jensen as the future Bible Study Fellowship director.

I had been asked to give something of my life story, how God began Bible Study Fellowship and gave us His pattern in answer to prayer in the early fifties in San Bernardino. Therefore it was a special delight to have two San Bernardino members of that first class and early teaching leaders sitting near the front—Mrs. Horton Voss and Mrs. Joy Sharp. There were so many whom I had taught in classes in the Bay Area, and who were my partners in leadership in the early days.

Seeing such a huge audience of leaders and class members, both men and women, enhanced the sense of oneness and wonder at all God had accomplished during these twenty-eight years.

The teaching leaders as well as area advisors were all on the platform. After introduction of the teaching staff members and my introduction of Mrs. Rosemary Jensen as the new general director, each teaching leader introduced his or her class members. As they stood, it was a wonderful exhibition of deep unity, changed lives, and the power of God's Word to give such expansion without any advertisement at all.

The intense mood of attention of these thousands of women and men was very moving, and in spite of my cancer, I was totally upheld by their prayers for an address of over an hour.

In order to accommodate all who could attend, each class had been given a number of free tickets. As the audience left, there were baskets at the back for voluntary gifts toward expenses: they were all covered. Afterward, we held a praise meeting with the teaching leaders.

Then Alverda, Rosemary, and I went home. We were prepared for a family dinner with all the area advisors that evening. It was to be held at the lovely old Claremont Hotel in Berkeley. I was anxious to be present before time to see that everything was well organized. But Rosemary kept urging me to wait. Finally we arrived at the hotel looking for our special private room. It was in complete darkness. Suddenly lights went on, and Alverda and I were amazed to find the room filled with more than a hundred people singing "Happy Birthday"! So many friends were there: the board of directors; Dr. Earl Palmer, pastor of our church; my niece, Dr. Margaret Watson-Williams and her husband; special friends such as Dr. Robert Young, whom I had not seen for years. Miss Marguerite Carter, who was now retired, had been asked by the board to put on a major celebration banquet, and she made it a delightful occasion by bringing in so many of our personal friends. Alverda and I were both speechless with surprise. All the staff was there and sang a special song to us, and Dr. Earl Palmer spoke, as well as Dr. Ernest Hastings who acted as master of ceremonies. Dr. Grant Whipple, president of our board, announced some special gifts for our retirement, and we were filled with gratitude for their thoughtfulness and all the lovely experiences of that memorable evening.

This was the first of other regional meetings. The largest took place a month later where about 7,000 met in the Anaheim Convention Center, next door to Disneyland.

Again we needed to combat the rock concert of the night before by cleansing the atmosphere with the song "Precious Is the Blood of Jesus." Also outside and above the banner, "To God Be the Glory," was an advertisement for milk. "You need milk each day" made for a good opening remark!

This was one of the best regional meetings. People came from Phoenix and San Diego, and the San Diego Men's Teaching Leader, Mr. Tom Springer, was an excellent organizer and leader. (He is now with the "Ozark Conferences" movement in Arkansas as manager.) I spoke for two hours, not realizing the time, but no one moved, and several new class members were converted. An interesting thing about Anaheim is that it was the first time a meeting was videotaped.

Following this, we went to Little Rock, Arkansas, where we who had never seen a tornado watched one brewing ever closer in a green-colored sky. Happily, in God's providence it passed by the city. It was wonderful to be with Dr. and Mrs. Wenger, and again the large crowd came from far distances.

The Fresno Regional Meeting was also a delight. After that, the Santa Barbara Regional Meeting was held in a theater. The advertisement for our meeting and a secular sign was somewhat misleading as both were linked together. "Bible Study Fellowship" and "The Big Sleep"! It made a good icebreaker before the message.

The Seattle Regional Meeting of about 6,000 was the last held in 1980. Miss Hertzler and I were already in San Antonio. With all the problems for the new general director, moving of staff members, and weeks of orientation for new teaching leaders, the original plans for other regional meetings had to be canceled for that year.

Seattle stands out in several ways. Like Little Rock, the city represented one of the first classes formed outside the Bay Area. The meeting in the arena was held on the day before Mount St. Helens erupted. We all left by plane at the time when the eruption was at its peak, and the pilot flew us as near to the scene as he dared. We realized afresh something of the power of God in creation.

These regional meetings will always stand out in my mind. It is one thing to hold retreats for leaders only, but when one looks at thousands of class members, of whom so many have been converted through the God-given pattern of Bible Study Fellowship and sacrificial dedication of leaders, one realizes how great is the power of God's Word. One has a small glimpse of the New Humanity He is everywhere preparing for eternity. Every one of them would say, "Did not our hearts burn within us as He opened up to us the Scriptures?"

Before most of the regional meetings, Miss Hertzler and I were preoccupied with our own move to San Antonio. I had already been presented with a Texan hat, a picture of blue-bonnet flowers, and a hobbyhorse, and Alverda and I had painted San Antonio to the staff in glowing colors. Now there remained the problem of our finding a house in San Antonio and selling our own. Dr. and Mrs. Jensen kindly entertained us again in December, and we found a house suited to our needs in a quiet, lovely location looking over the fairway of a golf course. Even before we sold our Oakland home in the hills, we arranged to buy this home in San Antonio. Ordinarily homes in our exquisitely beautiful Oakland Hills were in great demand. However, when we returned home, we discovered that the bottom had fallen out of the real estate market because of high interest rates. Again in faith, we prayed that God would sell our house in time. In His providence a young Swiss builder who always wanted a house with a view like ours offered to buy it. It's marvelous to be able to relate that the escrows both closed one day apart!

CRISES AND CONFERENCES

God of the Heights, austere, inspiring,
   Thy word hath come to me,
O let no selfish aims, conspiring,
   Distract my soul from Thee.
Loosen me from things of Time;
Strengthen me for steadfast climb.

The temporal would bind my spirit;
   Father, be Thou my stay.
Show me what flesh cannot inherit,
   Stored for another day.
Be transparent, Things of Time.
Looking through you, I would climb.

Now by Thy grace my spirit chooseth
   Treasure that shall abide.
The great Unseen, I know, endureth,
   My footsteps shall not slide.
Not for me the Things of Time;
God of mountains, I will climb.

Amy Wilson Carmichael

In February 1980 we entered into what everyone knows is an horrendous task, that of moving. Miss Hertzler went ahead to get our new house ready. I stayed behind to prepare for moving two separate "apartments" and 1,500 books.

But the Lord sent me human "angels" to help. Some of the staff were able to give special time, but others of our class membership who had more free time simply poured out their energy and time to pack the books, important papers, and chinaware in special boxes.

Then came the moving day and another "angel," Mrs. Hornberger, stayed all day with me as we watched the large moving van being filled to the brim.

The reader can imagine the arrival at San Antonio, the piles of boxes between which we walked, and the unpacking and placing of those books! Yet never could one have experienced more loving help than we experienced in San Antonio when Bible Study Fellowship members whom we had never met poured in to help us get unpacked. They prepared food for us. They poured out their love in every possible way. They tried to initiate us into the intricate system of freeways of San Antonio, helping us to get acquainted with the necessary shopping areas.

Of course, the joy of getting to know new friends cannot lessen the sense of missing our dear friends in Oakland which we had made over the past twenty years.

Last week a letter was written by a well-known pastor and radio speaker, saying, "If anyone needs help in our church, look for Bible Study Fellowship members. They put into practice the teaching of John 13 and truly apply what the Bible teaches and our Lord's specific commandments."

This should always be the witness of a committed believer. We now live in a humanistic world without moral absolutes or moral values. The result is that our neighbors live a life of suffering because it is a life void of meaning. This is especially true of young people. We need to look for these needy ones on every hand and to serve them just as our Lord served others.

After speaking at regional meetings in the U.S., I was due to speak at a regional meeting in England in September 1980. Miss Hertzler and I had also been given a trip to Europe, so that summer we were enabled to get away to our beloved Switzerland, perhaps for the last time. During the months of mid-July and August, I drove 900 miles through our beloved mountains. We eventually stayed near L'Abri, where we again enjoyed the loving fellowship of Dr. and Mrs. Francis Schaeffer and other L'Abri friends.

It was a delightful respite. We had found a chalet high up in mountain meadows where the beautiful music of the cowbells soothed us to sleep each night. We roamed through carpets of flowers: tall pansies, pink campions, wild marguerites, gentians, anemones, and buttercups growing together in a glorious mass of beauty. We drove and walked through fir woods where one tree grows directly out of a rock, which I always call the "Rock of Ages."

Although my spine made itself felt, one could somewhat anesthetize it by the joy of such beauties of God's creation. The enjoyment and rest had renewed us both, and we eagerly looked forward to meeting my relatives and friends and renewing relationships with our Bible Study Fellowship members in the north of England.

We landed in England at the end of August 1980. We were somewhat travel weary, and my low bed was tightly made up (English fashion) and firm against the wall. I unwisely used all my energy to pull out the low leg at the bottom of the bed. Alas! I fell back on my back heavily. The pain was agonizing. Miss Hertzler immediately called the hotel manager, and as God would have it, the hotel doctor was already almost at the hotel. I had not long to wait. After an injection he ordered an ambulance and engaged a private room in an English hospital not far away.

Most ambulance men in England belong to what we call the "Cockney Fraternity." Their use of language is their own, and they are noted for happy, friendly humor. They kept us amused. I enjoyed their comments. For example, as I was carried down the corridor to the elevator, feeling the bumps, I clutched a little tightly to the arms. They said, "Don't yer worry, Miss, we only reckon to drop 'em on Sundays." This and many similar remarks helped the journey to the hospital.

My eleven-day stay in the private hospital was enhanced by the grace of God. There were X-rays and considerable sedation, but all of my English family came immediately to see me after Miss Hertzler had sent them the news by telegram. Dr. Schaeffer alerted the "Greatham L'Abri" and they came too—always with flowers. They were also a great help to us when we felt we needed to return to the U.S.

Miss Hertzler visited me several times a day, but when it came to Sunday, I did not want her to miss the beautiful worship service of All Souls, Langham Place, where the Reverend Michael Baughen, the pastor, is a dear friend. He had spoken twice to our triennial retreat for teaching leaders. All the same, Miss Hertzler felt very much alone in an English church. But God had His special provision for her. She was met at the door by a gentleman quite well known to me. (I had introduced him and his artist wife to Dr. Grant Whipple, the beauties and particularly the wild life of the Great Western mountains and the great white oaks, which she had painted and exhibited with great success.) This gentleman asked Miss Hertzler if she were a visitor. When she told him our connections and my predicament, he said, "It is my turn to lead prayers this morning." So I was prayed for by the entire church. In the church there was also a group of Bible Study Fellowship members from Santa Barbara who gathered around Alverda, who came back to me uplifted by the fellowship and this evidence of God's lovingkindness.

The well-known Dr. John Stott (founder and former pastor of All Souls, Langham Place) gave the sermon that morning. He took time to have a long and encouraging phone conversation with me as he was leaving for a speaking engagement in Germany the next day. Later in the week, the Reverend Michael Baughen and his wife, Myrtle, came to the hospital for a delightful and enriching evening. I asked them about the work of All Souls, Langham Place, where the church had been completely renovated and all expenses were met in answer to their most urgent prayers. Once when Michael Baughen and a friend were desperately praying for an urgent financial need, the answer came in an envelope, pushed in the door during their prayer.

From the beginning I had hoped I would still be able to keep my speaking engagement in northern England for the regional meeting. However, my doctor said this would be impossible at this time. Then I began thinking of returning to the U.S. We knew we could not change planes as we had traveling to Europe. Our dear L'Abri Greatham friends came to our aid. Previously unknown to us was a plane of the British Caledonian Airline which went directly from London to Houston. Miss Hertzler checked and found it was a 747, which has a number of seats in the middle. My doctor said if I would go by ambulance and stretcher to the airport, and could lie down all the way in the plane, I might risk the travel.

We all prayed. Again the lovingkindness of the Lord was extraordinarily present. Miss Hertzler, struggling with changing airlines in unknown London, managed to purchase tickets. My kind doctor arranged that not only was I taken by ambulance to the airport, but into the plane itself. The ambulance man saw to tickets, luggage, and passport inspection without either of us having to do anything.

The plane was half-empty and I was able to lie down on a complete middle row. There was another empty row where Miss Hertzler could assist me. Prayer and pills helped and we made it to Houston.

There again, all customs regulations and passports were handled for us. Our Houston teaching leaders and friends were allowed on the now-empty plane, as well as the men from a Christian ambulance company. I was grateful to be with our caring Bible Study Fellowship family again. The next day two men of the San Antonio staff, Mr. Bob Owens and Mr. Steve Gately, arranged a station wagon with heavy mattresses (all seats removed) and drove me to San Antonio while

Alverda returned by plane. It was a wonderful experience of God's continual lovingkindness.

I was taken to two different hospitals in San Antonio. At the Methodist hospital the orthopedist was an earnest Christian and very interested in the text in my "Daily Light" for that day; "I am the Lord that healeth thee," which I have clung to ever since.

One day when I had been returned home, as surgeons felt it unwise to try to operate on the cancerous areas of my spine, I was suddenly in acute pain. Dr. Jensen came to see me. I returned to the hospital. More X-rays were taken, an emergency operation was performed, and a cancerous tumor in the colon removed. This led to six months in bed, mostly at home. This book which was supposed to have been completed in 1980, was left on the shelf until February 1981!

I should describe two more memorable conferences, one of which indirectly led to the writing of this book.

The International Congress on World Evangelization at Lausanne. The first was in 1975. I was then invited to the International Congress on World Evangelization held at Lausanne, Switzerland, July 16-26. More than 4,000 participants, observers, and guests from 150 countries attended. Heads of missions, representatives of countless organizations, pastors, and theologians of all major evangelistic organizations were there.

We mingled among men and women of all races, many in colorful garb—all there for one purpose—world evangelization. The atmosphere of love was overwhelming as we sat in the great auditorium of the beautiful Palace of Beaulieu. We listened to messages translated into six languages from such well-known speakers as Dr. Billy Graham, Dr. John Stott, Dr. Francis Schaeffer, and Malcolm Muggeridge.

The theme was "Evangelization of the World Now." We heard how amazingly God is bringing to Himself members of the Third World. The application was, "What part am I as a Christian *personally* having in fulfilling the Great Commission:

'Go ye into all the world, and preach the gospel to every creature,' (Mark 16:15)?"

I thought of the millions of young people in so-called Christian countries who think only of getting married and having a family in their home country and never know the joys of reaping fruit among the vast field of pagans who still have never heard the name of Jesus.

We had many deeply moving moments—one when the Congress began by singing "Alleluia, Alleluia." After the closing message by Billy Graham and a solemn communion service, we streamed out, singing, "Alleluia," until we reached the corridors.

We met members from many countries in the refreshment and meeting hall. Out in the foyer was a clock which ticked off every day the population increase, making us aware more deeply of the great need of the world. It was there that we met Dr. Stoddard (former pastor of the Walnut Creek Church and a member of our board), who visited with us in our chalet after the Congress. He drove us to Chamonix, France, where we had the thrilling and unforgettable experience of crossing Mount Blanc Glacier by cable car.

Chicago Summit Conference of ICBI. Another unforgettable conference was that of the Summit Conference of the International Council on Biblical Inerrancy. This conference took place October 26-28, 1978, in Chicago.

For some time I had been vaguely concerned about the growing lack of confidence even among professing evangelical pastors of the final authority of the Bible, and the fact (accepted in past generations) that it was entirely without error. Harold Lindsell's book, *The Battle for the Bible*, published by Zondervan in 1976, opened up this whole question. Some time later there was a small conference at Mt. Hermon, where the subject was discussed by outstanding theological scholars.

After meals there were discussions to which a few of us, including myself, were invited. As a result of this, Dr. Jay

Grimstead organized a group of leading Bible scholars to get together to form an inner council of sixteen persons to emphasize by various methods the importance of the inerrancy of Scripture in our day. Later a larger advisory council of leading evangelicals was also formed.

After the inner council was formed, I was surprised and delighted to be invited to become a member. The president of this council presently is Dr. James Montgomery Boice, the well-known radio speaker and author. I happen to be the only woman on the council, although Mrs. Karen Hoyt, as director of the administrative division, an extremely important posision, is always present.

The summit meeting of the International Council on Biblical Inerrancy was held at the Hyatt Regency O'Hare Hotel in Chicago. There were 300 invited to this summit meeting besides the council and advisory board. Most of these were men from thirty-four seminaries, thirty-three colleges, numerous churches, and Christian organizations; denominational leaders and heads of publishing houses were also present.

These were extremely full but mind-stretching and inspiring times, especially the plenary sessions. There were about a dozen of our Bible Study Fellowship people—area advisors and teaching leaders—who had been invited and were also enriched by the "elective sessions."

During the conference, small groups were assigned to work on "Nineteen Articles of Affirmation" of the inerrancy of Scripture, from every angle of controversy. It was interesting that when every member of the audience was given a copy of the final summary, about 90 percent of the audience signed the Affirmation document.

Since there is a serious slide from belief that the Bible is "without error" (in the original documents) both in seminaries and in churches of our day, this council (I.C.B.I.) was formed to stress the importance of holding to the belief of the early church, a belief which continued until the eighteenth century. It is an irenic council. Many "born again" persons are trapped by liberal scholars and fail to see the importance of this belief on which the Bible Study Fellowship stands strongly. Dr. Francis Schaeffer describes the "slide" as a "watershed" and believes that in the next generation the continued erosion concerning belief in the authority of the Bible as God's *inbreathed Word* (see II Tim. 3:16, Greek Translation), could cause belief in the Bible to be lost. The work of the summit and continued work of the council is to produce detailed and scholarly statements (geared also to lay persons) on the inerrancy of Scripture. Scholars also hold debates with seminary students and professors to this end.

Although in the Bible Study Fellowship we have many agnostics, unbelievers, liberals, and persons of different faiths, we find we do not have to overly emphasize that the Bible is without error. By the time class members have studied and discussed the problem passages for themselves, they become aware of the innate authority of this Word of God (see Heb. 4:12), and most experience conversion.

One interesting connection with I.C.B.I. is that as a result of speaking at a meeting for I.C.B.I. in San Diego, I was approached by Dr. Hawley, editor-in-chief of Tyndale House Publishers, to write this autobiography.

THIRTY

GOD'S MIRACLES
IN SAN ANTONIO

Behold, I will do a new thing; now it shall spring forth; shall ye not know it? [Isaiah 43:19].

Miss Hertzler and I had moved from our home in Oakland in February 1980 because we both felt this was God's will and would indirectly help to preserve the sense of continuity of the work of Bible Study Fellowship.

Yet what a joy it has been to both of us to watch the outworkings of God's miracle. God continues to reveal His purpose for the future of the work to the new (1980) general director, Mrs. Rosemary Jensen, in a remarkable way.

After the offer of the land in 1978, the first absolute necessity was to ascertain whether there was fresh water at the property. Most people involved trembled as they drilled into the ground lest water with sulphur in it would spring up. Instead the well contained the purest water.

Mrs. Rosemary Jensen is a woman of prayer. Also the Bible Study Fellowship staff has always prayed on their knees every morning, with a half day of prayer established monthly. Their diligence in prayer yielded amazing results.

The next important item was to choose an architect to recommend to the board. Mrs. Jensen discovered that the very best architect in the whole region was Mr. Paul Hesson. His daughter was in a Bible Study Fellowship class, and "it so happened" that two weeks before Mrs. Jensen felt led to approach him, he had become a member of the men's evening class taught by Dr. Jensen. When Mrs. Jensen asked him whether he would consider her recommendation of him to the board, he was deeply interested in the project.

On December 4, 1978, Mr. Paul Hesson came to Oakland to see the Skymount buildings and work flow, and was very impressed. We all felt a real fellowship with him and confidence in his ability. Before he arrived, Miss Hertzler and her staff in Oakland had already worked many hours on tentative drawings of plans for the future buildings. When Mr. Hesson came to Oakland, he consulted her about the project. The production staff, under Miss Hertzler's leadership, eventually drew up a very large-sized tentative floor plan for the production department, with the same arrangement as the one at Skymount, since the "work flow" it provided had proved very satisfactory. The new Production Building Mr. Hesson designed has the same "work flow" pattern, including the modules, where pallets piled with completed lessons flow by gravity on rollers to the shipping room.

The board of directors was interested in Mr. Hesson's projections, and agreed to employ him. The Bible Study Fellowship owes much to his excellent ideas and artistry of design which combined the natural beauty of the tree-covered region with the construction of the buildings. The beautiful, tan San Antonio rocks found at the site were combined with cedar to achieve this result.

At first there were many seemingly insurmountable obstacles. One concerned the road of access to the property. There was only a rough, rocky trail bulldozed out to make a temporary road for access to power lines belonging to the county.

When a group of us, together with the board of directors, tried to get through to the property in large trucks, we wondered how the Bible Study Fellowship could ever meet the expense of a road. Yet nothing could be started on the "land" until there was a road of access.

Mrs. Jensen's prayer league all prayed. Then Mr. Hesson heard that the City Public Service Board was building an access road from the coast, where there is a nuclear installation (nearly 200 miles away), for access to power lines in San Antonio. Eventually, perhaps after many months, this access road would reach up our hill; but the Bible Study Fellowship desperately needed it now. A member of the City Public Service Board (whose wife was in Bible Study Fellowship) knew of the Bible Study Fellowship predicament. Because of prayer, the City Public Service Board was persuaded to start from our hill instead of from the coast! This in itself was a miracle. Another miracle was that the heavy cost of moving their equipment from the coast to San Antonio was met by a close friend of Bible Study Fellowship (now with the Lord).

Mrs. Jensen and Mrs. JoAnn Goetting contacted Mrs. Goetting's uncle, Mr. H. B. Zachry, who is one of the world's most renowned contractors. With Mr. Zachry's tremendous resources, Mr. Hesson knew he could build that road better than anyone else. He generously offered to build it "at cost."

I shall never forget driving along that road with Mrs. Jensen (in a truck, of course) as far as one could go while it was being built. As I watched those huge bulldozers and Caterpillars removing immense rocks with ease, I thought of God who removes mountains. "Thou shalt thresh the mountains, and beat them small, and shalt make the hills as chaff" (Isa. 41:15).

In this I found a message for all of us who have spiritual mountains that hinder access to God's purpose. God has ways of making them as nothing (see Matt. 17:20).

This was in the spring of 1980 when San Antonio usually has rain. Mrs. Jensen's "prayer warriors" prayed that it would rain only on weekends, and it did! That road was finished *within three weeks,* in April 1980. Mrs. Jensen named it "Wilderness Way."

Then began the construction of buildings. Mr. Fred Goetting, a brilliant engineer, worked with Mr. Hesson and Mr. Harvey Hancock, who was the main contractor. Soon the foundations were poured. Mrs. Jensen's "prayer league" prayed for no rain while the foundations were laid. In the end some San Antonians said, "Please stop your people praying; we need rain in San Antonio!"

When a person now drives up that beautiful road and turns right onto the Bible Study Fellowship property, an exquisite view of tree-covered hills awaits him. The buildings are barely seen except the outline of the huge Production Building and of a high Prayer Tower with the Cross above it. The wide expanse stretches for miles and one has a sense of peace and glory.

It took over a year to build and furnish the property. Meanwhile most of the Oakland staff came and settled in San Antonio. Mrs. Jensen's gift of blending the experienced Oakland staff and new San Antonio staff into a group of twenty-four staff members, united, was the result of her dependence upon the Lord Jesus Himself. His provision of key persons to fill key positions came by His personal call, which was confirmed by Mrs. Jensen's official appointment.

For example, Mr. Richard Walenta (who is a well-known contractor) and his wife had been so changed through Bible Study Fellowship classes that they both loved Bible Study Fellowship with a deep affection. Many of our Bible Study Fellowship members have felt the call to the mission field, and are now in such areas as France, South Africa, South America, the Philippines, and other areas. Mr. and Mrs. Walenta began to feel that he might be able to use his gifts to help others on the mission field also. Then he heard of the Bible Study Fellowship need. After prayer, such was the couple's love for Bible Study Fellowship and the sense of God's leading that he and his wife wrote, offering his services. They were just what was most needed at the time. Although in Seattle he had ten acres of beautiful land and had recently completed his home on it, he left it. All the Bible Study Fellowship had to offer this contractor was a trailer in which to live with their two children. They were really "pinned" in on the property, being caretakers responsible for it for about a year, until their caretaker's lovely home was finished. Yet never was there any complaint about the lonely, nonstop responsibility. One thanks God for their attitude of dedication.

Many other key workers were brought into the work in answer to prayer, but the names of our present God-given staff and the story of their call are too numerous and much too extensive to recount here. However, there is one person on the present staff of Bible Study Fellowship whose name must be included. Mrs. John Hamilton (Pearl) had been with me in Oakland since 1958. Over the years she became my right-hand assistant, particularly in the area of leadership training. When the headquarters moved to San Antonio, she also moved there with her entire family in 1980. Her twenty years of experience in important areas of the work have been invaluable to the new general director, who appointed her deputy director.

A temporary business building had been rented for the staff in San Antonio while the buildings on the "land" were being constructed. This was delightful, for we were able to have fellowship with the staff, although the writing of this book took up much of my time.

Somehow Mrs. Jensen and her staff managed to keep pace with the increasing applications for new classes or replacement of teaching leaders. Six orientations of teaching leaders and substitute teaching leaders were held before the new buildings were erected. Applicants were housed in homes of the San Antonio staff and friends and meetings were held in the Jensens' home.

At the same time, the production of lessons for classes—printing, collating, and shipping—continued with a greatly reduced staff in crowded space in Oakland. Since there were 300 classes by 1981, each representing up to 450 members, and a need for extra lessons for new members, this meant shipping every quarter over 70,000 lessons to four countries (not to speak of the many other materials each Bible Study Fellowship class needs). There were only seven persons left in Oakland to do all this. But as usual a small array of volunteers, organized by Miss Anna Kingsbury, helped.

Mrs. Jensen would go to Oakland once a month to coordinate the work and encourage these faithful staff workers. They faithfully refused other offers of employment until the San Antonio property was ready in May of 1981, when the huge press and all furniture were moved to the new buildings.

Mr. Bob Owens, our business manager who had moved from Oakland to San Antonio, handled the main responsibility of selling all the Oakland property, including the three orientation houses. The selling of these properties at a difficult period for real estate sales again proved that God's faithfulness for this financial input was very necessary

The new buildings are unusually beautiful. One very experienced board member said, "Incredible!" when he saw them. He remembered the first view from the helicopter of both road and property. To see the beautiful design of buildings set on a hill in the midst of cedar and live oak trees is to marvel at our Creator's wisdom given to Mr. Hesson, Mr. Hancock, Mrs. Jensen and others. There are eight buildings occupying 52,000 square feet in all. The Production Building alone represents 27,000 square feet.

Imagine these buildings made of the beautiful tan-and-white rocks found on the road and property, set in the midst of cedar trees and live oaks. There are covered walks and small patios around each building, landscaped for beauty. Then picture the ninety-five acres of trees, the little patches of meadows, and the trails where one can walk and be alone with the Lord.

Three staff women, headed by an interior decorator, Mrs. Eleanor Craven, went to Dallas and managed to procure beautiful furniture at special prices. There are three lovely orientation houses, each capable of holding eight candidates for new classes. There is a beautiful dining room, living room, and kitchen accommodations. The dining room is filled with round tables seating six, with chair seats in a blue design. The living room is comfortable with sofas, chairs, and has a stone fireplace with a cross set in the midst. It is a perfect place for conversation.

One day during the prayer session, Mrs. Pearl Hamilton, who is a musical member of the San Antonio staff, prayed for a piano. What was Mrs. Jensen's surprise when the following day (out of the clear blue!) a lady called in asking if there was a piano in the new building. She then said she wanted to give a Steinway grand piano to the work. While Mrs. Jensen and Mrs. Hamilton were overwhelmed with delight as they saw this beautiful grand piano in the store, there was a telephone call. The lady who gave the piano called her sister in Houston and said, "I have given a Steinway grand piano to the Bible Study Fellowship. Why don't you give them an Allen organ!" This she was eager to do, and she telephoned accordingly. They went home walking on air! Both beautiful instruments are now installed and being used to the glory of God.

Set above the leadership training and administration buildings is a three-story Prayer Tower with a high Cross set above the roof. When the laborers placed the Cross at the top, at once there was a complete hush as it was installed. The staff climbs up to the third floor of this tower each morning and for the day of prayer. Prayer has always been the key for all the work of Bible Study Fellowship.

One cannot describe the buildings without mentioning the large army of volunteers from Bible Study Fellowship classes who continually gave their services. When the buildings were finished and the landscape full of debris, 100 women and men of the Bible Study Fellowship class in Austin came and spent a whole day picking up debris and putting their findings into huge garbage bins. They worked hard all day with much joy and fellowship.

As in Oakland, so in San Antonio, the Bible Study Fellowship has many regular volunteers. Recently Mrs. Betsy Wray, who is the coordinator for volunteers, held a training day and 125 volunteers came. These now come on different days and work in the shipping and collating department, helping in the office and other areas. How we thank God for them.

I have been describing God's miracles regarding the great enlargement of the physical facilities to meet future needs. Yet one's greatest sense of contentment has been in watching the spiritual progress of the work under Mrs. Rosemary Jensen's direction. We share the same ideals for the basic pattern of the work and continue to enjoy a close fellowship. At the same time, God has given her several fruitful innovations. It is good to see the unity of the staff from Oakland and San Antonio, the pleasure of the board of directors, and the wonderful financial provision through designated gifts so that the organization is completely free of debt. Mrs. Pearl Hamilton, deputy director, has greatly helped Mrs. Jensen in the building up of this unity.

I was privileged to take part in a recent innovation in June 1981. Mrs. Jensen recognized a need for teaching leaders to receive extra instruction to mature their theology and leadership. She invited teaching leaders from the southwest to attend an "Institute" in the new buildings. There was only room for thirty persons. They were housed in the new orientation houses, enjoyed close fellowship with the staff, and were entranced with the beauty of the new buildings.

Four such institutes have become an annual affair. They are a great help to the teaching leaders and bring them in close touch with the headquarters and staff. Key evangelical scholars give lectures on the particular series which the leaders expect to teach the coming year. Mrs. Jensen, Mrs. Hamilton, and I take part in the teaching, also.

When we on the board of directors first looked at this untouched property gift in 1978, we certainly never envisioned the development of the property and the beauty and symmetry of the building complex. This reminds me that when I had the first five women I did not envision the expansion of the work and all the miracles and changed lives God has brought about through the power of His Word in Bible Study Fellowship classes.

And "His truth is marching on!"

He who led them through the desert
Watched and guided day by day
Turned the flinty rocks to water
Made them brooks beside the way—
He will bring them where the fountains
Fresh and full spring forth above.
Still throughout the endless ages
Serving in the joy of love.

T.P.

THE DEDICATION OF THE NEW SAN ANTONIO HEADQUARTERS

Thou art worthy, O Lord, to receive glory and honour and power: for thou hast created all things, and for thy pleasure they are and were created [Revelation 4:11].

The morning of September 12, 1981, was a memorable one for all who attended the dedication ceremony for the new Bible Study Fellowship headquarters in San Antonio.

As cars streamed up into the hills, the carillon in the Prayer Tower was pealing forth beautiful hymns. As we entered the room of the huge Production Building where more than 500 people gradually gathered, the sense of expectation and excitement was high.

The platform was beautifully decorated with shrubs and flowers, and the beauty of the multicolored choir robes of Bible Study Fellowship members from different churches blended together as harmoniously as their beautiful voices contributed to the program.

All of the board members and Mrs. Jensen, Miss Hertzler, and I were on the platform with other speakers. Above them hung (as usual in Bible Study Fellowship gatherings), a beautifully lettered banner—"To God Be the Glory."

Some early history of Bible Study Fellowship was given

vivaciously by Mrs. Harold Gudnason, whose husband was one of the original board members. Following the presentation of the keys of the building by the architect, Mr. Paul Hesson, to Dr. Grant Whipple, chairman of the board, I had been asked to give the prayer of dedication.

Dr. Grant Whipple then surprised Miss Hertzler and me with the announcement that although the name of the whole complex had not yet been chosen, two buildings had been named. He said that at the entrance of the main building there was a plaque that read, "The Johnson Center, To the glory of God in honor of Audrey Wetherell Johnson, Founder of Bible Study Fellowship." Also, at the entrance of the Production Building there was another plaque reading, "The Hertzler Press, To the glory of God in honor of Alverda Hertzler, first Administrator of Bible Study Fellowship." We both were completely overwhelmed.

We had been asked to give "a response" and had wondered—to what? Now we knew and what words could express our deep appreciation for such a lovely honor.

Mrs. Rosemary Jensen then gave an inspiring outline of the vision she has for the future of Bible Study Fellowship, and she described some new ventures planned.

Mrs. Lois McCall gave an excellent review of Dr. and Mrs. Schaeffer's contribution to the Christian world, and she introduced him as one of the world's renowned theologians.

Before he began his address, Dr. Schaeffer expressed his deep interest in the work of Bible Study Fellowship and that he and Mrs. Schaeffer had valued the friendship of Alverda and me over the years.

Dr. Schaeffer's message was one of the most outstanding ones I had heard him give. It was divided into three sections: (1) why study the Bible at all; (2) the importance of Bible Study Fellowship in which thousands have the opportunity of studying the whole Bible from one end to the other (Dr. Schaeffer graciously stated that this has its impact on the whole church of Jesus Christ); (3) the importance of the fact that we must truly live daily under its teaching—otherwise the first two points would be rendered meaningless.

Following his challenging address, the room resounded with praise as the audience sang "To God Be the Glory."

The audience was then invited to a luncheon which was served at tables arrayed under the trees and in the dining room. After the luncheon, everyone was given the opportunity to view the buildings and the beautiful grounds.

The joy of witnessing the involvement of the Bible Study Fellowship board on the platform, the beautiful music from BSF class members from all over San Antonio, and most of all the message of Dr. Francis Schaeffer as well as the presence of Mrs. Edith Schaeffer, combined to make it a memorable event in the annals of Bible Study Fellowship. I rejoiced to see Mrs. Rosemary Jensen come into her own, working together with the members of the Oakland staff who have so beautifully united with the San Antonio staff to become a wonderful team. It is thrilling to realize all God has wrought during the last two years.

THIRTY-TWO
A NEW ERA

We give thanks to God always for you all, making mention
of you in our prayers: remembering without ceasing your work
of faith, and labour of love, and patience of hope in our
Lord Jesus Christ, in the sight of God and our Father
[1 Thessalonians 1:2, 3].

Perhaps the climax of my relationship with the Bible Study
Fellowship teaching leaders, who have given such devoted,
sacrificial, and fruitful service to God since the early years of
the fifties, was reached when Mrs. Rosemary Jensen held her
first teaching leaders' seminar in January 1982. There were
343 Bible Study Fellowship men and women teaching leaders
and area advisors present, most of whom I counted as very
dear friends throughout the years when I was in office.

The seminar was held near Austin, Texas, at a beautiful
resort on the shores of a lovely lake. Leaders came from
Australia, England, Canada, and from over three-fourths of
the United States.

Dr. Alan Redpath from England was the main speaker. He
spoke several times on Christian maturity. His messages were
profoundly blessed to everyone present.

This was the first time many of the teaching leaders had

seen the new headquarters. When Mrs. Jensen took them all back by bus to San Antonio to see the new headquarters and to hear of all the miracles which revealed the hand of God upon the work, they were deeply impressed and rallied loyally to her leadership. Joyous and awed reports filled the seminar halls upon their return to Lakeway late in the afternoon.

As the teaching leaders (from whom I had been separated for two years) came to me to express their feelings so lovingly, I was deeply moved. They assured me of their prayers for the writing of this book since my illness has made it difficult to write as I would have wished. We looked back over more than twenty years and we knew that the bonds God had forged between us could never be broken. Many had entered the Bible Study Fellowship work when it was very small. They all poured out their lives sacrificially every week on each of the five study series. They have watched unsaved individuals come to know Christ, family lives changed, and many new converts eventually led into full time Christian work. They have trained leaders and seen little children from non-Christian homes come into a real relationship with Christ.

During the twenty years we have been together at regional retreats and seminars and been refreshed and strengthened by one another's testimonies. We have prayed and wept together over a leader's sorrow as though he belonged to our own family. Such ties can never be broken.

I was overwhelmed with love and joy to be with them. Yet the time of person-to-person conversation was necessarily short. We comforted one another with the realization that in heaven we will have all the time we need to be together.

As I prepare to close this story of my life, I want to close with my deepest thankfulness to all the leaders I have known, as I continue to pray for their ministry until Christ comes.

To what are we committed? Not to Christian work but to God's will; to be and to do what He has foreordained for us to accomplish (Eph. 2:10).

Yesterday one of the orientees asked what he could pray for

me. I realized that my great longing is to "finish my course with joy."

Each of us is called to serve our own generation, and then God calls us to Himself. When God removes workers, He gives others. How deeply thankful I am that He now continues His work under such godly leadership as that of Mrs. Rosemary Jensen.

The torch of leadership of a work passes from one hand to another, but the eternal value of the work is according to the measure of the fullness of the Holy Spirit and the power of the living Word of God.

Lord of all life, below, above,
Whose light is truth, whose warmth is love,
Before Thy ever blazing throne
We ask no luster of our own.

Grant us Thy truth to make us free,
And kindling hearts that burn for Thee,
Till all Thy living altars claim
One holy light, one heavenly flame.

Oliver Wendell Holmes, 1809–1894

Left: A. Wetherell Johnson, 1950, at the beginning of BSF.
Right: Miss Hertzler's home where first BSF class met.

Miss Alverda E. Hertzler, 1974.

Wetherell Johnson in 1969.

Top: Laird Avenue home, where first leaders' meetings were held.
Bottom: The Bible Study Fellowship Production Department in Oakland.

Wetherell and Mrs. Rosemary Jensen, May 1980.

The Mt. Hermon Teaching Leaders' Seminar, 1979. Front center is Wetherell Johnson; left of her is Michael Baughn (All Souls Church, London) and his wife; on the right is Alverda Hertzler; immediately behind Miss Johnson stands Rosemary Jensen with her husband, Dr. Bob Jensen (wearing glasses).

The dedication of the new headquarters, 1981.

The Oakland Regional Meeting, December 1979.

IV

Guidelines for the Christian Life

THIRTY-THREE

THE JOY OF
BELONGING TO CHRIST
BY CONVERSION

*Verily, verily, I say unto you, He that heareth my word, and
believeth on him that sent me, hath everlasting life, and shall
not come into condemnation; but is passed from death unto life*
[John 5:24].

As I look at the secular world today, and read its books, I am
aware that most individuals experience an increasing sense of
emptiness and meaninglessness of life under the humanist
viewpoint which prevails in our society.

I remember from my school days two teachers talking
together. One was a committed Christian; the other had no
use for religion. The non-Christian said, "Yesterday and
every Sunday I visit a hospital for crippled children. I give
money to charities. Therefore when my time comes to leave
this world (if there is an afterlife), I expect St. Peter will let me
in. After all I have tried to live a good life, even though I do not
go to church."

The Christian teacher replied, "Jesus Christ said, 'Without
me ye can do nothing' (John 15:5). He also said, 'I am the way,
the truth, and the life: no man cometh unto the Father, but by
me' (John 14:6)."

I have talked with many young people (especially those

coming from divorced families) who live lives of quiet despair, which is a factor in the increase in suicide. Without a relationship with the living God, life is truly meaningless, and there is no lasting salve for sorrow.

I experience a deep sympathy for persons who recognize that all the learned philosophical statements of this world ultimately deprive life of any eternal meaning.

Hundreds of letters arrive at my home from Bible Study Fellowship class members. Probably as many as one third of our class members are unchurched or have never asked Christ into their heart before coming to class. These persons pour out their story of previous ways in which they tried to find happiness, yet experienced a heart hunger which nothing could assuage. Now they write to me to tell me how they found the Lord, their inexpressible joy, and the changed family life.

They have discovered that the secret of life lies in their relationship with the Creator of the universe as their heavenly Father. Their underlying sense of guilt has been taken away by their acceptance of the fact that the Lord Jesus Christ on the Cross carried their sins and the punishment of rebellion toward God. They rejoice in an intimate fellowship with the living Christ who was raised and is in Heaven preparing to return for His own children.

Their life is no longer without a goal. They now know that the eternal God (Who chose to create every human being "in His image"), has a purpose for that person to fulfill. They consciously move toward a glorious eternity planned for believers in the Lord Jesus, those who have been "born of the Spirit" (John 3:6) and are called sons and daughters of the living God.

One often hears these remarks; "I'm not a religious person, but I think that if whatever you believe makes you happy and you are sincere, that is good for you." "If there is a God, so long as I am kind to others and try to do good, St. Peter will let me in." "After all, if at death I am snuffed out, why not live it up while I am alive?"

People speak of "passing on" at death into the great "hereafter," vaguely imagining that this great hereafter will be similar to the present world but somehow better.

To reject or to ignore God, the Creator of the universe, Who originally created man in His own image, and to reject the Lord Jesus Christ, God's unique Son Who carried all the punishment for the sins of the world on the Cross, is ultimately the most fatal choice one can make. Not only does such a person lose the unique joy of having intimacy with the eternal God as heavenly Father in this earthly life, one's *eternal destiny*, "Heaven or hell," is also at stake, since the God Who gave you life makes demands from the human being He created.

Therefore such statements as, "There is no God," "I only am master of my fate," "If I live a reasonably good life, I expect to be accepted in the hereafter, if there is one," are actually to choose to blind one's eyes to the only eternal reality.

These ideas mostly describe an atheist's attitude. Atheists like Nietzsche, Spinoza, and Hegel of a former day refused to believe in any God. "Man is supreme in the universe, and makes his own fate" is their creed. Bertrand Russell stated regarding himself, "I believe that when I die I shall rot, and nothing of my ego will survive."

However, perhaps most unbelievers in our present society are more like I was at one period of life (described in an earlier chapter). I was an "agnostic." I did not know whether there was a God or not. I did not believe in Christ's Resurrection, Virgin Birth, or His miracles. Nor did I consider the Bible as God's revelation of Himself.

Yet, whenever I gazed at the billions of galaxies in the starry universe, moving with such mathematical precision that people on this planet can send a spaceship to the moon and calculate its arrival within minutes, my intellectual reason was boggled by the idea that this immense, starry universe just came into being by chance—a big bang that "just happened."

Again, to believe that my complex personality and intricately designed body developed by chance from protoplasm evolving "by mutation and natural section" simply represses the normal reasoning which all human beings possess. Romans 1:18 (NIV) describes such thinking as "suppress[ing] the truth by their wickedness, since what may be known about God is plain to them, because God has made it plain to them."

Whittaker Chambers, in his autobiography, *I Was a Witness*, describes his experience as a child in a rigidly atheistic home. One day he asked his mother, "Who made all this—the world, the stars?" His mother replied in extreme anger, "Who told you to ask this? Who has been talking to you?" Whittaker replied, "Why no one, I just thought that someone must have made it all." After having lived as a Communist spy during the McCarthy period, Whittaker Chambers later in life became an earnest Christian.

One day in my perplexity, I looked at the stars on a dark night in my room and said, "God, if You are there and will reveal Yourself to me, I will commit myself to live according to Your philosophy."

I have often suggested to agnostic young intellectuals to take up my challenge to God. Some of them have done so and discovered that God always answers the sincere cry to Him of a genuinely perplexed soul. Others refuse to go as far as to "commit themselves" to the truth if it is revealed to them. These continue to live in darkness. After all, in the long run, belief in God, the Creator, is not so much an intellectual question as a moral issue of commitment to light given.

There is a little known fact concerning the famous atheist, Voltaire, who once knew the truth but rejected it totally. He went so far as to prophesy that within two years after his death the Bible would be universally unknown! Yet Voltaire, on his death bed, called for a priest to whom he wished to confess his sins.

A very brilliant atheist of our own day, Will Durant, who died in January 1982 at the age of ninety-six, adopted Voltaire as his hero—"the greatest man who ever lived" he called him. Will Durant decided to leave the seminary and to adopt the humanist philosophy of today. He had a brilliant mind, and most intellectuals have studied his astounding books, "The History of Civilization" series. The story is told in the January 22, 1982, issue of *National Review* that on his death bed, he too, like Voltaire, confessed his sins to a priest.

What tragic, wasted lives those two exceptionally gifted men lived in regard to eternal values. Where will they spend eternity? Our God is not mocked.

The results of this philosophy today is called "humanism" (that is, the notion that there are no absolutes). Society and your own decisions are the only "absolutes," and we can see the effects of this in the terrible deterioration of society. Immorality, pornography, terrorism, crime, universal divorce, abortion, and the degraded civilization we all deplore is the logical outcome of life without God-given absolutes of right and wrong.

According to polls, most Americans say they believe in God, the deity of Jesus Christ, and the Bible. However, the majority of them do not know what the Bible says. Many have no personal relationship with Christ. Many follow the increasingly degraded lifestyle of our day. They have never made a solemn commitment to Christ, received eternal life from Him, and with repentance been delivered from the guilt of past sins. Such a concept is not real faith. To attend church does not necessarily mean that one has received Christ into one's heart as a *life* decision with all its implications.

What must one do to know the joy of sins forgiven and peace with God? What must one do to have a personal relationship with Him as a living Father? How does one consciously receive eternal life? John 17:3 states: "And this is life eternal, that they may know thee the only true God, and Jesus Christ, whom thou has sent."

Perhaps the reader, like many nonbelievers or nominal Christians who attend our Bible Study Fellowship classes, may ask the same questions, "What do you mean by a 'born again Christian'?" "How can I be sure I am 'saved'?" "What will happen to me if I chose to go on as I am, and not commit myself to Christ?" "Is it true that all I have to do is believe?" "I was brought up in a good home. I have attended a church all my life. I take communion. I guess I must be a Christian. What more is necessary for the joy of assurance of which you write?"

My reader friend, if you want to experience the joy of knowing God personally, the joy of complete freedom from guilt because the Lord Jesus carried all your sins on the Cross and was raised again without them, if you want to fulfill the purpose for which God created you, if you want to know in assurance that you have received eternal life from Jesus Christ (John 10:27, 28, NIV), will you consider some of the following steps?

I suggest that you go alone to your room (or wherever you can be alone and can speak aloud and kneel). Take your Bible so that you can underline certain verses. Ask God's Holy Spirit to interpret these verses to you, and to help you.

Remember God is listening to you. Tell Him you are confused, but pray that He will give you assurance that you have eternal life. Take the following steps:

Confession of Sin and Cleansing. Have you ever thanked the Lord Jesus because He carried all your sins on the Cross? Read I Peter 2:24, 25, II Corinthians 5:21, and I John 1:8, 9.

At this point confess that you are a sinner (perhaps confess special sins He brings to your mind).

Following this, *thank God that He has forever justified* you, that is, made you in grace *"just-as-if* I'd never sinned." Read Rom. 3:23, 24.)

Know where you stand about sin. Christ went to the Cross for you. Consider these passages:

Romans 5:12
Psalm 139:23, 24
Romans 6:23
John 8:24

John 3:16
Romans 3:23
1 John 1:7–9

Say to yourself: "I am a sinner who will perish in hell if I do not believe that Christ carried my sin and died for me" (John 3:16). It is absolutely necessary to confess your sins and as much as possible to honestly name them.

You must understand that the blood of Christ cleanses you because Christ died in your place for this reason. Read:

Isaiah 53:5, 6
Matthew 26:28
Romans 5:8
Hebrews 9:14, 22
Hebrews 10:17, 20
I Peter 1:18, 19
I Peter 2:24

Your sins are either on you or on Jesus. The choice is yours to make! If we receive the cleansing of Christ, God says we are justified in His sight (Rom. 5:9).

Repentance. Acts 3:19 calls for repentance from sin. This means to turn or return. It is applied to *turning* from sin to God. It means to change the direction of life from that of following your way, and sinful ways of the world, to *turn* life in a new direction of obedience and commitment to God. Actually, it involves "a change of mind."

Our Lord Jesus began His public ministry with the message, "Repent: for the kingdom of heaven is at hand" (Matt. 4:17). Paul speaks of repentance toward God and faith toward our Lord Jesus Christ.

There is no salvation apart from commitment to repentance for past sins and faith in Christ's cleansing (of those sins by His death on the Cross).

Thank the Lord Jesus for His cleansing from sin and believe that you are cleansed in God's sight.

Receive Jesus into Your Heart By Faith. Consider whether you have ever solemnly received Christ through the Person of the Holy Spirit into your heart. Read Revelation 3:20, Acts 2:38, Acts 4:12, and John 1:12 and deliberately ask Him to come in. He will not mock you. He promises to come into your heart forever when you solemnly ask Him to do so.

Thank Him for coming in to live in your heart. This is to be "born again," when God solemnly accepts you as His own child. When Jesus comes into you through the Person of the Holy Spirit, a new creation takes place, and new desires to live to please God (II Cor. 5:17).

This also means that you have received eternal life! You are now sealed with and stamped with God's name upon you. Read Ephesians 1:13.

This is to be saved (Rom. 5:9).

Solemn Commitment. Having repented and been cleansed from your past sins, your next step is to commit your whole life to God, as a person "spiritually alive from the dead." By His grace you will live by His strength and serve Him in everything. Read Romans 12:1, 2.

Prayer. It may help you to use the following prayer:

> Lord Jesus, I know I have sinned. I know I am lost unless You save me. I thank You because I believe and I thank You for carrying my sin. Cleanse me with Your own precious blood, Lord Jesus. I ask this with all my heart. . . . Come into my heart. You have promised to come in when my sins have been confessed and removed and I ask You to come in as my Savior and Lord. . . . Lord, I take Your gift of eternal life and thank You for it. I thank You now because You have come in. Amen.

I suggest now that you might wish to pray your own prayer and tell God what is in your heart.

Assurance. Ask yourself, "Has He come in?" "Do I have eternal life?" "Is He here in my heart?" Remember—faith is a choice! I am sure a joy will enter your heart and a realization that an eternal transaction has been made.

Witnessing. God asks you to confess with your mouth what He is to you (Rom. 10:9, 10; Matt. 10:32, 33).

You have now taken your first step into a life of joy in God of assurance of His undertaking for you in this life (whatever trials may come). You look forward to an unspeakably joyous life in eternity forever with God, the Lord Jesus Christ, and everyone else who is His own child.

> *O happy day that fixed my choice*
> *On Thee, my Saviour and my God:*
> *Well may this glowing heart rejoice,*
> *And tell its raptures all abroad.*
>
> *'Tis done, the great transaction's done;*
> *I am the Lord's, and He is mine;*
> *He drew me, and I followed on,*
> *Charmed to confess the voice divine.*
>
> *Now rest, my long-divided heart;*
> *Fixed on this blissful centre, rest;*
> *Nor ever from my Lord depart,*
> *With Him of every good possessed.*
>
> *High heaven, that heard the solemn vow,*
> *That vow renewed shall daily hear:*
> *Till in life's latest hour I bow,*
> *And bless in death a bond so dear.*

Philip Doddridge (1702–1751)

THIRTY-FOUR

THE JOY OF KNOWING GOD THROUGH READING THE BIBLE

Thy words were found, and I did eat them; and thy word was unto me the joy and rejoicing of mine heart: for I am called by thy name, O Lord God of hosts [Jeremiah 15:16].

The personal conviction from *faith* that one has been created "in the image of God" (Gen. 1:26, 27), gives a sense of dignity and meaning to my existence. To know that the Lord Jesus Christ, the eternal Son of God, lived a human life on earth meeting obstacles, making friendships, and obeying His Father, gives confidence of God's intimate understanding of human life. The realization that Christ bore the punishment—indeed, that He bore *my* sins on the Cross (Rom. 4:24; I Pet. 2:24)—gives freedom from guilt and is to be aware that the way to communicate with God is open all the time.

This leads to a deep desire to know all the facets of the personality of God and His eternal Son, the Lord Jesus Christ.

In His grace, God has communicated through human prophets and apostles His purpose for the human race He created. His acts in history, which also reveal His justice and other aspects of His character, and His unsearchable love are given in the Bible. If I am to enjoy a conscious *meaningful life*, I must choose to study the whole Bible. The believer, who is indwelt by Christ through the Person of the Holy Spirit, has a spiritual "interpreter." He combines with my intellect to give me a great intellectual and emotional delight in understanding what God has communicated and applying it to myself. (See I Cor. 1:18, 19.) First Corinthians 2:12 (NIV) states: "We have not received the spirit of the world but the Spirit who is from God, that we may understand what God has freely given us." First Corinthians 2:14 (NIV) states: "The man without the Spirit does not accept the things that come from the Spirit of God, for they are foolishness to him, and he *cannot understand them*, because they are spiritually discerned."

Knowing God *through the Bible* (as well as in other ways) has become the essence of my life. I believe that the biblical illiteracy of Christians today is largely responsible for many of the evils in so-called "Christian lands." Promiscuity, general immorality, divorce, and lack of true education and discipline of children are the results of not having objective absolutes. "The salt has lost his savour" (Matt. 5:13). Many young people live lives of frustration (as I once did), finding that human philosophies without hope of life after death lead to a sense of inward loneliness.

I recommend to any biblically illiterate person (whether a professing Christian or an unbeliever) to take a Bible correspondence course or to go to some class like that of Navigators or Bible Study Fellowship which requires students to give individual study to the entire Bible. Without personal Bible study one cannot enjoy a *unique intimacy* with Christ. To know Him is life eternal (John 17:3). God also states that "Man doth not live by bread only, but by every word that proceedeth out of the mouth of the Lord doth man live" (Deut. 8:3).

Seeing that God's purpose for every human being He brings to Himself is that "I" may be conformed to the image of Christ (Rom. 8:29), I need to look at Him continually, in the Bible. The Bible promises that as I look at Christ I shall be transformed to His image from "character to character" or "glory to glory" by the Holy Spirit (II Cor. 3:18). The Bible is said to be "The word of God, which is living and active. Sharper than any two-edged sword, it penetrates even to dividing soul and spirit, joints and marrow; it judges the thoughts and attitudes of the heart" (Heb. 4:12, NIV).

The Bible is not an "idol" as some people often treat the Koran. It is the God-inbreathed revelation of Himself to His creatures. Second Timothy 3:16 states that God's Word is "in-breathed" (the exact translation of the Greek). Through reading it as the Word of the living God, I receive life and life abundant when I choose to apply its precepts and promises to my life.

This represents a conscious intimacy with God. I am *listening to a Person*. I then begin to understand His dealings with mankind since human life was created, man revolted against God in the first tests (Genesis 3), and all mankind inherited the "genes" of our ancestors—Adam and Eve. I begin to understand God's infinite holiness, wisdom, power, and unsearchable love. I find the *true meaning of life.*

It is good to read one or two chapters of the Old Testament and one or two chapters of the New Testament every day. It is also good for a Christian to consider his time of twenty-four hours each day and think through his priorities.

In regard to daily Bible study, I would like to make several suggestions:

1. *Settle on a good time for every day.* I suggest one new to Bible study should start by making a settled appointment with God to listen to His voice, as you read His revelation of Himself in human language. In my early Christian life I took 6:00 A.M. for my daily appointment with God and got myself a strong cup of tea or coffee to make my mind awake.

This week (January 1982) I received more than 100 letters from Bible Study Fellowship class members telling me that the morning time with God was the very "nicest time of their whole day."

343

2. *Pray for God's help in reading.* Before you read at all, ask God to reveal to your mind the supernatural importance of what you read as well as that which your intellect comprehends (I Cor. 1:18, 19; 1 Cor. 2:12).

3. *After reading a chapter, try to remember main facts.* After you have read a chapter, lift up your head, and first try to enumerate the main facts you have read. For example, using Matthew 1 as an example, you might think in paragraphs such as these:

1. The genealogy (1–17)
2. The problem of Joseph (18–20)
3. The meaning of the name of Jesus
4. Joseph's obedience

4. *What did facts mean to persons involved?* For example, ask yourself: "What did this mean to Joseph and Mary?"

5. *Try to discover the lesson received.* Ask yourself, "What lesson do I learn from this chapter?"

6. *Application to life.* Ask yourself, "How can I apply this to my own life?"

In other words, in every chapter you read, you actually ask yourself four questions: What does it say? What did it mean to people of that day? What does it mean to me? What am I going to *do* about it today?

The Bible is its own authority. It is God's reliable communication in human language of His will, translated from the Hebrew and Greek languages into the many English versions we use today.

God communicated, "in-breathed," the original Scriptures to prophets, disciples of the Lord Jesus, and later apostles such as Paul. To quote II Timothy 3:16, "All Scripture is God-breathed and is useful for teaching, rebuking, correcting, and training in righteousness, so that the man of God may be thoroughly equipped for every good work" (NIV).

As any believer, after praying for the help of the Holy Spirit who lives in him, studies the Bible, God's authority becomes real to him. He reads the Bible as God Almighty's living communication to man. Increasingly, the study becomes a delight, a means of guidance for life, and a direct communication of the Almighty Father Who loves you *and in this way makes you know His love.*

In regard to the numerous translations from the earliest Hebrew and Greek manuscripts into English—I suggest you read any of the following. The more modern is the *New International Version.* The Bible translated for easy understanding is *The Living Bible.* Some older people, like myself, prefer the *King James Version.* Any of these will build up your character and conformity to Christ as you read them.

You may, like many, find it helpful to jot down in a little book thoughts on each passage so that they stay in your mind. God has spoken to you. He says, "Let Me hear your voice," and we must say with the Psalmist, "My voice shalt thou hear" (Psa. 5:3).

I remember when I first started to seriously read the Bible. I was reading John 2. I asked myself the third question, "What does this mean to me?" At once I remembered the text in the passage, "Whatsoever he saith unto you, do it." I knelt and asked God what He wanted me to do that day. God answered me in my thoughts, "I want you to talk to one of your work companions about Me." I did so, and God's blessing resulted.

THIRTY-FIVE

THE JOY OF THE
BELIEVER'S PRAYER LIFE

Be careful for nothing; but in every thing by prayer and
supplication with thanksgiving let your requests be made known
unto God. And the peace of God, which passeth all under-
standing, shall keep your hearts and minds through Christ Jesus
[Philippians 4:6, 7].

No one will deny that one of the greatest joys of human life is
the experience of a loving relationship. To have a friend who
knows the worst about you, yet loves you just the same, is
rare. God wants to be this kind of a friend to Whom you
continually resort.

Even though God our Father and the Lord Jesus Christ are
presently invisible to us, we can enjoy a genuine personal
communication and relationship by reading what God says
and replying to Him aloud in prayer.

However, this relationship has to be developed. How much
more glorious than the best relationship on earth is this
genuine experience (by one's choice and God's promises) of
talking to the eternal Father Who has forgiven your sins
(because they were laid on Christ on the Cross) and Who
loves you.

My heavenly Father desires to hear my voice in worship,

adoration, gratitude, and a pouring out of my need, my suffering, my inadequacies, and my fear. God always hears my cry. Sometimes His answer comes at once. Sometimes He tells me to "wait patiently" for Him, and then He will grant to me an answer.

Perhaps because prayer is so powerful, it is also the most contested exercise in the believer's life. The saintly poet, Frederick William Faber (1814—1836), expressed the struggles most believers have experienced concerning distractions in prayer. Faber struggled almost in despair and then experienced deliverance and joy:

> Ah, dearest Lord, I cannot pray
>   My fancy is not free
> Unmannerly distractions come
>   And force my mind from Thee.
>
> I cannot pray; yet Lord Thou knowest
>   The pain it is to me
> To have my vainly struggling thoughts
>   Thus torn away from Thee.

However, Frederick William Faber, struggling with a painful illness, found his answer and expresses God's answer to Him in many other beautiful poems.

> Jesus! Why dost Thou love me so?
>   What hast Thou seen in me
> To make my happiness so great
>   So dear a joy to Thee?

The Bible includes what I call a "prayer manual" in the book of Psalms. There are innumerable examples of prayer, praise, worship, desperate petitions, and prayers of consecration in the Psalms. The prayers of the Psalms were uttered by men, but all the Bible words (in the original languages) were ordained by God to be recorded in the Bible. (See II Tim. 3:16, 17.)

Although written many centuries ago, individual Psalms, especially those of David, represent poured-out prayer of repentance for sin (Psa. 51), praise to God (Psa. 84), and love (Psa. 16 and 63). David states, "Morning by morning, O Lord, you hear my voice. Morning by morning I lay my requests before you and wait in expectation" (Psa. 5:3, NIV). Sometimes the Psalmist is in despair and writes Psalms which express one's emotions better than the suffering person of today can utter.

Once in China when I was in the depths of depression I remember reading Psalm 142 and feeling some comfort in the expressed language of sorrow. I continued to read Psalm 143 on the same theme. Then suddenly I came to Psalm 144:1, "Blessed be the Lord my strength, which teacheth my hands to war, and my fingers to fight." Suddenly I was lifted clean out of my depression, knowing that God was my strength and would teach me what to do and think in my present circumstances. Many a time has that wonderful Psalm come back to mind.

There are prayers of David against wicked men (who were also against God). Today I find power in using these prayers as weapons against Satan whom Jesus calls the "prince of this world."

Prayer also includes intercession for others. One prays for one's family, pastor, friends in need, and especially persecuted Christians such as those in China, Russia, and Poland.

I find the five main prayers of Paul for his converts wonderful to use for myself and others. They are God's prayers inbreathed and written by Paul, overshadowed by God's Holy Spirit in a unique way.

1. Ephesians 1:15-23
2. Ephesians 3:14-21
3. Colossians 1:9-14

4. I Thessalonians 3:9-13
5. Philippians 1:9-11

It is wonderful to use a secret weapon of power for others. No one knows about it, but it is thrilling to see results in changed lives of those for whom you have secretly prayed. Some people will be with you in eternity because you responded to God's call to pray for them.

Prayer, as far as possible, should have a set time every day—an appointment made with God. If possible, pray *aloud* to God. It makes you sense the Person listening to you more distinctly. Of course there are often times during the night or day when emergencies come, when we are overwhelmed with God's goodness, or when we praise or pray silently to Him.

The "model of prayer" is the prayer by which the Lord Jesus taught His disciples to pray (Matt. 6:9–13). We use our own words but follow our Lord's pattern of speaking to our Father—a pattern of worship, dedication, confession, and joyous faith. For example:

1. God is my Father! (I worship You as the Lord of the universe in Heaven.)

2. I hallow Your holy name. (I will keep that name sacred today and commit myself to live a good, holy life to the best of my ability. "Name" in Scripture always refers to a *person*.)

3. I pray that Your kingdom may come. (I also include specific, known needs of countries and individuals for which You remind me to pray that they may come into Your kingdom.)

4. I commit myself to do Your will *today on earth* as the angels do in heaven. (This includes asking what is His will for me today.)

5. I pray concerning personal, earthly needs—food, money, shelter.

6. I confess my sins and deliberately choose to forgive those who have wounded me or treated me unjustly.

7. I pray for deliverance from temptation along the lines I need most.

8. I rejoice, worship God, and praise Him for His power and glory and the inheritance reserved for me in eternity.

Sometimes it is good to pray walking in a secluded place where one cannot be heard. Sometimes the majesty of God or one's grief over sin is so great that one wants to lie prostrate before Him to pray.

Sometimes, as was my case, one cannot find *words* to express loneliness, depression, disappointment, and desire, as well as joyous praise to God. Always one can find words in the Psalms that express the deepest praise and worship, the tears and cries to God, the thankfulness for deliverance. These words of David's prayers give an outlet of expression to God. I read at least one Psalm every day.

In my early life as a committed Christian I wrestled with distractions. When I prayed one day, I discovered II Corinthians 10:4, 5 which states: "(For the weapons of our warfare are not carnal [worldly] but are mighty through God to the pulling down of strong holds;) Casting down imaginations, and every high thing that exalteth itself against the knowledge of God, and bringing into captivity every thought to the obedience of Christ." I placed my finger upon these verses (as I prayed on my knees, with the open Bible in front of me on the bed). I said to God, "I am using your weapons of 'promise and prayer.' Please prove these are mighty to bring my present distracted thoughts 'captive to the obedience of Christ.'" And it worked! Every time I prayed I would use that promise until God trained me in prayer.

It is important to follow the example of the Psalms, and after earnest or agonizing petition, to look into one's heart to see if one has faith, real expectancy, that God will do something about the situation.

Note the beginning and ending of many Psalms. Often one begins with a cry of need, but the same Psalm ends in thankfulness for deliverance. Read Psalm 4:1, 2 compared with verse 8; Psalm 7:1–7 compared with verse 17; Psalm 13:1 compared with verses 5 and 6. I remember once praying in urgency, then I began again with the same petition. Suddenly I said to myself, "Do I expect God to do something, whatever *He* sees best, or not?" I discovered I did not expect this. I simply "hoped against hope"! Then I went back on my knees and followed David's example of giving praise to God in that I knew He would answer my prayer in His own way—and He did. "Without faith it is impossible to please Him." The English have a little proverb: "Blessed is the man that expecteth nothing, for he will not be disappointed!"

Sometimes we wrestle with doubts. I remember a great victory where God convicted a friend in an important position, who openly confessed her departure from God. On return home, I discovered that this person had reneged on the confession. I was overwhelmed that God's victory had been changed to defeat.

I went to God and bluntly said, "God, I'm sorry but I don't believe You always answer prayer." Immediately after I had spoken those words aloud, I corrected them. "God, I do believe but I don't understand." God then gave me His loving assurance. He said, "My child, *wait* for Me. I have not finished." My very voicing of unbelief (to God alone) delivered me. I started to praise Him. Later I had another interview with the person who was completely delivered from her difficulty.

My point in writing this is that when we come to God in intercession (that is, asking things from Him for myself or others) we must not be afraid to *speak out* our doubts honestly. *Immediately* He answers to our heart and we are filled with praise for our own Father as we lean on His shoulder and know He will work in His own way.

I suggest that the position of kneeling is a great help to prayer. This is my position toward the eternal Creator.

If I am in the mountains or by the sea, I sometimes walk. Prayer is wonderful there because of the beauties of God's creation.

Sometimes one cannot speak for *joy*. I have everything in Him and the joys of eternity too.

In Psalm 73:23–28 (NIV), the praying believer states: "Yet

I am always with you; you hold me by my right hand. You guide me with your counsel, and afterward you will take me to glory. Whom have I in heaven but you? And being with you, I desire nothing on earth. My flesh and my heart may fail, but God is the strength of my heart and my portion forever. . . . As for me, it is good to be near God. I have made the Sovereign Lord my refuge; I will tell of all your deeds."

May you and I experience a continual growth in the delights of real communion with God by confident praise.

THIRTY-SIX

THE JOY OF CONFIDENCE THAT ONE LIVES IN THE WILL OF GOD

I will instruct thee and teach thee in the way which thou shalt go: I will guide thee with mine eye [Psalm 32:8].

Life has rich meaning when I have a personal conviction, confirmed by God that my work and important relationships are in tune with my Creator's purpose in creating me as a separate individual. This is to sense real fulfillment.

Ephesians 2:10 states: "For we are his workmanship, created in Christ Jesus unto good works, which God hath before ordained that we should walk in them." Notice, it is not "any kind of good works" which I might selfishly choose to do, but the good works which God has prepared for me to do.

One often feels uncertain, perhaps overwhelmed, when one is faced with a necessity to make a vital decision. For example; choosing a career, finding a marriage mate, deciding on which seminary or college to attend. Sometimes one has to make decisions which will affect the lives of other people. Either one is apt to postpone the decision and live in confusion of indecisiveness, or one makes the decision without confirmation of God's direction in it and afterward worries as to whether the decision was wise. If one is a Christian, one is tempted to wonder if that decision was the direct will of God.

355

Knowing the inadequacy of sinful man's wisdom, God has made provision for His children's most important need of direction. Throughout the Bible God has promised to guide His own children in answer to prayer and a definite seeking of His guidance: Proverbs 8:14 declares, "Counsel is mine, and sound wisdom: I am understanding; I have strength." Proverbs 3:5, 6 (NIV) states, "Trust in the Lord with all your heart and lean not on your own understanding; in all your ways acknowledge him, and he will make your paths straight." Psalm 25:9 (NIV) says, "He guides the humble in what is right and teaches them his way." Psalm 73:23, 24 (NIV) states, "Yet I am always with you; you hold me by my right hand. You guide me with your counsel, and afterward you will take me to glory." James 1:5–8 (NIV) makes a specific but conditional promise, "If any of you lacks wisdom, he should ask God, who gives generously to all without finding fault, and it will be given him. But when he asks, he must believe and not doubt, because he who doubts is like a wave of the sea, blown and tossed by the wind. That man should not think he will receive anything from the Lord; he is a double-minded man, unstable in all he does."

God is our Father. He loves His child to ask Him for wisdom (guidance) in any situation where a decision has to be made which is important or causes anxiety to His child.

Guidance in regard to general lifestyle is given very clearly in the Bible. God gives clear information concerning Christian life. God also gives very specific prohibitions.

On the positive side, the believer is actively to seek to be conformed to the image of Christ (Col. 3:1–10). The believer is to offer his everyday life as a living sacrifice, holy and acceptable to God (Rom. 12:1). He is to refuse to be conformed to the lifestyle of the world around him (Rom. 12:2). When the Christian lives by these directions, he will increasingly *prove* that God's will is "good for him" and pleasing to him. (See Rom. 12:2 [NIV] and [KJV].)

If you carefully read the New Testament, you will find that

the Bible gives clear prohibitions concerning life. Therefore you need not pray for guidance where you have clear commands in Scripture concerning the situation. For example, do not pray about marrying a non-Christian, about premarital sex, adultery, homosexuality, divorce, or drunkenness (Eph. 5:12 and II Cor. 6:14).

The Bible also gives general lines of guidance in regard to women's dress (specifically, that it must be modest). First Peter 3:3-5 in *The Living Bible* states: "Don't be concerned about the outward beauty that depends on jewelry, or beautiful clothes, or hair arrangement. Be beautiful inside, in your hearts, with the lasting charm of a gentle and quiet spirit which is so precious to God. That kind of deep beauty was seen in the saintly women of old, who trusted God and fitted in with their husbands' plans." This means that a Christian woman does not dress (or undress!) provocatively to tempt men to disobey the commandment of the Lord Jesus (Matt. 5:28). In God's sight the woman is also responsible if she makes a man to "commit adultery with her in his heart." A man or woman must always remember that God wishes him or her to appear to others as one who has been created in the image of God. We are God's ambassadors to a lost world and we represent Him.

The Bible tells us we must not lie to one another, or bear malice (see Eph. 4:25 and 5:3-7). The Bible also declares that "as a man *thinketh*, so is he." Therefore there are certain books, movies, television shows, and undesirable jokes about which one needs *no extra guidance*. You know this is not God's will for you.

The entire Bible sets basic moral standards for Christian lifestyle. These are *not* burdensome. God makes the believer to have great peace of heart as these guidelines are obeyed. If we have disobeyed, we confess our sin to Him, and He cleanses us from it and changes our mental attitudes. First Thessalonians 5:22 states: "Abstain from all appearance of evil." God's Word, the Bible, will come to our mind sooner or later with conviction when we turn away from His moral law given in the Ten Commandments, the Sermon on the Mount, Psalm 119, and many other passages.

Dr. Tozer once compared the Bible to a watch. He said, "When you have a watch, you do not need to ask God what time it is."

However there are many decisions which deeply affect one's own life or the life of another (especially if one is in an administrative position), concerning which the Bible gives no specific direction. For example: Should I speak at this meeting or not? Which seminary should I attend? Should I go to Africa or China as a missionary? Which *Christian* person should I choose or accept in marriage or as a close associate in the Lord's work for which I may be responsible? Which of two jobs should I choose? Where should I spend a vacation? Each of these decisions (some important and some less important), could have imponderable results. Intimacy with my own Father Who "counts the hairs of my head" and knows what consequences will follow any decision, requires that I consult Him by prayer and looking for God's practical confirmation of His wisdom and *direct guidance.*

God promises in James 1:5–8 to give wisdom if we deliberately ask for it and do not doubt that He will give it.

The question every Christian asks is "How can I be sure that I do *not* confuse God's answer with my own desires?"

In my experience, after I have prayed for God to give me wisdom in a decision, I look for three practical confirmations that God has given me His answer. If I do not have *at least two* of these three, I normally continue to wait for proofs for full assurance.

Each of these three confirmations can be also counterfeited, so one needs to be aware of that hazard.

First, confirmation may come as one reads God's Word, or a text comes to mind as one prays. I have already given several examples of clear direction given by God, regarding going to China, starting a Bible Study Fellowship class, and others in the earlier pages of this book.

A young woman friend who is quite frail in health and has a family to care for pours out her life in practical helpfulness wherever she sees a need. Lately, however, her health had been failing and friends were concerned that this trouble might be caused by too much activity. She prayed to know God's will about this. One day as she stood in her kitchen, not even thinking about this problem, a verse came most clearly to her mind. It was Ephesians 2:10 in *The Living Bible.* She remembered reading it but was uncertain where to find it in the Bible. It reads, "It is God himself who has made us what we are and given us new lives from Christ Jesus; and long ages ago he planned that we should spend these lives helping others." God gave her His answer. She still pours out her life to help others and God is increasing her strength. Her heart was filled with His peace.

This is one form of confirmation which is directly God-given. However the Christian needs to recognize a hazard. Shakespeare has said, "Satan doth quote Scripture to his purpose." One needs to recognize that if one *wants* a special answer, anyone can find a text completely out of context to suit the situation which could be wrongly used to satisfy a desire. Therefore a second confirmation of God's leading is advisable.

I believe second confirmation comes from sound reasoning. God does not bypass our intellect and common sense in making decisions.

For example, a father might ask God for guidance if offered a new position in another locality. Should he move there or not? After prayer, as he thinks over God's direction, guidance might come in very practical ways. For instance, he might discover that there is a good church where his children will be blessed; there is availability for transportation when needed; there are convenient shopping areas; the climate is good; the neighborhood is good; and his wife is in agreement.

Such reasonable confirmations would be a likely answer to his prayer to God for His wisdom and guidance.

However again one must remember the hazard (our own

desires). God wanted Jonah to go to Nineveh. Jonah found a boat, found a berth, Jonah had money to pay for it, the weather was good when Jonah went on board in the opposite direction from Nineveh. Yet Jonah (even with all those good circumstances) *knew* that he was moving against God's inward clear command. Therefore do not depend entirely upon favorable circumstances. Look for more than one confirming sign of God's direct guidance.

Another reasonable confirmation might arise from advice given by godly, trustworthy people who are completely aware of the entire situation.

My third confirming sign, and perhaps that which is to me the strongest confirmation of God's guidance, is a *deep sense of peace* whenever I consider one particular decision or choice.

Colossians 3:15 states: "let the peace of God rule [or arbitrate] in your hearts." Such a peace may be indescribable, but it is very real.

The hazard to watch is that one could mistake a false sense of comfort, pleasure, and desire for God's peace.

To conclude, I have found by experience that God often gives me all three confirmations. If I have only one, I wait in prayer for further confirmation that this decision is of Him (especially if I have very strong leanings in one direction according to my own desire!).

Seeing that every believer will have to give account to God as to how he has used his time, to be assured of guidance is all important. It gives a profound sense of peace and a joy that one *knows* one is walking with God. (See I Cor. 3:13–15; II Cor. 5:10; Rom. 14:22.)

Life becomes very meaningful and confident when we are sure we are walking in the direction God has given us. This is especially true when difficulties arise in the path. One says to the Lord, "Lord, seeing that You led me to do this, I am trusting You to guide me as to how I handle this unexpected development."

There is a beautiful verse in Psalms which we almost invariably used in China. It is very descriptive. It says, "Behold, as the eyes of servants look unto the hand of their masters, and as the eyes of a maiden unto the hand of her mistress; so our eyes wait upon the Lord our God, until that he have mercy upon us" (123:2). In China the master or mistress does not need to talk to the servant in front of guests. The Chinese servants are taught to watch silently the hand or motion of their mistress to be ready all the time for instructions or satisfaction.

So our spiritual eyes, too, wait upon the Lord, to see what He will have from us.

THIRTY-SEVEN
THE JOY OF REWARD FOLLOWING TRIUMPHANT SUFFERING

Now no chastening for the present seemeth to be joyous, but grievous: nevertheless afterward it yieldeth the peaceable fruit of righteousness unto them which are exercised thereby [Hebrews 12:11].

I have stated that the Christian life is the most fulfilled, joyous, and satisfying life a person can ever live. Every person alive was created in God's image (Gen. 1:27) and to fulfill God's purpose in creating him. Therefore to fulfill that for which I was created, I need to share God's thoughts, experience His emotions of joy, pity, or "righteous" anger, and choose to exercise my *will* in making decisions to obey Him.

However, the question arises, "If Christians are the children of the living God and serve Him, why do they suffer the same afflictions as nonbelievers?" Indeed some well-meaning preachers seem to proclaim that if you become a Christian, your troubles will be over. As long as you keep close to God, fulfill His will for you, serve others, and bear fruit, you will live a gloriously happy life on this earth in preparation for the more glorious life to come.

But this is not being realistic. Christians do suffer afflictions of sickness, of pressure, of depression (often due to weariness in God's service), and ask that question, "Where is my God?" Psalm 10:1 says, "Why, O Lord, do you stand far off? Why do you hide yourself in times of trouble?" (NIV).

For that matter, nonbelievers ask another question, "Why does God allow suffering at all?" (although it is true the man on the street allows punishment of criminals and understands suffering in such cases).

The Bible answers this overall question very clearly, especially in Romans 8. Ever since the "fall" into rebellion, the deliberate sin of our ancestors, Adam and Eve (recorded in Gen. 3), the whole of mankind and the world suffers the consequences.

Every person's "genes," so to speak, include a bias to sin from birth. Today we still live in a fallen, frustrated world because of sin. (Read Rom. 8:17–33, which gives the clue to the general suffering of mankind.) "We know that the whole creation has been groaning as in the pains of childbirth right up to the present time" (Rom. 8:22, NIV). "That the creation itself will be liberated from its bondage to decay and brought into the glorious freedom of the children of God" (Rom. 8:21, NIV).

Suffering is inescapable under the present cosmology in which Satan, whom Jesus called "the prince of this world," plays a large part. For example, a child may play with fire and be burned. That is the child's fault. Yet a person may also slip on a banana skin and be seriously hurt, or a car may run into you on an icy road. One can suffer a heart attack or develop cancer. A beloved husband or wife dies, or a man for reasons not his own loses his position and is out of work for a long period of time.

There are pressures, afflictions, and trials which come upon all men in one way or another because in this day and age we are still under the system resulting from the "fall." Physical death is inevitable and is tied up with what is theologically called "original sin." "The wages of sin is death; but the gift of God is eternal life through Jesus Christ our Lord" (Rom. 6:23).

For the non-Christian, afflictions and suffering are an intolerable burden. In contrast, for God's own child, afflictions allowed by his heavenly Father have an eternal value.

It is important for the true Christian to ask the *spiritual* questions: "Who am I?" "Why was I created?" "What is my destiny?" This is a tremendous help in understanding how to cope with present-day trials.

According to biblical teaching, it is clear that from the beginning, God's divine interest was in *man* whom God created in His own image.

God's ultimate purpose in creating man in His own image was to create a people who would be conformed to the likeness of His own Son, the Lord Jesus Christ, to be "His Bride" who is destined after suffering to reign with Christ (Rom. 8:16–18).

The believer is to be an eternal companion for God's beloved Son. Therefore, seeing that the believer is destined to "judge angels" and share Christ's throne (I Cor. 6:3, Rev. 3:21), he needs to be disciplined and trained.

The Christian must understand who he is. His destiny is to reign with Christ. His present life in this world is to bear fruit by revealing to the world his hidden strength given by the Lord to endure. The joy, even during suffering, is that this suffering is not wasted but working for a special reward. Second Corinthians 4:17, 18 in the Amplified version states: "For our light, momentary affliction (this slight distress of the passing hour) is ever more and more abundantly preparing and producing and achieving for us an everlasting weight of glory—beyond all measure, excessively surpassing all comparisons and all calculations, a vast and transcendent glory and blessedness never to cease! Since we consider and look not to the things that are seen but to the things that are unseen; for the things that are visible are *temporal* (brief and fleeting), but the things that are invisible are deathless and everlasting."

In Ephesians 3 (NIV), when Paul was speaking of the "mystery" (partly hidden in former Old Testament ages), he stated in verse 10, "[God's] intent was that now, through the church, the manifold wisdom of God should be made known to the rulers and authorities in the heavenly realms, according to his eternal purpose which he accomplished in Christ Jesus our Lord." In Ephesians 3:13 (NIV), Paul continues, "I ask you, therefore, not to be discouraged because of my sufferings for you which are your glory." This is followed by one of Paul's prayers, which to me is the most wonderful of them all.

Seeing the exalted position to which God has called us, seeing that our Lord Jesus (Who was sinless and perfect) "learned . . . obedience by the things which he suffered" (Heb. 5:8) and "offered up prayers and supplications with strong crying and tears" (Heb. 5:7), why should Christ's follower be immune from suffering?

Hebrews 2:10 (NIV) states: "In bringing many sons to glory, it was fitting that God, for whom and through whom everything exists, should make the author of their salvation perfect through suffering." Then follows verses which are most moving—"Both the one who makes men holy and those who are made holy are of the same family. So Jesus is not ashamed to call them brothers." In verse 13 Christ is quoted: "Here am I, and the children God has given me." Verse 14: "Since the children have flesh and blood, he too shared in their humanity." Verse 16: "For surely it is not angels he helps, but Abraham's descendants. For this reason he had to be made like his brothers in every way." Verse 18: "Because he himself suffered when he was tempted, he is able to help those who are being tempted."

All these verses prove that temptation, trials, and suffering are a part of our training, but work for us an eternal weight of glory *when we choose* not to fix our emotions on present visible suffering, but fix our thoughts on the eternal glory and reward, which cannot be ours without some measure of suffering.

Hebrews 12 is a classic passage on this subject—especially temptation to sin, which is suffering.

We are called to "throw off every sin or lifestyle which hinders, and to run with *perseverance* the race marked out for us." Hebrews 12:2, "Let us fix our eyes upon Jesus, the author and perfecter of our faith, who for the joy which was set before him endured the cross, scorning its shame, and sat down on the right hand of the throne of God."

The eleventh chapter of Hebrews speaks of key men of old who triumphed in suffering. The first verse of Hebrews 12 gives an encouraging word in that these heroes of the faith represent a "cloud of witnesses." *The Living Bible* translates Hebrews 12:1, 2 as follows: "Since we have such a huge crowd of men of faith watching us from the grandstands, let us strip off everything that slows us down or holds us back, and especially those sins that wrap themselves so tightly around our feet and trip us up; and let us run with patience the particular race set before us."

Try to imagine the encouragement of the men and women of Hebrews 11, knowing what it is to suffer and watching us with encouragement "to see how we make out"!

Later the writer of Hebrews states that sometimes trials are a means of *discipline*. Hebrews 12:11 (NIV): "No discipline seems pleasant at the time, but painful. Later on, however, it produces a harvest of righteousness and peace for those who have been trained by it" (i.e., chosen to accept it from God).

Paul shows a different aspect of this in Romans 5:2 (NIV), "And we rejoice in the hope of the glory of God. Not only so, but we also rejoice in our sufferings, because we know that suffering produces perseverance; perseverance, *character*; and character, hope. And hope does not disappoint us, because God has poured out his love into our hearts by the Holy Spirit."

To me Paul's sufferings and troubles seem almost unbelievable. (Read II Cor. 11:16–30, NIV.) However in II Corinthians 4:7 he explains that the glory of Christ Jesus living within us is like a treasure in jars of clay (our bodies and personalities). This is so that no one will glorify us, but see

367

that we are what we are by the supernatural power of God. This simple outline of II Corinthians 4:7 shows the pattern of suffering in the Christian life:

Hard pressed—Not crushed
Perplexed—Not in despair
Persecuted—Not abandoned
Struck down—Not destroyed

(Read also II Cor. 6:3–10 with Paul's emphasis on rejoicing.)

There is a power in suffering when there is a willingness to die to self through the Cross of Christ. Second Corinthians 4:12 (NIV) states, "So then, death is at work in us, but life is at work in you."

Imagine a sponge full of life-giving water. Only when it is squeezed does this life-giving water pour out upon other lives.

I write this to the reader not as though I have attained this triumphant way of handling suffering, for I so often fail to triumph in Christ as I should, and I praise God that He lifts those who fall.

However, "I press on toward the goal to win the prize for which God called me heavenward in Christ" (Phil. 3:14, NIV).

God said to Paul (when he prayed for deliverance from "a thorn"), "My grace is sufficient for you, for my power is made perfect in weakness." Paul replied, "Therefore I will boast all the more gladly about my *weakness* so that Christ's power may rest upon me."

The Christian's suffering throws him upon God more than any other experience. Suffering is necessary for the decentralization of self and a deeper development of love toward God Who is the source of all comfort.

As we receive comfort from God, we experience that such comfort is adequate. This experience of God's adequacy enables us to comfort others in suffering, either by realistic prayer for them or personal help.

We should not ignore the ancient book of Job which gives

another clue to the mystery of suffering. Job was a "good man," and he loved God. God pointed Job out to the evil adversary, Satan, who said, "Just take away his things and watch Job turn away from God." God allowed this. Then came the test of physical suffering (but God limited this: "Touch not his life"). Job could not understand the reason for all his troubles. Job never turned from God. Job was egotistical (chapters 29, 31, etc.). However, when God answered Job, Job said, "My ears had heard of you but now my eyes have seen you. Therefore I despise myself and repent in dust and ashes" (Job 42:5, NIV).

Job's discipline revealed to Satan that God's grace was sufficient to hold the loyalty of His own child however deep the affliction.

When Job prayed for his criticizing false comforters, the Lord made Job prosperous again and gave Job twice as much as he had before. God blessed the latter part of Job's life more than the first.

Perhaps as an example of this, I might share with you the "trials" which have accompanied the writing of this book.

Since my last major operation for cancer, I am still troubled with a cancerous area in my spine. I count on writing five hours a day from early morning. But when I write I have to bend my head and the upper part of my spine. This gives continuous pain, which I think sometimes hinders my thoughts.

Yet as I write I think of the future. I pray that some people reading this book may be blessed of God and even converted to Christ. This is not looking at the *now*, but looking at "eternal fruit." I know I need discipline for firming up my character, but there is the *special joy* of anticipated fruit to God's glory.

I should also mention that I have had a specially kind publisher whose editors have been very encouraging and gracious.

Let us all forget any failures and the past sufferings that are behind us. Instead, let us look for the fruit our loving Father gives to His children who are allowed to suffer.

From prayer that asks that I may be
Sheltered from winds that beat on Thee,
From fearing when I should aspire,
From faltering when I should climb higher,
From silken self, O Captain, free
Thy soldier who would follow Thee.

From subtle love of softening things,
From easy choices, weakenings,
(Not thus are spirits fortified,
Not this way went the Crucified)
From all that dims Thy Calvary,
O Lamb of God, deliver me.

Give me the love that leads the way,
The faith that nothing can dismay,
The hope no disappointments tire,
The passion that will burn like fire,
Let me not sink to be a clod:
Make me Thy fuel, Flame of God.

Amy Wilson Carmichael

THIRTY-EIGHT
THE JOY OF POSSESSING AN EVERLASTING INHERITANCE

But as it is written, Eye hath not seen, nor ear heard, neither have entered into the heart of man, the things which God hath prepared for them that love him [I Corinthians 2:9].

When our Lord Jesus was preparing to leave His disciples, He spoke of their future permanent abode. "There are many homes up there where my Father lives, and I am going to prepare them for your coming. When everything is ready, then I will come and get you, so that you can always be with me where I am. If this weren't so, I would tell you plainly" (John 14:2, TLB).

Like a child who is promised the wonders of a vacation far away, and longs for details, so do we Christians long for more details concerning our permanent abode living with God and His Son, our Lord Jesus Christ, forever and ever.

The last chapters of the Revelation of Jesus Christ to His servant, John the Apostle, give us a wonderful glimpse into the delights God has prepared for His own.

Leonard Verduim, in *Something Less Than God* states: "The plain implication is that from the earliest beginnings the divine interest was to reach its climax in man. . . . Man is pictured as the crown and capstone of the entire creative

371

enterprise of the Almighty: man is the goal toward which the whole undertaking moved. Verily, the Bible does not speak meanly of man."

Perhaps this vision of God's ultimate purpose in the creation of man is most vividly seen in the Epistles of Ephesians and Colossians. The believer is adopted by God and called a "son of God" (Eph. 1). The Church is the Bride of Christ (Eph.5). Ephesians 1:23 calls the Church the "fulness of him that filleth all in all," the Body of whom Christ is the Head. Colossians 3:4 states that "when Christ, who is our life, shall appear, then shall ye also appear with him in glory."

In Revelation 21 the Apostle John was given to see the "New Jerusalem" as a glorious city coming out of heaven from God (on to a *new earth*), as beautiful as a bride adorned for her husband. This is the fitting end that climaxes God's eternal purpose for His people.

Ephesians 3:9, 10 and Ephesians 2:6, 7 give glimpses of God's noble end for the man He created and for whom Christ died. We are to show to principalities and powers (angels and demons) "the incomparable riches of his grace, expressed in his kindness to us in Christ Jesus" (Eph. 2:7, NIV).

Satan's purpose throughout the history of man was to separate man from God. But God proves that His grace and His power, and also His love demonstrated at Calvary, are totally victorious to win the love and loyalty of all who are born again, in spite of Satan's machinations to draw men to himself and his system.

The old earth and humanity has been ruined throughout history by man's rebellion against God and the dominion of Satan. It is full of sorrow, illness, despair, death, and war. Only the believers of the Old Testament and the New Testament experienced an inner joy and triumph in God, and gave thanks to our resurrected Lord Jesus Christ as they passed through life as "pilgrims" of another land.

The new earth and heavens will be altogether different. *First*, God is openly and visibly living with men. He even has

His throne in the midst of His own children—day and night we are with Him. *Second*, there is no more sorrow (Rev. 21:4). God will wipe away every tear forever. *Death* is irradicated. There will be no more mourning, crying, or pain of any description.

As mentioned previously, the Apostle John was given to see the future new earth (with no oceans) and a new sky, for the present earth and sky had disappeared (Rev. 21:1, TLB).

Following this, John saw a new great city called "the New Jerusalem" coming down from God out of heaven. "It was a glorious sight, beautiful as a bride at her wedding" (Rev. 21:2, TLB).

Within the city is the God-redeemed new humanity comprising the believers of all ages. Presumably, this "New Jerusalem" is the capital city of the New Earth.

A completely new era has come in God's planning. We shall see Him; He will be dwelling with us all the time. (See Rev. 21:3.) We shall reign with Christ, actively serve Him, and perhaps visit the new starry heavens. Our world will be a new world of unending joy, peace, love, and meaningful activity.

Peter states that God "according to his abundant mercy has begotten us again unto a lively hope by the resurrection of Jesus Christ from the dead. To an inheritance . . . undefiled, and that fadeth not away, reserved in heaven for you, who are kept by the power of God."

The next time you are given a reserved place (for example, on a plane), remember the reserved place the Lord Jesus is keeping for you in Heaven and in the "New Jerusalem"!

As I study the Bible I envision a world of indescribable beauty. Glorious trees with fruit (as in Eden) and glorious rivers and lakes. I see myself making friends with lions and tigers and all of God's *new creation*. We shall also live with thousands upon thousands of angels; yet we for whom Christ died have a unique position forever and ever with our Lord as we "reign with Him."

There will be music, fellowship with all the saints, and all the time we shall be looking with undiminished joy at the Almighty God, Creator of universes, Who is our own Father.

Whatever new purpose God may have for future ages, we shall be working with Him forever and ever and ever.

What could be a more glorious prospect!